GENERATIONS AT WORK

Managing the Clash of Veterans, Boomers, Xers, and Nexters in Your Workplace

Ron Zemke
Claire Raines
Bob Filipczak

American Management Association

New York • Atlanta • Boston • Chicago • Kansas City • San Francisco • Washington, D.C.
Brussels • Mexico City • Tokyo • Toronto

Special discounts on bulk quantities of AMACOM books are available to corporations, professional associations, and other organizations. For details, contact Special Sales Department, AMACOM, an imprint of AMA Publications, a division of American Management Association, 1601 Broadway, New York, NY 10019. Tel.: 212-903-8316.   Fax: 212-903-8083.

Library of Congress Cataloging-in-Publication Data

Zemke, Ron.
    Generations at work : managing the clash of veterans, boomers, xers, and nexters in your workplace / Ron Zemke, Claire Raines, Bob Filipczak.
        p.   cm.
    Includes bibliographical references and index.
    ISBN 0-8144-0480-4
    1. Diversity in the workplace—United States.   2. Age groups—United States.   3. Conflict of generations—United States.
    4. Supervision of employees.   I. Raines, Claire.   II. Filipczak, Bob.   III. Title.
HF5549.5.M5Z45   2000
    658.3′0084—dc21
                                                                                99-33791
                                                                                CIP

Printing number

20 19 18 17 16 15 14

CONTENTS

GENERATIONS AT WORK

INTRODUCTION:

These Modern Times and the
Cross-Generational Workplace

Today's American workforce is unique and singular. Never before has there been a workforce and workplace—so diverse in so many ways. The mix of race, gender, ethnicity, and generation in today's workplace is stunning. The latter, generational diversity, and the tension and challenge, opportunity, and promise it presents are the focus of this book. There is a growing realization that the gulf of misunderstanding and resentment between older, not so old, and younger employees in the workplace is growing and problematic. It is a rift that will not heal itself or just go away, as so many organizations—those even aware of it— fervently hope. It is a problem based in economics, demographics, and world views that must be confronted to be solved.

Microhistory of the Problem

It is an oddly American set of dilemmas we describe and discuss here. The population of no other country in the world has come to this point and place in history quite the same way as the United States. A young country, as countries go, the United States has nevertheless been front and center in world-shaping events for a century and a half. Although a major participant in a century of horrendous global conflicts, the United States has never been invaded, conquered, or laid waste to, as have so many other countries. It has sunk as deeply into global economic depression as any country, but rebounded and bounced back faster and higher. It has weathered the socioeconomic storms of the century with remarkable resilience. The legacy of this lucky history was a beaming, can-do optimism that rode an economy that seemed indomitable through the third quarter of the century. This lasted until about 1980, when a new set of global economic behemoths emerged and the optimism turned to panic and self-doubt.

Today, as America is once again a, if not the, dominant global economic force, there is a more cautious, wary attitude in the halls of American commerce. To paraphrase Charles Dickens, we are living, organizationally and individually, in a best of times and yet a worst of times. It is particularly true in terms of the human drama of life on the shop floor and the cubical level. No job is "safe," no career assured in a work world where the pace of organizational acquisition, consolidation, and rapid directional change has been unrelenting for a decade. Every workplace has become a continuous, sometimes macabre game of musical chairs. Every employed person a survivor—but just for now. A simple cipher in a head count game where the only rule is: The fewer the better.

It should hardly be a surprise that in this environment there is a growing sense of individual and generational enmity. "Us" versus "Them" and "every man, woman, and child for himself" attitudes are easy to comprehend—and empathize with. It is easy to see why the "Us's" are often generational groupings. Oldsters holding fast to their decades of gains are increasingly being pitted for organizational survival against youngsters hungering for their own advancement and security. That they have closed ranks against one another is natural—even when those age group alliances are unspoken and informal and masked by generational name calling and categorization.

It is an atmosphere that does not bode well for effort, energy, and productivity, much less marketplace competitiveness. Yet, as we shall see, it is neither the inevitable outcome of our modern times, nor an irreversible situation. As we shall demonstrate through example, today's workplace can be a positive, productive, and compatible home for old, not so old, and young workers alike. It takes an aware and enlightened management determined to make it so.

The Generations

The generations vying against each other in today's workplace, as we depict them, are somewhat unique and a bit different than those commonly suggested by others. For instance, we define the Baby Boom generation as those born from 1943 to 1960. Others, particularly population demographers, define the Baby Boom as 1946 to 1964. Why the difference? We have factored in the "feel" as well as the "face" of a generational cohort in our definition. For instance, our research finds that people born between 1943 and 1946 have similar values and views as the "true" demographically defined Baby Boomers, those born between 1946 and 1964. Likewise, we date Generation X from 1960 rather than 1965. This again, comes from our research and conclusion that the 1960 to 1964 cohort act and think more like Generation Xers than any other group. Many individuals from these birth years we have confronted in interviews and discussion groups adamantly refuse to be labeled Boomers for any purpose. Therefore, our four generational groups are the following:

- The Veterans 1922–1943 (52 million people). Those born prior to World War II and those whose earliest memories and influences are associated with that world-engulfing event.
- The Baby Boomers 1943–1960 (73.2 million people). Those born during or after World War II and raised in the era of extreme optimism, opportunity, and progress.
- Generation Xers 1960–1980 (70.1 million people). Those born after the blush of the Baby Boom and came of age deep in the shadow of the Boomers and the rise of the Asian tiger.
- Generation Nexters 1980–2000 (69.7 million people to date). Those born of the Baby Boomers and early Xers and into our current high-tech, neo-optimistic time.

Note that our generations overlap at their end points. If we wouldn't utterly confuse everyone, we would overlap them by three or four years. There are no hard stops or road signs indicating when one generation ends and another begins. Please note also that we are aware of the dangers of stereotyping whether by generation or gender. To say, as we do, that the Veteran musical icons are the likes of Duke Ellington and Stan Herman, and the Boomer significants are Elvis and the Beatles does not mean to imply that a Veteran or an Xer will not appreciate the Beatles or Elvis. But the specific affections of a generation's formative years *do* bind them together in exclusive ways. To say, for instance, that Gen Xers are more attuned to rock climbing and extreme sports than Veterans, doesn't preclude the possibility of avidly rapelling grandmas. It does suggest, however, that aside from the passion for climbing inclines, the Veteran gram will have fewer attitudes and experiences in common with the Gen Xer than would another Gen Xer. Those common ties are self-reinforcing and self-sustaining and lead to within group cohesion.

How This Book Is Organized

This book, like the Gaul of another era, is divided into three parts. In Part One, "Dynamics of the Multigenerational Workplace," we explore the problems, pressures, and opportunities of the mixed generation workforce and workplace. In addition, we profile the four major generational groups and outline the unique wants, needs, and feelings of each. In Part Two, "Case Studies in Generational Peace," we look at five companies where a mix of generations is treated as an asset rather than a problem. They are a wonderful mosaic of the possible. As a bonus we introduce the ACORN imperatives from which these oaks of hope are rising.

In Part Three, "Advice-o-Plenty," we hear first from a panel of seven experts who tackle the plight of Charlie Roth, a manager with no skill and little wit for dealing with a department divided generationally. The icing on Part Three is twenty-one generation-based questions we hear most frequently in seminars and workshops—answered. The question and answer chapter is indexed separately for easy future access and reference.

Finally, there is an appendix section with an inventory you can use to evaluate the generational "friendliness" of your organization and a listing of resources you can use to further your understanding of generational differences.

Okay. With all that out of the way, we invite you to dive into the fascinating world of the mixed generation workplace—warts, perils, opportunities, and all.

A Few Words About Our Research

The three of us became interested in generational issues and have collected information separately and collectively for nearly a decade. As writers, consultants, speakers, and trainers, we have spent substantial time learning from those who are "in the trenches," facing intergenerational workplace issues on a daily basis. We have administered surveys and facilitated discussion sessions and focus groups to get a broad understanding of how the generations see themselves and each other. In addition to interviewing hundreds of managers and those who report to them, we have interviewed the leading experts on the sociology of generations. Our findings have been corroborated by the growing body of research about generations done by organizations like the Higher Education Research Institute at the University of California at Los Angeles, Yankelovich Partners in New York, the National Center for Educational Statistics in Washington D.C., and Northwestern Mutual Life Insurance Company in Milwaukee.

PART ONE

DYNAMICS OF THE MULTIGENERATIONAL WORKPLACE

CHAPTER ONE

OLD FARTS AND UPSTARTS:

Crisis in the Cross-Generational Workplace

"In a great barroom conversation with John Parry Barlow, cyberspace pioneer and former lyricist for the Grateful Dead, the conversation shifted to Xers and Nexters. 'You guys hate us, don't you?' he asked. He meant my generation, the Xers, hate his generation, the Boomers. I had to agree, even though he is a Boomer and I enjoyed him as much as anyone I'd met. But there we were, diplomats representing warring factions, understanding that, outside of the conflict, we would get along just fine and might even be friends. It was a generational moment."

—BOB FILIPCZAK

There is a problem in the workplace—a problem derived not from downsizing, rightsizing, change, technology, foreign competition, pointy-haired bosses, bad breath, cubicle envy, or greed. It is a problem of values, ambitions, views, mind-sets, demographics, and generations in conflict. The workplace you and we inhabit today is awash with the conflicting voices and views of the most age- and value-diverse workforce this country has known since our great-great-grandparents abandoned field and farm for factory and office. At no previous time in our history have so many and such different generations with such diversity been asked to work together shoulder to shoulder, side by side, cubicle to cubicle.

Yes, there have been multiple generations employed in the same organization before. But, by and large, they were sequestered from each other by organizational stratification and the structural topography of a manufacturing-oriented economy. Senior (older) employees, who were mostly white and male, worked in the head office or were in command positions in the manufacturing chain. Middle-aged employees tended to be in middle management or high-skill, seniority-protected trade jobs. The youngest, greenest, and physically strongest were on the factory floor or were camped out in specific trainee slots that they more or less quietly endured for significant periods—junior accountant, sales representative, teller, assistant manager. Their contacts were primarily horizontal, with people like themselves or, at most, one level up or down the chain of command. Generational "mixing" was rare and then significantly influenced by formality and protocol. Senior employees did not share their reasoning or ask for input for their decision making. Juniors, when they had complaints or doubts, kept them to themselves or at least to those on their own level, and then usually discussed them only "off premises."

In today's postindustrial info-centered work world, social and physical separations are no longer powerful barriers to generational mixing. Frequently, senior employees are older today than senior employees were "back then," and these older employees are inhabiting positions once "manned" by younger employees. The new, more horizontal, more spatially compact workplace has stirred the generations into a mix of much different proportions. According to Walker Smith and Ann Clurman of Yankelovich Partners, widely recognized authorities on consumer trends, "New market trends wrought by generational differences are causing business upheavals, bringing new categories (of work) into being at warp speed and causing old ones to shrink or disappear."[1]

Here in an era when even the most profitable businesses are striving to run ever leaner and meaner, there are three very distinct generations vying for position in a workplace of shrinking upward opportunity. They will soon be joined by a distinct and yet again different fourth generation. The old pecking order, hierarchy, and shorter life spans that de facto kept a given generational cohort isolated from others no longer exist, or they exist in a much less rigid, more permeable manner. Merit is overcoming time in grade, or any other variable, as the deciding factor in advancement. One outcome of this largely accidental generational blending is creativity, or at least it can be. People of different perspectives always have the potential to bring different thoughts and ideas to problem solving and future opportunity. An unfortunate outcome, one that mitigates against positive creative synergy, is intergenerational conflict: differences in values and views, and ways of working, talking, and thinking that set people in opposition to one another and challenge organizational best interests. Unfortunately, dissension between groups that are different is an almost wired-in part of human nature, according to diversity experts such as Norma Carr-Ruffino of San Francisco State University, who says that not understanding others' perspective on the world "can be stressful, confusing, and frustrating."[2]

The sounds of generations in conflict are heard around the water cooler, across the cafeteria table, at the coffee bar, and on the e-mail whine boards of 1,001 corporations and public servers.

- "They have no work ethic. They're just a bunch of slackers."
- "So I told my boss, 'If you're looking for loyalty, buy a dog.'"
- "A hiring bonus! Wet behind the ears and he wants a hiring bonus! At his age, I was just grateful I had a job."
- "I have a new rule. I will not attend meetings that start after 5 P.M. I have a life."
- "He's been out of training and in the field for six months and he wants a promotion—a promotion!"
- "She wants a 'career map.' Hell! I don't even know if there will *be* a customer relations department this time next year."
- "He asks me, 'Do you have an e-mail address?' I felt like telling him, 'since you were in diapers, buddy!'"
- "If I hear 'We tried that in '87' one more time, I'll hurl in his wrinkly, old face."

More importantly and ominously, the gripes, complaints, and underlying fundamental differences are not heard across the conference table or discussed and dealt with in any constructive fashion or forum. Like death and taxes, they are assumed to be immutable and irreparable, and, consequently, they are never openly addressed. In the "old," rigid, highly regimented organization, that may not have mattered. In the "new" organization, they can be devastating. They nonetheless fester, cause tension, and lead to unnecessary, at times disabling, personal, departmental, and organizational conflict.

Bridging the Gaps

In truth, generation gaps are neither new nor forever insurmountable. The "Archie Bunker—Meat Head" differences of the 1960s divided many a family and society in general. The rancor between hawks and doves, flower children and traditionalists, seemed, at the time, destined to shake apart the nation forever. In the 1920s, the "flapper" era, symbolized and chronicled by the likes of F. Scott Fitzgerald, was yet another period when the gulf between old and young seemed forever unbridgeable. Earlier still, in the immediate pre-Civil War period, the United States was rife with generational conflict. The realignment of political loyalties and political parties in the 1850s—with younger, more progressive Americans flocking to the then brand-new Republican Party—planted the seeds for the bloody domestic strife that was to follow. Earlier still, as any history book will readily confirm, Socrates of ancient Greece was slipped that hemlock highball not because of his annoying habit of answering a question with a question, but for riling up the youth of Athens and driving a wedge between them and their elders.

What is new and different is that the new generation gap is tripartite and soon to become a four-way divide. There are already, as we speak, three generations at odds in the workplace. Also, unlike other eras, the power relations are not a simple, straightforward matter of the older generation having all the marbles—resources, power, and position—and the younger generation in revolt and anxious over access to, and control of, those resources. The once "natural" flow of resources, power, and responsibilities from older to younger arms has been dislocated by changes in life expectancy, increases in longevity and health, and disruption of a century-old trend toward negative population growth, as well as changes in lifestyle, technology, and knowledge base. A world that once seemed linear is no longer. Life for every generation has become increasingly nonlinear, unpredictable, and unchartable.

In times of uncertainty and anxiety, differences between groups and sets of people, even generations, become tension producing and potential flash points. We increasingly live and work in a world of high stakes, winners and losers, high tensions, diminishing commonalties in values, and changing social contracts and compacts. And, ironically, we increasingly live and work in a world where the sheer numbers of us and the interdependent and virtual nature of the work we do often depend on and demand collaboration and compromise, not just independence and virtuosity. It means an explicit need exists for overcoming and understanding generational and communication differences to create positive ends for the organization and the individuals who inhabit it.

Demographic Imperatives

The legions of ancient Rome were composed of ten cohorts each: cohesive units of 300 to 600 men who trained, ate, slept, fought, won, lost, lived, and died together. Their strength was their ability to think, act, and, more importantly, react as a unit. Though composed of individuals, training and socialization equipped them to behave as if of a single mind when called to battle. Social demographers, students of the effects of population on society, use the term *cohort* to refer to people born in the same general time span who share key life experiences—from setting out for school for the first time together through reaching puberty at the same time, to entering the workforce or university or marriage or middle age or their dotage at the same time.

Demographers such as David K. Foot of the University of Toronto see demographics as critically influential in how we see ourselves as individuals and judge ourselves to be: "Most of us think of ourselves as individuals and underestimate how much we have in common with fellow members of our cohort."[3]

To borrow an example from Foot, the seventy-year-old person who is an avid rock climber is a unique individual. So is the twelve-year-old opera lover. Just the same, says Foot, "The chances are good the young opera lover will rent his first apartment, buy his first car, get married at about the same age as his peers."[4] Both the timing and texture of most life events are highly, though perhaps not obviously, influenced by the backdrop of demographics. Members of a cohort who come of age in lean times or war years think and act differently than those born and raised to their majority in peace and plenty.

A word about stereotypes. We are all individuals; there are a multitude of ways each of us differs from all others in our generation or even from our own family group. To be effective with other human beings, we must know them as individuals—their unique background, personality, preferences, and style. However, knowing generational information is also tremendously valuable; it often explains the baffling and confusing differences behind our unspoken assumptions underneath our attitudes. The seventy-three-year-old web master who creates rock and blues digital music doesn't fit the stereotype of the World War II era senior citizen, yet he was forever touched—as were all members of his cohort—growing up during the Great Depression, hearing about the disaster at Pearl Harbor, and feeling the pride and patriotism that were part of the fabric of the mid-1940s.

Just as important as the obvious sociological, political, and economic conditions a cohort faces is the impact of the size of the cohort itself. Throughout the nineteenth century, the population of the United States was on a slow decline. Births and immigration combined were failing to create the numbers necessary for simple replacement. America at the turn of the century was a land of opportunity... great opportunities waiting to be realized and there for the taking, with scant competition for them.

As the century turned and the landscape became tamed, the country grew prosperous, birth rates began rising, and what was once a trickle of immigration became a flood spurred on by hard times in Europe. Prosperity spurred birth rates and unprecedented growth. By the advent of the Great Depression, the United States had reached a population of 123 million people. As the devastation of the Depression set in, birth rates were again falling, a trend not to be reversed until the end of World War II, fifteen years later.

By 1946—with half the planet reeling in the aftermath of the largest, most costly war in history—the United States, one of the most intact of the survivors, was poised for another era of unprecedented economic growth and prosperity—and births.

Veterans of World War II and those born during the war years found themselves in a workforce and workplace of rich opportunity, a situation not to be substantially diminished for a generation until the rise of the vaunted Japanese productivity machine in the 1980s. Birth and immigration rates again paralleled economic growth. It seemed, at least in contrast to prewar years, that once again there was an unlimited future for those with the will and determination to seize it.

Today the United States is a country of 250 million people of greater vigor and greater life span than ever before. But it is also a country of complex demographics and subtle but critical economic influences. A simple example: The last-ins of the contemporary workplace, the so-called Generation Xers, are arguably the most highly educated, technologically savvy cohort group yet to enter the workforce in significant numbers. Many of them have knowledge and skill that is highly valued in today's workplace. At the same time, they exist in a workforce of limited upward mobility that none of the preceding generations can quite comprehend. Baby Boomers—those immediately preceding the Xers—for whom the concept of career planning was essentially an exercise in choice, have no understanding of, or sympathy for, the Gen Xers who face a landscape of very different opportunities. The force of the Boomers' own demography is lost on them. They see and hear the pessimism of the liberal-arts Xer who believes he or she is condemned to a future of "Would you like fries with that, sir?" but do not comprehend that a lack of ambition or willfulness is a factor of only minor import. Likewise, the Baby Boomer manager is stunned by the elite Xer, the one with a sterling high-tech portfolio who demands a hiring bonus and idiosyncratic benefits, or who puts his feet on the desk during the interview and says, "Tell me why I should work for you." The forces behind the hard-edged steeliness and determination to "get mine now—when it's there" are, again, lost on the Baby Boomer for whom life, work, and team are interchangeable terms. For Boomers, work is definitely not a dispassionate game to be played toward personal, idiosyncratic ends.

The upshot of these and dozens of other star-crossed intergenerational scenarios is wariness and mistrust. Boomers see Xers as alternately greedy and lazy, suspicious and self-serving, loners and cynics: all overgeneralizations and the work of stereotypy, and a negative eddy of wasted energy. Xers, for their part, see Boomers as obsessive, dictatorial, "my way or the highway," a little naíve, a little soft: again, stereotypical overgeneralizations, but nonetheless existent perceptions.

How Generations Differ

In addition to the coincidence of birth, a generation is also defined by common tastes, attitudes, and experiences; a generational cohort is a product of its times and tastes. Those times encompass a myriad of circumstances—economic, social, sociological, and, of course, demographic. Particularly telling are a generation's defining moments: events that capture the attention and emotions of thousands—if not millions—of individuals at a formative stage in their lives. An old adage holds that "People resemble their times more than they resemble their parents." The first headlines to inspire and awe, to horrify and thrill, to send the imagination soaring or cause dark contemplation and heated conversation, do much to shape the character of a generation. The music that members of a cohort hear, the heroes they share, the passions they agree or disagree about, and their common history shape and define a generation. And because generations share a place in history—in time—and have events, images, and experiences in common, they develop their own unique personalities. Not that every individual fits that generation's personality profile to an exact "fare thee well." Some embody it; some spend a lifetime trying to live it down. Either way, all members of a generation are deeply affected by the personality of their cohort group—their generation.

DEFINING EVENTS	
1930s:	Great Depression
	Election of FDR
1940s:	Pearl Harbor
	D-Day
	Death of FDR
	VE Day and VJ Day
	Hiroshima—Nagasaki
1950s:	Korean War
	TV in every home
	McCarthy HCUAA hearings
	Rock `n Roll
	Salk Polio vaccine introduced
1960s:	Vietnam
	Kennedy elected
	Civil Rights movement
	Kennedy/King assassinations
	Moon landing
	Woodstock
1970s:	Oil Embargo
	Nixon resigns
	First PCs
	Women's Rights movement
1980s:	Challenger explosion
	Fall of Berlin Wall
	John Lennon shot
	Reagan elected
1990s:	Desert Storm
	Oklahoma City bombing
	Death of Princess Diana
	Clinton scandals

Generational commonalties cut across racial, ethnic, and economic differences. As unique as people's individual experiences may be, they share a place in history with their generation. Whether they were raised by neurosurgeons or a single mom, whether they grew up on "the Res," in "the Hood," or on a military base, whether they wore designer jeans or hand-me-down shoes, they all share with their generation what was in the air around them—news events, music, national catastrophes, heroes, and heroic efforts.

To a certain extent, even immigrants have much in common with those in their generation who grew up in the United States. Although he grew up south of the U.S./Mexico border, a forty-five-year-old Mexican immigrant in El Paso shares commonalties with his generational cohort born and bred in the United States. He, too, was touched by JFK and his early departure from this life... he dreamed of his favorite girl when Elvis sang "Love Me Tender" just like his cohorts up north... he was just as amazed as the rest of the world when a man took his first steps on the moon. Certainly the twenty-two-year-old son of Taiwanese immigrants in Los Angeles is different in many ways from other Gen Xers, but he shares a whole set of sociology, trends, and heroes with his native-born counterparts. This is more true today than ever before, as we increasingly become a world community via the World Wide Web.

Equally powerful in shaping the views and values of a generation are the first, nervous, sometimes traumatic days in the labor market. A cohort that joins the workforce begging for jobs feels very differently about life and work from one that joins the workforce when jobs are going begging. The effort needed to bring in that first job makes a lasting mark.

A first job that is a first choice and a stepping stone in a carefully planned career has a distinctly different feel and impact than a job that is a consolation, a disappointment, and a subsistence meal ticket.

The three generations that occupy today's workplace and the fourth generation that is entering it are clearly distinguishable by all these criteria—their demographics, their early life experiences, the headlines that defined their times, their heroes, music, and sociology, and their early days in the workplace. Their differences can be a source of creative strength and a source of opportunity, or a source of stifling stress and unrelenting conflict. Understanding generational differences is critical to making them work *for* the organization and not against it. It is critical to creating harmony, mutual respect, and joint effort where today there is suspicion, mistrust, and isolation.

The Players

The four generations of the American workplace on the cusp of the twenty-first century span a remarkable slice of American and world history. Three major wars, economic booms and busts, social upheavals, rocketing technological achievement, presidential impeachment, and the first steps beyond the boundaries of our planetary bonds are among the milestones that have directly and indirectly shaped the temper of their and our times. They and we have experienced directly and indirectly, and many have lived through, more significant history than perhaps any set of generations that have strode the face of the planet before us.

The four generations of today's workplace addressed here cover nearly eighty birth years, from 1922 to 2000. They are the *Veterans*, 1922–1943; the *Baby Boomers*, 1943–1960; the *Generation Xers*, 1960–1980; and the *Nexters*, those born 1980 and after. Each of these four generations, their formative forces, values, and views, their workplace aspirations and dreads, their hopes and fears, their delights and disappointments, will be addressed in separate chapters.

The thumbnail sketches preview those in-depth treatments, and they should assist the reader in anticipating the broader context in which each exists and the conflicts and clashes that ensue from their differences.

The Veterans (1922–1943)

George and Dorothy are the Dole/Bush/Kennedy/Carter generation. Tom Brokaw calls them the "Greatest Generation" (Fig. 1-1). Bebop-pers and bobby soxers, Rosie the Riveter, and "Don't sit under the apple tree with anyone else but me" compose the heart of this cohort group. All but the youngest came of age before and during World War II, but before the official arrival of the vaunted postwar Baby Boom, and they are the true traditionalists and last of the gray flannel suits, the corporcrats. Think "American values," and you've got their number—civic pride, loyalty, respect for authority, and apple pie. They attend more symphonies than rock concerts, watch more plays than play in pick-up softball games, and eat a lot more steak than tofu.

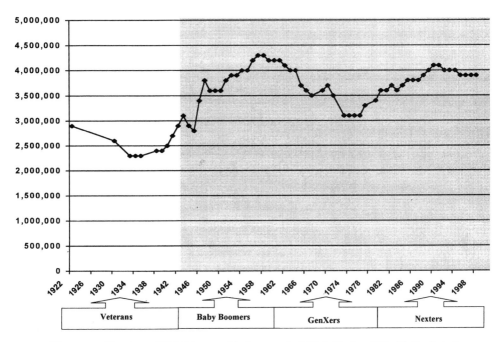

Figure 1-1. Number of U.S. Veterans births recorded (U.S. National Health Statistics).

These aging hangers-on of the workplace are the classic "keepers of the grail" of yesteryear, and they are a pain in the backside for action-oriented Boomers and technology-crazy Xers. They are also an irreplaceable repository of lore and wisdom, practical wiliness, and more than a few critical organizational contacts. Though they are nearing the end of their work-a-day-world conscription, they are still, and yet, good soldiers and solid, no-nonsense performers. If they'd only cut out the Moses act and admit the writing on their tablets now says "Bayer," they'd be a lot more interesting to be around and their advice would be more palatable: like spending time with a wonderful Gram and Gramp, sans the cookies and milk. And, oh yes, those Gray Panthers control a significant part of the optional spending economy, own billions of dollars of Sun Belt real estate, are a staunch political force via the American Association of Retired Persons (AARP), and will continue to be a force well into the twenty-first century. They are still power brokers in U.S. big business, holding the majority of CEO slots in the vaunted Fortune 500 companies. They will not—are not—going gently into that good good-night.

The Baby Boomers (1943–1960)

Tom and Linda, the postwar babies, are graying; and many of their compatriots are looking forward to the unbearable lightness of fulfillment at the end of the tunnel (Fig. 1-2). They'd really rather not be seen as the "problem" in the workplace, though they frequently are. After all, they've been defining everyone else as "the problem" since "Don't trust anyone over 30" was the rule of cool. And, to this day, they define the generational world as "pre-us," "us," and "post-us"when they look to make sense of it. They've never met a problem they couldn't bluff, blunder, or power through, and then pronounce themselves master of and write a book about. If it wasn't invented in the 1970s or 1980s, it can't have a decent return on investment (ROI). "Ready for my *Fortune* cover close-up, Ms. Liebovitz." Their never-flagging "Me first, me last, me only" theme is wearing as thin as their hair. That's the dark side.

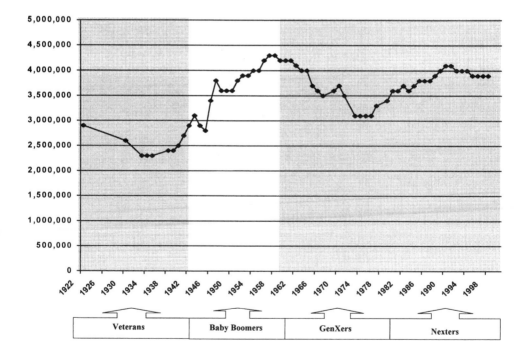

Figure 1-2. Number of U.S. Baby Boomer births recorded (U.S. National Health Statistics).

At the same time this is the cohort group that invented "Thank God, it's Monday!" and the sixty-hour workweek. Boomers are passionately concerned about participation and spirit in the workplace, about bringing heart and humanity to the office, and about creating a fair and level playing field for all. They are, after all, the civil rights, empowerment, and diversity generation. Their energy and enthusiasm, and their ability to become engrossed in cause occupations, have made the business of business the most dramatic story of the last quarter of the twentieth century. And now that Madam Hillary has made turning fifty officially cool, they have a new workplace motto: "Hell no, we won't go." Or was that "Don't trust anyone under fifty"? Or "Life begins at fifty"? Or "This *is* what fifty looks like"? Stay tuned; they will redefine old and cool and important and success a half a dozen or more times before they are done with the world they've sworn to make over in their own Sharper Image.

The Xers (1961–1980)

Breathes there a cohort group with a soul more dark or with such an edgy skepticism about them? Devon and Li are discouraged and disheartened. And they are also technologically adept, clever, resourceful, and willing to work in the same electronics warehouse from dawn until dusk. The Xers are a deeply segmented, fragmented cohort (Fig. 1-3). From the hypertraditionalists who revere and wallow in pseudo-1950s Fifth-Avenue views, values, and dress styles, to the leather-jacketed, Black Stockings who labor to reinvent Beat–and who wear dark glasses after midnight–they are a perplexing lot to work with. Their need for feedback and flexibility, coupled with their hatred of close supervision, is but one of the many conundrums they present to employers. At the same time, they are personally adept and comfortable with change; after all, they've changed cities, homes, and parents all their lives. They are, indeed, the new change masters. And they are much more inclined to keep their own counsel than are their Boomer predecessors. Xers are very clear about the meaning of the word "balance" in their lives: Work is work. And they work to live, not live to work. And where they live can be a shock to Boomers who try to get to know them and "grok" their kool. Especially when their idea of kool can run from "The Partridge Family" to Heroin Chique.

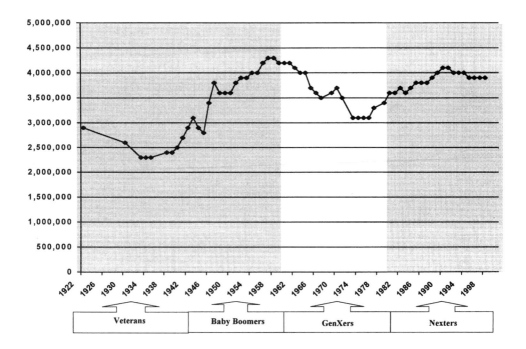

Figure 1-3. Number of U.S. GenXer births recorded (U.S. National Health Statistics).

At the same time, Xers as individuals are more positive about their personal futures than their pessimism and reluctance to be as overtly "gung ho" at work as the Boomers they dislike would indicate. They believe opportunity exists for them, just not on Veteran or Boomer terms. Note please: Bill Gates—a Boomer—hadn't yet founded Microsoft at age 24. Marc Andreessen, the cofounder of Netscape Communications, was worth $54 million by the age of 24, a factoid not lost on the ambitions of hardcore Xers.

Caution: Just as there are Boomers who don't want to be identified with either the Hippie or the Yuppie subspecies of their cohort, there are Xers who categorically reject the label and, more importantly, the dark, cynical, fragile image. As we tested our cohort definitions and delimitations, we encountered a substantial number of mid-1970s-born "Xers" who objected strongly to being called "Xers" and who, indeed, report that they reject out of hand the "Xer" ethic. More on this interesting important subgroup, these "proto-Nexters," later!

The Nexters (1980–2000)

Call this Group 3.5.1, the newest version on the market. Brandon and Crystal are among the smartest, cleverest, healthiest, most-wanted *Homo sapiens* to have ever walked the face of the earth. Their parents see themselves as devoted parents sacrificing to bring this new generation to adulthood. Think soccer moms and Little League dads, and nonstop rounds of swimming meets and karate classes and dancing lessons and computer camp and...you get the picture. They're an optimistic bunch, and what their parents think *is* important to them. In fact, they think their parents are cool. Some Nexters even know the word "cotillion" and like the idea. They have new, easy attitudes toward gender stereotyping and their place in time and space. They express doubt over the wisdom of traditional racial and sexual categorizing, and they have Internet pen pals in Asia who they can, and do, contact at any hour of the day or night. Barriers of time and space appear to have a different, less absolute meaning for them. They aren't confused by the international dateline or perplexed by relativity (Fig. 1-4).

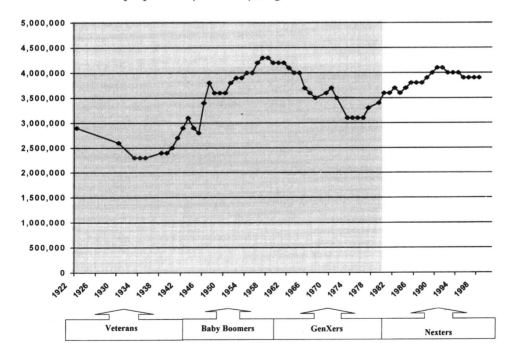

Figure 1-4. Number of U.S. Nexter births recorded (U.S. National Health Statistics).

Table 1-5.

Popular Names Generation	George and Dorothy The Veterans	Tom and Linda The Baby Boomers	Devon and Li Generation Xers.	Brandon and Crystal The Nexters
Also known as...	Traditionalists GIs Mature WW II Generation The Silent Generation Seniors	Boomers	Xers Twenty-somethings Thirteener Baby Busters Post-Boomers	Millennials Generation Y Generation 2001 Nintendo Generation Generation Net Internet Generation
Birth Years	1922–1943	1943–1960	1960–1980	1980–2000
Defining Events and Trends	Patriotism Families The Great Depression WW II New Deal Korean War Golden Age of Radio Silver Screen Rise of labor unions	Prosperity Children in the spotlight Television Suburbia Assassinations Vietnam Civil Rights movement Cold War Women's Liberation The Space Race	Watergate, Nixon resigns Latchkey kids Stagflation Single-parent homes MTV AIDS Computers Challenger disaster Fall of Berlin Wall Wall Street frenzy Persian Gulf Glasnost, Perestroika	Computers Schoolyard violence Oklahoma City bombing *It Takes a Village* TV talk shows Multiculturalism Girls' Movement McGwire and Sosa
Visible Members	Harry Belafonte George Bush Jimmy Carter Geraldine Ferraro Phil Donahue Sidney Poitier Lee Iacocca Gloria Steinem John Glenn	Bill Clinton Hillary Clinton David Letterman Oprah Winfrey Jane Pauley Bill Gates Rush Limbaugh P.J. O'Rourke Mick Jagger	George Stephanopoulis Douglas Coupland Kurt Cobain Jewel Brad Pitt Michael Jordan Matt Groening Neil Stephenson Michael Dell Adam Werback Meredith Bagby	Kerri Strug Macauley Culkin Chelsea Clinton Tara Lipinski LeAnn Rimes
Music of Their Early Years	Swing Big Band Glenn Miller Duke Ellington Benny Goodman Tommy Dorsey Bing Crosby Kate Smith Ella Fitzgerald Frank Sinatra	Rock 'n Roll Acid Rock Elvis The Beatles Rolling Stones Grateful Dead Beach Boys Jimi Hendrix Janis Joplin Bob Dylan Supremes Temptations	Disco Rap Reggae Elton John Bruce Springstein Tina Turner Bon Jovi Michael Jackson Guns'n Roses U2 Prince	Alternative Rap SKA Remix Jewel Puff Daddy Alanis Morrisette Toni Braxton Will Smith Savage Garden Spice Girls Hanson Garth Brooks Backstreet Boys

The few now in the workforce—think fast food, grocery store car-ryout, yard work, babysitting, and web-page building—seem bent on being what one sociologist calls "Good Scouts," willing to work and learn. Of the three older generations, the one with which they feel the most affinity is the Veterans. Indeed, it appears the Nexters could be-come a new-fangled version of that civic-minded group. The view that says generations cycle and recycle back on themselves may be con-firmed with this latest cohort of confident, achievement-oriented young people, or so it seems right now. (Table 1-5 summarizes the early influences on the four generations.)

The Challenge

These four generations—Veterans, Boomers, Xers, and Nexters—have unique work ethics, different perspectives on work, distinct and pre-ferred ways of managing and being managed, idiosyncratic styles, and unique ways of viewing such work-world issues as quality, service, and, well...just showing up for work.

Managing this melange of ages, faces, values, and views is an in-creasingly difficult duty. For one thing, few Americans are able to un-derstand their own generation in context. Canadian pop culture ob-server Marshall McLuhan is purported to have observed, "We don't know who discovered water, but it probably wasn't a fish." Whether the citation is correct or not, the sentiment is. It is difficult to look at one's own life as part of a segment, trend, era, or generation. We each feel too unique and individual—an overarching American value—and too iso-lated to be a simple "statistic"! According to William Strauss and Neil Howe, authors of *Generations*, "people of all ages feel a disconnection with history. Many have difficulty placing their own thought and ac-tions, even their own lives, in any larger story."[5] It is diversity manage-ment at its most challenging. The obvious markers of race and sex have less clear impact on the differences and signal less in the way of differ-ential treatment than do generational differences. As business grows more and more competitive—and companies continue to rightsize, reengineer, and de-layer—frustrated managers are confronted with a Gordian knot of questions. Questions such as:

- How can I get my older employees to sit down and discuss projects with my younger ones, when they can't even share a cup of coffee without snarling at each other? (Or even agree on what a cup of workplace coffee *is*?)

- How can I convince my young employees to listen to their older counterparts when they don't see anything relevant in the older employees' experience? And when my oldsters insist on communicating like World War II generals?

- Some of my most valuable people are just turning fifty, and *they've* laid down the law: forty-hour workweeks—period. Meanwhile, my boss is breathing down my neck to produce, produce, produce; *and* our competition has *mandatory* overtime? What can I do to woo these diverse troops back onto the treadmill? And how can I make them like it?

- A customer just called. He said one of my sales reps—a new, young, technology-savvy hotshot—just told him, "Look, this is obviously the best system out there. If you're too damn dumb to realize it, maybe I should be talking to someone else." Now what do I do?

- A brand-new MBA-type I went to bat for during the hiring process wandered into the second day of the new manager's class two hours late. When the instructor challenged him, he gave him one of those looks and said, "My people have a different time sense than yours. Get used to it." And the CEO was there. And the new kid was a highly recruited, tech type from an ethnic group we need better represented in our workforce. Now where am I?

In Chapter 6 we will look at five cross-generationally friendly companies and their efforts to make moot the problems of generational hostility and its accompanying productivity drains. In Chapter 8 we explore the twenty-one most frequently asked questions and griped-about intergenerational problems, and suggest some answers and solutions.

What follows is a more extensive look at the generational rifts that are dividing today's workplace, the conditions that cause and perpetuate them, and some ways of minimizing—if not extinguishing—them.

We begin with a portrait of each generation, what we and others have learned about their preferences in managing and being managed, leading and working. Then we discuss the implications for helping generations survive and thrive together in today's hectic and high-tension cross-generational workplace.

CHAPTER TWO

THE VETERANS:

What Will the Colonel Do Now—Work? Retire? Consult?
GEORGE AND DOROTHY BORN BETWEEN 1922–1943

"The difficult we do at once;
the impossible takes a bit longer."

—MOTTO OF THE SEABEES

They are the generation whose vision and hard work created the United States as we know it today—a bold, powerful, prosperous, vital, modern democracy with all of its inherent challenges and paradoxes. Viewed as a body, their accomplishments are staggering. "I am in awe of them" writes Tom Brokaw in his book, *The Greatest Generation*.[1] They did indeed have "a rendezvous with destiny" as Franklin Roosevelt so aptly put it. They shook off the Great Depression and rejuvenated a failing economy. They won a world war and hammered out a lasting peace. They built a durable national infrastructure of interstate highways, bridges, and dams. With skillful mothering and masterful teaching, they raised the largest generation of American children.

They built a space program and landed a man on the moon. They created miracle vaccines, and wiped out polio, tetanus, tuberculosis,

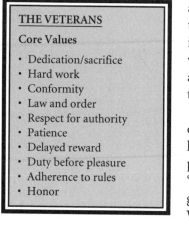

THE VETERANS

Core Values

- Dedication/sacrifice
- Hard work
- Conformity
- Law and order
- Respect for authority
- Patience
- Delayed reward
- Duty before pleasure
- Adherence to rules
- Honor

and whooping cough. Today they hold three-quarters of all the financial assets in the United States. Their total net worth is over $7 trillion, and they have a combined personal income of more than $800 billion.

Their mind-set has so dominated our culture that every other set of beliefs is weighed against theirs. When people argue that we need a return to "family values," they mean we need to go back to the morality of the Veterans. When managers say young employees today lack a work ethic, they mean they don't have the work ethic of the Veterans. When we say, "Parents aren't teaching values in the home anymore," what we really mean is they're not teaching Veteran values. It's the "great American value system," a perspective on the world so pervasive that a large percentage of all generations continue to embrace it today, or rebel against it.

This is the basic Kennedy/Carter/Dole/Bush generation, born before 1943. They're variously labeled the Traditionalists, Matures, Silents, Loyalists, GI Joes, and Seniors. They account for about 25 percent of the work population, where their numbers are shrinking as they move ever more quickly into retirement, part-time work, grand- and great-grand-parenthood, and Sun City. These powerful elders of the workplace—Lee Iacocca, Jack Welch, Mary Kay Ash, Lou Gerstner, Warren Buffett—are the classic "keepers of the grail" of the organizational history and founding tenets. They understand and are comfortable with alternative "big pictures." They are solid, reliable, no-bull performers. With the rising need for skilled labor, unemployment at its lowest in history, and a frightening shortage of good people, the best, the brightest, and the most sprightly among them are quickly being re-recruited by companies that once willingly offered them "early-out" packages.

"Tempered by War, Disciplined by a Hard and Bitter Peace"

The children of the 1920s and 1930s grew up in hard times. If anyone has earned the right to tell those stories that begin, "I walked three miles to school, uphill both ways through the snow and wind...," it's these folks. In 1929, the Stock Market crashed and the bottom fell out of the American economy. The early 1930s ushered in the Great Depression. Nine million Americans lost their life savings. Eighty-six thousand businesses closed their doors for good. More than two thousand banks failed.

Millions of workers lost their jobs, and, by 1932, about fourteen million people were unemployed—nearly one of every four workers. In the preceding decades, the country had become accustomed to abundance; suddenly, the sight of ragged and hungry people waiting in line for soup and sustenance became commonplace. President Herbert Hoover's efforts to turn the economy around failed. "Prosperity is just around the corner," he kept saying, but no one was convinced, and it wasn't to be so. Then the Dust Bowl added insult to injury. The farm economy was already reeling when the worst drought in U.S. history burned up 300,000 square miles of Great Plains crops, turned the soil into dust, and ended forever a way of life for millions. Hundreds of thousands who had tended the soil and fed a growing nation became rootless wanderers blown before the winds that blew away the very soil they had lived on and lived for.

It was a "do without" era, but America's new generation of hardy scouts had gumption—to get things done...to accomplish any worthy goal...to "bear any burden, pay any price." The Empire State Building was the very incarnation of the spirit of the times. The nation's conscience whispered, "Do it big," and, despite—or because of—the times, construction began on the tallest skyscraper in the world. It was com-

---

THE VETERANS

Seminal Events

1927	Lindbergh completes first transatlantic flight
1929	Stock market crashes
1930	U.S. Depression deepens
1931	*Star Spangled Banner* becomes national anthem
1932	Lindbergh baby kidnapped
1932	FDR elected
1933	The Dust Bowl
1933	The New Deal
1934	Social Security system established
1937	Hindenburg tragedy
1937	Hitler invades Austria
1940	United States prepares for war
1941	Pearl Harbor; United States enters World War II
1944	D-Day in Normandy
1945	FDR dies
1945	Victory in Europe and Japan
1950	Korean War

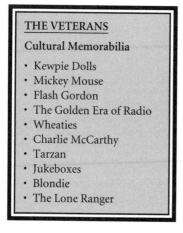

THE VETERANS

Cultural Memorabilia

- Kewpie Dolls
- Mickey Mouse
- Flash Gordon
- The Golden Era of Radio
- Wheaties
- Charlie McCarthy
- Tarzan
- Jukeboxes
- Blondie
- The Lone Ranger

pleted in May 1931, and although it went virtually unoccupied through the depression years, it stood as a monument to grandness—the biggest, the tallest, the best that American enterprise could construct and that the grit of American labor could create.

If older members of the Veterans seem tight with a dollar and somehow risk averse, it is the legacy of the days when a handful of change was all that stood between many a family and an empty larder, and not even banks were trustworthy. Likewise, they can be excused for preferring cash on hand to a portfolio of high-risk junk bonds.

In March 1933, a new American leader was inaugurated. President Franklin Delano Roosevelt had promised in his campaign to put the nation back on track. Enlisting the youth of the country, he instituted the New Deal, which established the Farm Credit Act, the Civilian Conservation Corps, the Tennessee Valley Authority, and thirteen other major bills for creating a modern national infrastructure, preventing another stock market crash, creating new jobs, and restoring the economy. Largely successful, he helped people to feel involved by broadcasting what he called "fireside chats," and, most important to this generation, he restored confidence in government. He reinvented government, shaping it as "the solution" to catastrophic woes, a value and belief instilled in most Veterans and lasting well into the 1990s.

The entertainment industry soothed the suffering psyches of children and their families, serving up a brief escape from the harsh realities of their lives. In 1939, eighty million people spent fifteen cents each week to see not only a feature film, but a newsreel, cartoon, and short subject. According to FDR, it was a "splendid thing that for just 15 cents an American" could "go to a movie and forget his troubles." The silver screen raised their spirits by transporting them to Tara, Oz, and The Ritz. Garbo, Hepburn, Grant, Gable, Astaire, Rogers, and Tracy gave them glamour, glitz, and hope. It was also, of course, the beginning of the golden era of radio. Nearly every home had a set, and when families sat down at the dinner table, the repast might not be a sumptuous meal, but it was accompanied by the magic of live shows—"The Shadow," "The Lone Ranger," and "Amos 'n Andy"—along with the big-band sounds of Goodman, Ellington, and Miller. Kids escaped to comic books, and their greatest hero was Superman. He was powerful, masculine, and logical, with a "can do" attitude. Always upbeat, he didn't let the bad times get him down. The message was to "ac-cen-tu-ate the positive."

In the late 1930s, Americans watched in horror as European parliamentarianism gave way to the tyranny of social democracy and totalitarianism; Hitler's troops marched into Austria, Czechoslovakia, Poland, Scandinavia, France, Romania, Bulgaria, Yugoslavia, and Greece. By July 1940, the only free European nation not in Hitler's grasp was England, where air raids became a regular phenomenon. Out of the troubles in Britain emerged one of the most colorful and dynamic heroes of an era that was to produce an abundance of bigger-than-life heroes—the new Prime Minister Winston Churchill. They were dark times, but Churchill stood for the same sense of determination that was and would continue to be an American and British generational hallmark. "I have nothing to offer but blood, toil, tears, and sweat," he proclaimed. He was fondly caricatured as a bulldog and was adored on both sides of the North Atlantic.

As mentioned earlier, generations catalyze around a "defining moment," an event so momentous that all members of the generation can tell you forever after where they were when the event took place. These moments are so significant that, until we die, we can remember with precise acuity the weather, the scene, even what we were eating and wearing. For most members of this generation, the defining moment occurred at 7:49 A.M. local time on the morning of Sunday, December 7, 1941, when 183 Japanese carrier-based dive bombers and fighters attacked the U.S. Naval Base—and the bulk of the U.S. Pacific Fleet—at Pearl Harbor, Hawaii. As individuals in the Mountain and Pacific time zones awoke, and midwesterners and easterners returned from church, they joined family and neighbors around the kitchen table to listen with horror as events unfolded and were announced on the radio. The next day, President Roosevelt labeled it "a date which will live in infamy." He declared war and called on the well-practiced "can do" spirit of the nation so that, "with the unbounding determination of our people, we will gain the inevitable triumph."

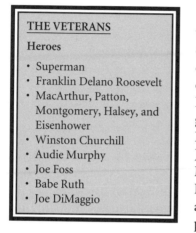

The new generation responded with gusto, inspired by a whole new set of real-life heroes—men whose wits, courage, and commitment were tested in Europe, Africa, and the South Pacific. Men like Bernard Montgomery, Lieutenant General Dwight Eisenhower, Lieutenant Colonel James Doolittle, General Douglas MacArthur, and Admiral William Halsey were revered by the new generation of soldiers. Soon the war had produced heroes from among the Veterans' own cohort: George S. Patton, Audie Murphy, Mark Clarke, and George Marshall. Some said the initials GI stood for "galvanized iron," metal heated to unbearably high temperatures and molded into something strong and durable. Others thought GI stood for "general issue" or "government issue"; indeed, it was a time when conformity and obedience to central authority were considered a national necessity. "Loose lips sink ships" was the watchword of the day; it seemed there were Fascists everywhere looking for ways to destroy the world, even in the Saturday movie serials. President Roosevelt urged the young to discard the concept of "each individual for himself" and to embrace instead the concept of "a broad highway on which thousands of your fellow men and women are advancing with you." The civic mind believed that standardized things were the "best," "most modern," "advanced," and "efficient"—and the Veterans marched in formation. It is fitting that they wore uniforms more than any other cohort, from their Boy Scout greens, to their Civilian Conservation Corps (CCC) uniforms, to their fatigues and dress blues and whites in World War II.

By late 1944, the Allied forces were beginning to break Hitler's iron will in the European theater and to thwart the Japanese in the South Pacific. While young men in their twenties fought for freedom on land, on sea, and in the air, the young women at home sacrificed and served as well. Rosie the Riveter and fifteen million other American women answered the call for production, turning out ships, tanks, airplanes, and weapons at unprecedented rates. The war effort at home involved doing without, and this generation of women did it good-naturedly, creatively, with flair. Living on rations, they "used it up, wore it out, made it do, or did without," conserving coffee, sugar, rubber, nylon, and gasoline. Finally, in 1945, peace had been earned: in Europe in May and in the Pacific in September. World War II was over, and a new era was about to begin, one in which the Veterans had earned high rank and set a tone of accomplishment they would pursue with the vigor of a war effort for the next fifty years.

Born Too Late: The Sandwich Group

When considering the Veterans, it's important to remember that the generation's two halves were not created equal. Those born before 1930 set the pace, while their younger cohorts moved quietly into the parade. Those in the older set were just the right age to answer the call to serve in World War II. They're the ones who fit comfortably into the sociology we've spoken of here, and they do so proudly.

On the other hand, the second-halfers, the Sandwich Group, born primarily in the 1930s, were not old enough to serve. They waited at home while the cohort ahead made big sacrifices to create a brighter future. Some of these second-halfers will tell you they wanted the war to go on and on, so that when their time came, they could prove themselves as worthy as their older brothers. With Hiroshima and Nagasaki, though, the war came to an abrupt halt, and the younger group has had to live in the shadow of all that their older cohort stood for and accomplished. Though many second-halfers did, in fact, serve bravely and with distinction in the Korean War, it has simply never "counted" in quite the same way as service in World War II.

They don't feel worthy of accepting the mantle the older cohort wears so proudly. Yet they can't identify completely with the Boomers who came along just behind them. In fact, they are positioned, both historically and demographically, in a trough between the two. Growing up in very different eras and separated by conflicting basic beliefs and values, the Veteran and the Boomer personalities sit in stark contrast to one another. The Sandwich Group rests in a trough between. They've never had their own president. The United States went straight from Veteran George Bush to Boomer Bill Clinton. Likewise, they are much fewer in number than those born the decade before or after them. As a result, they've grown up with no real sense of generational place, deeming themselves unworthy of Veteran status and unwilling to call themselves Boomers—only sensing they are "tweeners," whatever that may mean.

Many did, in fact, act as forerunners, pacesetters, and trendsetters for their boisterous younger cohorts. Think of Ray Charles, Jane Fonda, and Gloria Steinem. They campaigned for John Kennedy, joined civil rights marches, and protested the war in Vietnam. In fact, the Sandwich Group supplied all the major leaders of the modern Civil Rights movement, including Martin Luther King, Cesar Chavez, and Russell Means. And it was from their ranks that the leaders of the feminist movement of the 1970s came.

Sociologically, they found themselves in between, as well. The country's mores around sexuality and marriage were shifting, and none felt the brunt of it so much as these second-halfers. As the Boomers mounted the soapbox to offer lip service to open marriage and free love, this group actually experimented, and then paid the price, in the shadows, getting sent off to the Florence Crittendon Home for Unwed Mothers to bear the baby the elders were ashamed to acknowledge.

But the second-halfers learned valuable skills in in-between land. Nobody can "get along" quite the way they do. Unlike the Boomers, they can listen to an Archie Bunker without getting emotionally involved, easily, and with humor. They are fair and impartial, with great communication skills and a deep belief in the power of dialogue. They don't mind being placed in the role of mediator. Torn as many are between Veteran and Boomer values and sensibilities, they are more comfortable with mediation than with direct, aggressive advocacy.

Today, they are transforming elderhood, forcing all the younger generations to redefine when "old" happens and what it looks like. After all, it was Gloria Steinem, a Sandwich Group member, who, when she turned fifty, grew so tired of hearing she didn't "look" fifty that she had a t-shirt made that read, "This *is* what 50 looks like." Get over it.

The Veterans' Generational Personality

They formed their view of the world in the shadow of hard times and the bright light of America's triumph over them. They took up the challenge to rebuild the nation, the economy, and even war-torn Europe, to build a foundation that would allow future generations to live out the American Dream worldwide—or so they truly believed. As they came of age, the nation was in transition from a primarily agrarian way of life to a manufacturing mind-set.

- *Veterans like consistency and uniformity.* Birdseye introduced frozen foods—comfortably consistent, uniform, standardized— in the 1930s. Manufacturing offered not only consistency but conveniences that made everyday life easier and more pleasant. Household objects, from dinnerware to dishwashers, took on a sleek new look. In 1934, nylon was developed; in 1935, the acrylics Lucite and Plexiglas burst onto the market; and in 1937, polyurethane and polystyrene promised to revolutionize equipment, housewares, and gadgets. No wonder the World War II era family friend in the 1960s movie "The Graduate" takes the fresh-faced young Boomer aside at his graduation celebration to whisper "just one word" into his ear—"plastics." A generational icon and symbol of triumph of man over the vagaries of nature.
- *Veterans like things on a grand scale*—niftier, more new fangled, bigger, better. The new technologies allowed Americans to become far more mobile; transportation quickly became faster, less expensive, and more available. The New Deal had created a network of rails on which aerodynamically streamlined and affordable trains carried mom, dad, sister, and brother from Los Angeles to Tampa to see Aunt Tilly. But, by the end of the war and rationing, everyone pined to travel by car, and now that automobiles were mass produced and sold at prices that middle incomers could handle and were eager to commit to, the personal automobile became the symbol of freedom, prosperity, and accomplishment, the antithesis of mass transit, troop movement, schedules, and timed group transportation. Individuality was reasserting itself. Auto courts, motels, and service stations sprung up along the brand new interstates to give these liberated drivers a place to rest their road-weary heads and replace their fraying fan belts. In the late 1920s, Lindbergh had flown solo from New York to Paris, raising the bar on air travel. By 1932, Douglas Aircraft was producing planes designed for passengers instead of cargo. During the war, aircraft easily and routinely spanned the Atlantic and soared above the Himalayas. The nation was moving toward a bright future of bustling enterprise, and it was doing it on wings and wheels of manmade steel.

Some of their favorite films were giant epics like "The Bible," the huge blockbuster "Gone With the Wind," and the kaleidoscopic productions of Busby Berkeley. Government always has and likely always will play a big role in their lives, and they have placed their faith in big institutions. One-third of all members of this generation are war veterans. The GI Bill helped them pay for college educations, and VA loans assisted them in buying their first homes. Never mind that the GI Bill was actually initiated to keep them out of the workforce while a peacetime economy developed, or that the VA home loan program was a resuscitator for a housing industry that had gone comatose during the war. To the Veterans, it felt like government was coming to their personal rescue and aid; and peacetime government grew to meet that perception of peacetime partner. Unprecedented numbers of Veterans worked in government jobs. Currently, Social Security and Medicare are paying the largest pensions and providing the most wide-ranging medical care in U.S. history to today's senior citizens. The circle is complete, cradle to grave.

- *Veterans are conformers.* They learned from their Boy Scout leaders, President Roosevelt, and their drill sergeants to stay in line, be "a regular guy," and "do the right thing." They started young; the men married at twenty-three and the women at twenty—a full six years earlier than today's averages—and they started their families right away. The trumpet call to produce postwar Baby Boom babies was sounding, and 94 percent of all American women responded with an average of three plus children each. The roles of the sexes were crisp and clear, and both men and women accepted them without much question. "Gals" took very seriously their job of creating a wholesome and comfortable home for the mister and the kids. They'll tell you it was the best job they ever had— best working conditions, best pay, most rewarding. Their men were macho guys whose mettle had been tested and who now were busy building a better society. Men were men, modeled after John Wayne—left brained, rational, with confidence in the scientific method: it's true if it can be proven so, with numbers, in black and white. They were taught clear rules about which topics were and were not appropriate for conversation, particularly in a "mixed" group that included "ladies."

- *Veterans believe in logic, not magic.* They prefer conversations that stay with "appropriate topics," and they often find their Baby Boomer adult children prone to make conversation uncomfortable with talk of feelings and "too personal" information. They much prefer to watch violence on TV or in the movies than to be subjected to love scenes, especially those with graphic sexual content.

- *Veterans are disciplined.* Veterans get as frustrated as everybody else with things like general confusion, poor service, inconsistent leaders, and poor directions, but they're far more willing to put up with it than their younger cohorts. They'll suffer silently. The word "snafu"—"situation normal, all fouled up"—grew out of World War II experiences and became a popular phrase of the era. When an order didn't make sense, the automatic response was, "Who knows? Some general made it up," but it was uttered quietly to close confidants. It would've been disloyal to say it aloud and in public. It was simply the way the world worked, and this generation didn't, and doesn't, become irritated—at least out loud—with glitches. One member of the generation says it this way, "All of life's a force-fit. All you need to keep things going is a big hammer and some shims."

- *Veterans are past oriented and history absorbed.* After all, they helped conquer the Evil Empire and a malevolent dictator in order to create a promising future. They feel the future is created by history; when it comes time to make a tough decision, their tendency is to look at the past to find precedents: What worked? What didn't? They make their decisions based on that data. This mode of operation lends predictability and stability to their world, a world that seems to have grown increasingly more chaotic. It's true all generations become somewhat more focused on the past as they grow older, but for the Veterans, the past is an important part of their sociology. This is the final American generation to be part of what Alvin Toffler calls "the second wave," which centered on the development of commerce and industry and was guided by traditions and history.[2] The late Clare Graves, an industrial psychologist who pioneered a body of work regarding personal values and their effects on the workplace, noted that, as we shifted into the information age, people became more future oriented.[3] But the World War II generation was taught, and continues to believe, that the future is a product of history, that we have little control over destiny, and that we make our best decisions when we are guided by the lessons history offers.

- *Veterans have always believed in law and order.* The chaos of war and the thuggery of the depression taught them the value of law. Depression-era movies, such as "Public Enemy Number One," were a constant stream of morality plays that reinforced the law-and-order message. Today, they are more likely than any other generation to favor stricter laws and longer jail terms.[4] They have a much more definitive sense of right and wrong, of good and bad, than the generations to follow, who often see every question as having a field of correct answers. When Veterans went to school, they lost points for the wrong answer; the teacher wasn't interested in how they solved the problem, just that they got it right. They learned that divorce is wrong, and they've stuck with that notion. When the marriage was struggling, they hung in there, even if just for the kids, sometimes at high personal stakes. If life wasn't fun, "those were the breaks."

- *Veterans' spending style is conservative.* They have always saved and paid cash. Remember "layaway"? A gal saw something she really wanted in the department store, comparison shopped, pondered its purchase carefully, asked to have it "set back," made monthly installments, then finally picked it up after she made her final payment. Of course, the Veterans buy American. They're the most fiercely materialistic and brand-loyal cohort of consumers in the marketplace today. They tend to buy up inside a product line. For his first car, a guy just home from the

THE VETERANS	
Markings:	Conservative, somewhat "dressy" clothing: coats and ties or nylons; neatly trimmed hair; American cars; golf clubs; mixed drinks
Spending style:	Save and pay cash
What they read:	*Reader's Digest, USA Today, Time, Wall Street Journal*
Their humor:	*The Better Half*

war usually bought the lowest-priced Chevy. Then, for his next couple of cars, he traded up inside the Chevy line. Maybe for his next car, he changed over to a Pontiac or Olds. Then he upgraded in that brand. If he made it big, the ultimate purchase was a Cadillac if he'd started with a Chevy, or a Lincoln if he was a Ford man.

The power and influence of the World War II generation has just begun to ebb. For the last few years, nearly thirty thousand World War II veterans have died each month. Nevertheless, for nearly six decades, they were the only generation to support the winner of every election, from Franklin Roosevelt in 1930 to George Bush in 1988. In the political arena, count on them exerting their strength for at least another decade. Their influence in the workplace will likely remain for decades, long after they've retired and even died off. Here's why: The hierarchical method of running business was uniquely suited to armies and manufacturing. It worked best to have the brains at the top, in the executive ranks, and the brawn on the bottom, on the front lines. Top management, the generals, made the important decisions and passed them down the chain of command, where they were carried out without comment, respectfully and thoroughly.

Competition, the demand for speedy responsiveness, the information age, and the nature of workers themselves are, of course, challenging the old order. But, as much as we read about flattened organizations, empowerment, employee involvement, and democratic workplaces, the hard truth is that most operations are still, underneath it all, basically hierarchical. It's a tough change to make, a hard habit to break. Not only are managers having a hard time turning over information and decisions, but the average nonmanagerial employee is reluctant to get involved in many of the more challenging parts of management, like appraising the performance of fellow workers. When push comes to shove, most everyone likes to have someone to blame for the myriad of things that just aren't right, and bosses make perfect targets in the blame game. Thus, the most enduring workplace legacy of the Veterans is likely to be the old-style command-and-control leadership they learned in war, modified for peacetime, particularly manufacturing, and which they believe in their hearts is the only sane way to organize work—and society.

Though World War II was the great annealing event of the leading edge of this generation's youth, its emotional impact and circumstance and its value-shaping power are largely lost on later generations. Boomers understand it intellectually, and a few vaguely, mistily, recall it. Gen Xers know it as an historical data point and a textbook, multiple-choice, pop-quiz answer. Nexters know it from movies such as "The Thin Red Line."

Most, but not all, of those who actually served in World War II are disinterested, if not unable, to describe their experiences in any meaningful way. Those who try often are frustrated by their inability to characterize the experiences without oversimplifying or sounding braggadocio. How do you describe an experience that was alternately frightening, exhilarating, humiliating, boring, frustrating, and incomprehensible? Or make sense of the oft-heard GI Joe-ism, "I wouldn't trade the experience for a million dollars or do it over again for two."

So it is that Veterans have become indebted to Steven Spielberg for his film "Saving Private Ryan" and the portrayal of their experience in terms they could never summon.

Whether it is true—as media critic Neal Gabler contends—that "Saving Private Ryan" is "the bloody, heartfelt, cultural salve to the divisions and tumult that have riven this country throughout the postwar period" or simply entertainment, it tells a story the Veterans have had trouble conveying. It compellingly tells the tale of the last time this country was united in a common, moral cause. And it previews their later attitudes, feelings, and behaviors in the workplace. Given orders that sent them into frightening personal peril, they somehow survived. They learned to accept and follow incomprehensible orders ever after, and to expect their own orders to be followed as they themselves had in much more dire circumstances.

George: A "Regular" Guy

Most days, you can find George, 74, on the golf course or the driving range near his home in Green Valley, Arizona. George semiretired there a few years ago from the company he founded in 1960. Although he's no longer involved in the day-to-day operations of the business, he continues as chairman of the board and puts his mark on virtually every important decision. Make no mistake about it: George remains the most influential person in the company.

The defining moments of George's life occurred during World War II, when George flew a Hellcat off an aircraft carrier in the South Pacific. After returning from the war, he married his best friend's little sister, who had turned into a real beauty while he'd been gone, completed his college degree, began his family, and earned an MBA from Stanford. After eight years in the group department of one of the big national life insurance corporations, he set up a small benefits consulting firm, which developed into a thriving company of two hundred people. It would be fair to say that George had two life partners: his job and his wife. He became known in the trade as a no-nonsense guy with unquestionable ethics. He ran a tight ship where his employees revered him for his straightforward manner. There was never a question as to who was boss. George worked hard, putting in long days, a night or two a week, and an occasional weekend. And it paid off: The investments he made with his profits will pay the couple's bills and finance a very comfortable lifestyle for as long as they live.

Today, George maintains his business acuity, mostly. Faxes arrive in his office four or five times a day. He carries his cell phone with him on the golf course, though he grumbles mightily about the way it interferes with his game. A copy of the *Wall Street Journal* is delivered to his desert home driveway every weekday morning. He finds the whole concept of corporate layoffs and downsizing distasteful. He operates on the premise that he is responsible for his people; during lean times, he has always found a way to meet payroll. Having always been the leader and key decision maker in his own business, he's put off by what he calls "committee decision making" and many of the other recent business trends he hears about.

George is active in the Lions Club and attends his investment group's monthly breakfast. He reads AARP publications and regularly talks to his buddies on the phone about political issues that disturb him. George's wife has allowed him—home is her domain—to maintain his office in their home. Today, along with his World War II memorabilia, we'll find a desktop PC. He was a quick study when it came to learning computer basics, and he grasped the "big picture" with no problem. He occasionally sends and receives e-mails—and a couple of times he's read about a company whose stock he was interested in on their web site—but George would tell you that, in all honesty, he thinks this whole computer thing is overrated. He will admit that a lot of his friends see their PCs as super CB radios, regularly sending e-mails with "off-color" jokes and cartoons. Most of them track their investments online. And yes, the web is giving them better mobility and access to more information than their own parents had in their dotage.

George is enjoying his more leisurely lifestyle. But something that troubles him, though he's far too proud to ever say it, is that people in his old company seem to have begun to think of him as "old school." Not that he'd want to go back to work full time. He's glad to be free of the day-to-day stress and grind, but he would be delighted if his employees would tap into his expertise and experience more often. And it really ticked him off last Christmas when that cute little thing behind the counter at the airline advised him that she could request a cart to convey him from concourse A to concourse F. He isn't that old yet!

Dorothy: A Tweener

It is 8:00 A.M., and Dorothy, 61, is leaving her home in the Chicago suburbs to make her daily twenty-five-minute commute to corporate headquarters. It amazes her to think that her career has spanned nearly forty years. She has been with this company in a variety of positions for twenty-two of them. Today she is director of diversity, and it is likely she has reached the apex of her career. There is probably no other place for her but out. But that doesn't bother her much. Her investments have been solid, and she really has no plans to retire. She is relishing her current position and all the perks that come with it, and she will likely move into part-time consulting in another three or four years. She has friends who have gone that route, downsized their lifestyle a bit, and thrived on the result.

Dorothy grew up with four brothers and sisters in a middle-class home on Chicago's south side. She has always pushed herself hard, and she earned a scholarship to a rather highbrow eastern college, where she found herself outside the mainstream socially, but where she excelled academically.

After graduation, she took a service assistant position in the international division of a large New York City bank. In five years she worked her way into the international correspondence room and from there into the personnel department. All of which made her perfect recruitment bait for the Chicago bank where she works now. Soon after returning to Chicago, she found herself caught up not only in the emerging Civil Rights movement, but in the early women's movement as well. Those lessons became the foundation for her current career and her life.

Not long ago, Dorothy reached a personal milestone. She has found herself to be a role model and mentor for younger women all her life. She decided, as her sixtieth birthday approached, that she wanted to pave the way for her younger coworkers to think differently about turning sixty. She spoke with many of them as the birthday approached, assuring them that she was looking forward with delight to splurging and celebrating her maturity with her two sisters at a California spa.

Dorothy is an extrovert and a charmer. She is active in her church, the Urban League, and a half-dozen professional associations. Although her job has grown somewhat less demanding in the last couple of years, she finds herself busy nearly every night of the week with committee meetings, fund raisers, and community affairs.

Dorothy would call George one of the "good ol' boys" and would feel a bit uncomfortable finding herself lumped into his generational profile. Though she clearly isn't a Boomer, Dorothy doesn't identify with the World War II personality, either. She knows Glenn Miller, the jitterbug, and swing from the "old movies" and is surprised by the current swing-dancing fad, something she vaguely remembers her parents doing. She does exemplify the work ethic, loyalty, and discipline of her older cohorts, but she also has spoken up all her life for the Boomer tenets of participation, involvement, and fairness.

Dorothy, more than anything else, is a great communicator. She moves with ease into and out of distinctly different groups of people. She listens with heart, and she speaks in such a way that those around her stop what they're doing and focus on what she has to say.

THE VETERANS
On the Job
Assets
• Stable
• Detail oriented
• Thorough
• Loyal
• Hard working
Liabilities
• Inept with ambiguity and change
• Reluctant to buck the system
• Uncomfortable with conflict
• Reticent when they disagree

George and Dorothy on the Job

George and Dorothy, on the surface, appear to come from different worlds. Yet, when it comes to work, they are surprisingly alike. They are part of the cohort of Americans who were children before and during the major sociological event of their times—World War II. Their childhoods took place in an era of hardship and struggle, strong nuclear families, and faith in big business and government.

They share a belief in the intrinsic value of work. Both grew up in times when most people were trained once for life. The question, "What are you going to be when you grow up?" was valid; people didn't reanswer it every few years. Members of their generation held just one to four jobs over a lifetime. Both George and Dorothy tend to be conservative and loyal, and they honor history and the past. They differ slightly in their view of authority. George thinks the power of an organization sits at "the top," and Dorothy believes in delegating and getting the opinions of those who report to her; but both grew up in a hierarchical world. They understand it, know how to work with it, and have developed a certain comfort with it.

George and Dorothy both feel a bit uncomfortable with technology, though they've adapted to it differently. They dislike voice mail and prefer personal service. George doesn't have an ATM card, and he threatens to hang up if the phone isn't answered by a real person. His wife made their voice mail recording at home, and they haven't changed it in two years. Dorothy found herself forced a few years ago to adapt to faxes, voice mail, and e-mail, and she appreciates the ease they have added to her workday. She's developed excellent technical skills, but they didn't "come naturally" to her.

Working with George and Dorothy is different than working with members of younger generations. They see the world of work in subtly different, but important, ways. Working for them or with them, selling to them, or influencing their opinions requires understanding them: who they are, what forces shaped them, what is important to them, and what they want now. Even if you aren't *of* their generation, they're worth your time; after all, their way of thinking laid the foundation for everything the workplace is today. If history holds any lessons of value for today, George and Dorothy are the living repositories of that wisdom.

Their Work Ethic

Good or bad, it's fair to say that many, if not most, managers hanker for associates with the Veteran work ethic—at least the part of it that includes loyalty, dependability, and stick-to-it-ism. As employees grow increasingly more sophisticated, demanding rights and privileges, managers of all generations become more and more nostalgic for people who believe in "an honest day's work for an honest day's pay" and who aren't big on "rocking the boat." Many Vets' parents lost their jobs during the Great Depression, and the whole family experienced hardships. As a result, members of this cohort don't take a job for granted; instead, they're grateful for it. In their view, work is noble and ennobling; it is something to be revered. Their lives have not been easy, but that's okay. They worked hard to get things accomplished, and that's how they wanted it.

Their work ethic was hugely influenced by the manufacturing economy, a perspective most Boomers and Gen Xers, who grew up in the postindustrial world, would never experience and never really understand. The Veterans experienced uncertainty and insecurity during the Great Depression. The postwar manufacturing boom provided a certain security where there had been none before, but the Veterans knew there were no guarantees; they knew that they too were, by and large, interchangeable parts, just as they had been in the war. As they advanced in their careers and their corporations aged, these folks hung in there. When, in the 1980s, many long-time employees were "riffed," "reengineered," "laid off," and put out to pasture in the downsizing tsunami, the lesson was not lost on this generation. It confirmed much of what they knew and feared all along.

Just as they are loyal consumers, they are loyal employees—up to a point. Because of the world war and its aftermath, they are fiercely loyal to the United States and its products. They're the ones who responded with "Buy American" bumper stickers when, in the 1970s, the Japanese exported increasing numbers of automobiles into the U.S. market. Most Veterans would rather eat their shirts than drive a German or Japanese car, depending on the theater in which they fought. They have long memories. So it is with work. They tend to view a job as something to have over the long haul. They figure the company has made sacrifices for them, and vice versa, and many have stayed all the years required for that gold watch. They created the strongest union movement in history, banding together to organize their coworkers to overcome unfair labor practices, tyrannical bosses, and inhumane working conditions, in much the way they had joined together to overcome two tyrannies in World War II. But bosses wanting "more for less" isn't seen as sinful or a breach of a social contract. It is "just the way of the world," just one darned thing after another. There's always another battle to be fought.

Veteran employees grew up valuing obedience over individualism on the job. Find an old *Reader's Digest* from the 1930s and you'll see that following the leader was highly valued and was taught rigorously to America's children. Members of this cohort tend to feel confident in their own abilities, but they were taught to respect leaders and their institutions. As a result, you'll rarely find your older employees speaking out—loudly—against authority. This can be a welcome relief or a troubling challenge. On the one hand, it's great to have a good soldier who simply does what you ask without demanding your rationale. On the other hand, you may find that when your older employees disagree, their paths of communication are rather circuitous and indirect. They carry with them the residue of a value that says "I don't get it, but the big boys must. That's why they're in charge."

Veterans tend to get satisfaction from the work itself (though that satisfaction tends to come of doing a job well, rather than from seeing extraordinary meaning in the work they do). You won't find them focused, particularly at this stage in their careers, on climbing the corporate ladder. They'll leave that to their younger Boomer and Gen X counterparts. They also tend to get far less stressed out than other employees. Perhaps because their lives are a less complex balancing act now—most of their kids left the nest quite some time ago—they feel less rushed. And, of course, they never had the "you can have it all" ethic so prevalent among the Boomers. They know that, in fact, you can't have it all: duty comes before pleasure; hard work and sacrifice pay off over the long haul; and success comes quietly without a lot of self-aggrandizing hype and lip service.

Where They Work

Veterans, attracted to security and stability, went to work originally for big companies and government. Up until the last decade, manufacturing was particularly depen-

> **THE VETERANS**
>
> **Messages That Motivate**
>
> - "Your experience is respected here."
> - "It's valuable to the rest of us to hear what has—and hasn't—worked in the past."
> - "Your perseverance is valued and will be rewarded."

dent on this generation of workers. Today, most of the nation's senior business and government leaders are members of the Sandwich Group, filling the ranks of executives, senior officers, and board members. They've been attracted away from big cities. Members of the Veterans always tended to live outside the metropolitan areas, and, as they've aged, they have moved into rural areas, suburbs, and small towns. They tend to avoid the inner city, which feels chaotic and lawless to them, and disturbs their preference for law and order. Most members of this generation have small-town roots; in their elder years, they want to recapture that lifestyle.

The highest proportion of self-employed workers in the United States comes from the fifty-five- to sixty-four-year-old cohort. Working on a part-time or on a contractual basis, they are consultants, writers, researchers, and tinkerers. Many have found that their empty nests have created new, less pressured employment options for them. As they begin to make the transition from full-time career to full retirement, they find they are desperately needed in the job market, and that new technologies—PCs, fax machines, e-mail, and cellular phones—allow them to blend part-time self-employment with their leisure time.

The Workplace of the 1950s

To understand the Veteran associate or executive, it is helpful to keep in mind the workplace they first entered and that shaped their view of what "ought to be."

Division of labor	Executives supplied the thinking, made the decisions, and passed them down. Workers supplied the brawn, carried out the plans, and did most of the labor.
Rank and status	Seniority and age correlated.
Structure	A clear, well-defined hierarchy. People knew where they stood.
Advancement	Employees moved up the ladder, rung by rung, through perseverance and hard work.
Relationships	Formal, almost military-like. Employees called those above them on the organization chart by their last name, with "Mr." in front of it.
Authority	Call it respect, call it fear, call it a social norm—there was a clear distance between the boss and worker. They didn't often socialize.
Conversation	When people at more than one level were involved, conversations were limited to the work issue at hand. It was irregular to talk about one's personal life, especially about intimate issues such as problems with the "Missus," save over several drinks off premises, if then. Executives on the

	same level often discussed their golf swings, but that was about as far beyond the world of work as things went.
Boundaries	"Work life" and "family life" were separate and distinct.
Speaking up	When it came to asserting an opinion about one's own career or a business issue, there were certain unwritten rules about what and how a junior member could say what he wanted to say. He was best served by making rather oblique references to the topic on his mind, and he was likely to get answers couched in third-party language: "The company thinks very highly of you. We haven't seen a way to move you along just yet, but management thinks if you're patient, there will be a place for you at the top."

Their Leadership Style

In leadership roles, Veterans tend toward a directive style, which was standard operating procedure in the workplace they first entered. In many ways, command-and-control leadership and executive decision making was a good system; it was simple, clear, and evident, without all the complexities of getting the masses involved. It got things done, and it produced legendary leaders like Lombardi, Patton, and MacArthur.

Prevailing leadership theories began to change in the 1960s with the advent of "T-groups," theory X–theory Y, job satisfaction concerns, and encounter groups. But, in truth, early attempts at participative management and employee involvement were less than successful, more often than not causing frustration and poor morale. Most Veterans have never seen a compelling reason to change their leadership style, though many have learned to talk the game quite well. After all, their generation accomplished far more than the big-mouthed, big-dreaming Boomers ever have or will—ask 'em.

If the Veterans in your organization are in leadership positions, expect them to take charge, delegate, and make the bulk of decisions themselves. If called on it, they may apologize, but not with much enthusiasm. Expect, also, to be a bit surprised at how well some employees respond to this management style. There are a surprising number of Boomers and Gen Xers who like being able to leave their work at work at the end of the workday and appreciate a take-charge manager who allows them to do just that. Current research shows that Nexters are attracted to this style of leadership and may actually emulate it.

As Team Member

Don't count Veterans out when you're forming teams. After all, they grew up working as a team, and they're very civic minded. They watched the nation form teams that worked together to overcome hardships. They witnessed business and government come together during the New Deal to conquer the depression. They saw the power of union membership and collective action make dramatic changes in workplace dynamics, and they have seen the impact of the collective actions of all shape and manner of special-interest groups. The early Veterans have already made Gray Pantherhood a potent set of political alliances.

It's just that the teamwork has changed its look a bit in the last fifteen years in business, with a new sense of equality throughout the team. During their tenure, Veterans worked on many teams, but under strong leaders who told them exactly what to do, how, and when. They learned to conform to the needs of large efforts, as soldiers, citizens, and factory workers.

Recently, as consultants, we've seen very strong teams where the majority of team members were Veterans, or held a similar work ethic, and the team leader was willing to take a rather directive role.

On the other hand, we've seen such teams come apart when a younger team leader did not enforce rules, policy, and mutual agreements consistently, allowed the stress of continual change to affect the team, and failed to manage the generational differences of the team members.

A Word About Teams

All generations participate on teams of some sort. What sets the generations apart are the size, rules, and roles. For the Veterans, the team was huge—the U.S. Army, for example, with command and control rules, with highly specialized roles and a strong central authority figure. For Boomers, the group is community sized—"It Takes a Village"—interconnected like a commune, with shared leadership. The Xer team can be virtual rather than real and often involves no more than three people; it has the rules of a jazz improv group and no defined leadership. It looks like the Nexters will form huge civic-minded teams, much like the Veterans did, teams that include everyone. Neil Howe, a historical economist who studies generational cycles, predicts that the Nexter motto will be "No one gets left behind."[5]

If you want a more concrete model for guidance, just look at the kinds of sports teams each generation embraces. Veterans go for baseball and football, which have big teams with highly specialized rules and roles for each member. Boomers tend toward soccer and basketball, in which the teams are smaller and whoever has the ball is in charge. Xers tend toward solitary sports like rock climbing and roller blading. Expect to see a resurgence of large-team sports with the next generation.

Managing the Veteran

Managers of all ages tell us there are traits of the Veteran worker they absolutely treasure and that their older employees offer some unique challenges. The ease and pleasantry with which they deal with customers and their dependability top the list of attributes. Conversely, we hear that Veterans sometimes buck the authority of younger managers, that they are occasionally overbearing when directing others—possibly because of their "one right answer" tendency, and that they often get stuck in the "we've never done it that way" school of thinking. Whether George, Dorothy, and their counterparts report to you or work on your level, their wisdom, talents, and skills are unassailable, though sometimes their "hard won" truths are dated and irrelevant. With employee retention at the top of the list of contemporary cost-containment measures, it is wise to do all you can to keep them motivated, productive,

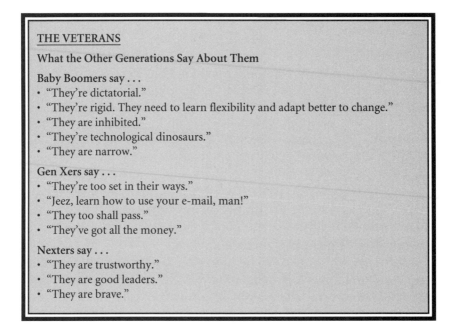

THE VETERANS

What the Other Generations Say About Them

Baby Boomers say . . .
- "They're dictatorial."
- "They're rigid. They need to learn flexibility and adapt better to change."
- "They are inhibited."
- "They're technological dinosaurs."
- "They are narrow."

Gen Xers say . . .
- "They're too set in their ways."
- "Jeez, learn how to use your e-mail, man!"
- "They too shall pass."
- "They've got all the money."

Nexters say . . .
- "They are trustworthy."
- "They are good leaders."
- "They are brave."

and employed by your organization. Take care in how attractive, and how many, early-out packages your organization offers.

Always keep in mind the workplace they first joined; it laid the foundation for the way they think of work today. The workplace of the 1950s was made up mostly of men. Gender roles were stereotypical; most of the women who worked were nurses, secretaries, paper processors, light manufacturing drudges, or teachers. Corporate men wore white shirts—only—and arrived and departed with their hats on. They've seen the changes, adapted to and adopted them, but they are not necessarily enamored of them. Their adaptations are of behavior, not attitude or heart. That, in and of itself, is important to remember: you can rely on them to change their behavior when requested and required. Do not expect their hearts to follow. Their attitudes and thoughts are their business, not yours.

If you're from a younger generation and managing a Veteran, it's worth learning from them about their background, experiences, work preferences, and personal needs. Go to lunch. Or breakfast. Or coffee. Break the paradigm, and earn their trust. It *will* take time. And don't expect to learn everything at one sitting.

Respect their experience, but don't be intimidated by it. If you grew up in a home where you learned traditional values, such as respect for elders, that's great, but don't let that respect get in the way of effective management. Go ahead and respect your older employees, but also remember that you're the boss for good reason. Be honest. Say the hard stuff when it needs to be said.

Some Key Principles

Recruiting

1. Don't limit your consideration of older employees to full-time employment only. The "all or nothing" transition patterns of the 1950s and 1960s—straight out of full-time employment, then cold turkey into retirement—are far less popular with them today than was the case a decade ago. A good proportion of these older workers are not interested in leaving the workforce entirely, and they welcome opportunities to share their lessons with others.

2. Be open minded and consider using older workers for part-time or project employment.

3. Messages that speak to family, home, patriotism, and traditional values touch the right buttons.

4. Let them know their age and experience will be considered assets, not liabilities. Phrases like "I could really use your help and experience on this project" ring the right bells.

5. Use clear enunciation and good grammar. Include "please" and "thank-you," and avoid profanity like the plague. (Surprisingly, these protocols are making something of a comeback among the youngest of employees!)

Orienting

1. Take plenty of time to orient Veteran employees, even if they are just part-time employees. They're far less comfortable than younger generations about just jumping in and learning on the fly. They prefer to know what to expect, what the policies are, and who's who.

2. Bring them up to date on the history of the department and organization. They appreciate and relate to your company "story": where the company came from and where it is trying to go. They like the "big picture," especially if it is wound around an interesting tale.

3. Emphasize long-term department and organization goals, and show them how they will be contributing to the long-term strategies.

Opportunities

1. Stress the long haul; communicate in terms of months and years, not weeks.

2. Keep in mind that, if your customer base includes a good percentage of seniors, your workforce should, too.

3. Keep gender roles in mind. Veterans grew up with clear distinctions between the roles of the sexes. And at no other stage of life do lifestyles of men and women differ so greatly as when they are in their sixties, seventies, and eighties. Because men tend to marry when they are a bit older, because men die younger, and because widowers often remarry, it is likely that Veteran men are members of a couple; often the women are single.

Developing

1. You are likely to need to train this group in technology. Veterans didn't learn about the computer in the two most common places: school and work. Those sixty-five and older tend to find technology intimidating and confusing. They appreciate logic, and the logic of technology isn't always obvious to them. One in ten has a PC at home (in the Generation X cohort, it's three of ten); less than one in ten watches videos regularly (for Xers, it's five of ten; and only two of ten have an ATM card (Xers it's six of ten).

2. Don't rush the training itself. Train in an atmosphere that is as free of stress as possible. Avoid situations where your older employees can "lose face" where others are watching or waiting.

3. Some Veterans are uncomfortable learning from a "wired twenty-year-old." Find older trainers or teach your younger trainers to speak the language of the Veteran.

4. Use large text in printed materials. The Veterans aren't the only ones who will appreciate the larger type. Boomers with fiftysomething eyesight will also be grateful.

5. A point of caution: Don't stereotype all Veterans as technophobes. Once trained, lots of members of this cohort take well to new technology and continue their learning; many will develop a fascination with it. Remember: They and their cohorts did invent the electromechanical and telephonic concept structures that make today's high tech possible. Computer technology didn't spring whole from the teeth of a Hydra or Steve Wozniack's brain. Daytime presence on the Internet is highly skewed toward retired seniors who have taken to the World Wide Web with glee.

Motivating

Ask those who report to you what personally motivates them. Even among the Veterans, personal preferences vary. If you are an Xer, you'll be surprised by the answers; they may seem very familiar.

1. Use the personal touch. Hand write a note. Veterans want to work in an atmosphere with living, breathing humans, not voice mail, e-mails, and faxes. Remember that the "hurry up and wait" many of them experienced in the military and in 1950s-style organizations led to idle chatter and socialization being an acceptable way of corporate life. When your assigned tasks were completed, there was time to kill and it was best not to have independent initiative.

2. Remember that traditional perks were visual symbols of status—the executive washroom, company cars, and up-front parking places. Although you probably won't be giving top performers their own restrooms, consider plaques and more traditional rewards for this cohort group. A photo of them with the CEO or an important visitor will likely find a place on their bookshelves or cubicle wall.

Mentoring

It isn't true that you can't teach an old dog new tricks, but it can be a challenge. Some Veterans have a hard time accepting coaching from markedly younger colleagues. Whereas your younger employees may be interested in advancing their careers, that motivation is likely to fall short with the Veteran group. They will be willing to learn new skills if you can prove the necessity for change in terms of corporate or department goals.

1. Consider finding for your Veteran employees a coach who is respected as a leader, possibly because of age and experience.

2. Coach tactfully. Be respectful. Ask permission to coach. Describe the performance issue and get agreement on the problem. Then suggest ways of improving behavior that focus on long-term goals.

3. Establish rapport by acknowledging the employee's background and experience.

This process is further explained in what Dr. Thomas Connellan calls the *Four Step Coaching Conference*.[6] It is outlined in detail in the following example.

Step 1: Position the Discussion

The goal is to not take the employee by surprise, but to give him or her the time to feel prepared, which is important to a Veteran.

"*Dorothy, I'd like to sit down with you later today to talk about new account openings. I'd like to work with you to get back on track. What time would work best for you?*" (*And of course this would be done out of earshot of other employees.*)

Step 2: The Discussion

During the discussion you should:
    Put the employee at ease:

"Dorothy, I know you are working on meeting your sales goal. I want to meet with you to make sure that all that work is going to get you where you need to go."

Describe the performance issue:

"As you know, the goal is four account openings a month. You are running between two and three through the first quarter. Does that square with your count?"

Get agreement on the problem:

"Would you agree that you need to find a way to improve on that record?"

Ask future-oriented, neutral questions:

"Is it possible to reach the four-account goal?"

"What might you try to get your closing rate closer to the goal?"

"How can I help you?"

Listen to and encourage employee ideas:

"That's a good thought. What else might you try?"

Step 3: Agree on a Course of Action

After you and the employee have discussed a number of possible remedies, it is time to narrow the field and pick a course of action.

"Well Dorothy, I think you've got some pretty good ideas here. Let's narrow them down to the one or two best and decide how to go forward from here."

Step 4: Set a Follow-Up Date

A follow-up commitment on your part says that you want to know that the problem is solved. It also communicates to the employee that your concern isn't simply the whim of the day, to be forgotten tomorrow.

"Dorothy, when would be a good time for us to meet again and see how the plan is working?"

Current and Future Issues

It is perhaps ironic that these "oldsters" really have become a viable source of "new" labor. In the last three years, more than one million seniors have traded in their golf clubs for a Rolodex. Having learned to conserve during the Depression and World War II, they are the most affluent elderly population in U.S. history and the wealthiest population segment in the United States. They resent Boomer free spending and misuse of credit. They are nonplussed that their children and grandchildren continue to count on them for financial help—to indulge themselves, pay for college educations, and make down payments on homes and cars. Today's grandparents buy one-fourth of all toys sold in this country, yet they sometimes don't reap the rewards they thought they might. Their kids don't depend on them for emotional support or show the sort of appreciation they themselves would have bestowed on the offer of similar largess when they were the same age and at the same stage and circumstance in their lives. The Veterans tend to be rational beings, and their relationships with their kids have a certain hierarchy-like distance to them.

They still wield a lot of clout. They contribute to causes they support, they let lobbyists know where they stand, and they vote. Don't expect them to fade into the background anytime soon. They will remain a powerful force for years to come. Though some have traded walking for wheeling or need an extra "prod" to move about, their minds are still sharp and available for lease.

The Future

When it comes to energy, productivity, and innovation, don't overlook your Veterans. After all, Carol Shields won a Pulitzer Prize at sixty. Michelangelo produced the Medici Chapel at fifty-nine. Sculptor Louise Bourgeois was first recognized with a one-woman show at the Museum of Modern Art at 70 plus. Ward Garland, a 103-year-old refrigeration engineer, still works every day in Waynesboro, Pennsylvania; Waldo McBurney, 96, continues to run his own business, McBurney Honey, in Quinter, Kansas; and Nat Kaufmann, 88, is going on thirty years as a stockbroker for Wedbush Morgan Securities in Los Angeles.[7]

The number of "older people" in the United States is growing rapidly. Mortality rates have fallen sharply this century; as a result, there are now eight million Americans over the age of eighty. The average life expectancy is quickly approaching eighty. Thus, more and more people

FACT AND FICTION ABOUT OLDER WORKERS

Myths:	Facts:
1. They have more accidents and they get sick more often.	1. Older persons have fewer on-the-job accidents, and insurance claims by older workers are no different than for all employees.
2. They can't learn technology.	2. Seniors are willing students when the training is done right (respectfully, with low stress).
3. They don't want to work.	3. Many retirees say they'd prefer to be working, at least part time.
4. They're not as productive as younger employees.	4. The U.S. Department of Health and Human Services reports that older workers are every bit as productive as younger ones.
5. They're not as bright as their younger counterparts.	5. The American Management Association reports that psychologists find that intelligence remains constant until at least age 70.

will live twenty to twenty-five years after the usual retirement age. Actual retirement will become an unattainable luxury for some and simply a too-boring alternative for others. Meanwhile, a growth economy will continue to require qualified labor. For all these reasons, you simply can't afford to lose all your Veteran employees.

The problem is they tend to leave the workplace earlier than any generation before them. The reasons are rather baffling, because some experts estimate that a full half of all retirees would really prefer to work.

Perhaps they leave because of the dearth of incentives to keep them on board, because it is the company norm to retire at a given age, or it may be that they are unaware of the need for their services. And they simply may not have been asked to stay on. Or perhaps some overeager Boomers and Xers are tired of waiting for their next promotions, and they see the Veteran as an impediment to be pushed aside.

Innovative programs for keeping seniors in the workplace are beginning to emerge. The National Older Worker Career Center helps corporations and federal agencies to develop programs and options that appeal to workers fifty-five and older.[8] The U.S. Department of Labor has granted $250,000 to Green Thumb, a nonprofit organization that recruits low-income seniors, to fill jobs as systems analysts and network administrators; but such programs are leading-edge exceptions. In 1993, the Society for Human Resource Management and the American Association of Retired Persons surveyed one thousand companies to find out how many had retention programs tailored to older workers; only 28 percent did. Those organizations that make their workplace friendly to Veterans will outdistance their competitors by capitalizing on the skills, talents, and experience of a pool of workers usually overlooked and undervalued.

More than just an untapped source of second-career labor, today's older workers offer us a laboratory. As the Veteran demonstrates, modern health care and the economy have conspired to make older workers an enduring and valuable resource. This trend is not a short-lived phenomenon. Boomers, the next generation we'll talk about here, will not only live longer than the generations ahead of them, but, because of their poor savings record and their work ethic, it will likely be a chore to move them out of the workforce. In the United States, the number of workers fifty-five and older will increase 38 percent by 2005, according to the U.S. Department of Labor. What is learned from the Veteran, who has chosen to keep working, will form a valuable base of learning for the increasingly mixed-generation workplace of the next century.

CHAPTER THREE

THE BABY
BOOMERS:

Peter Pan Grays at the Temples

TOM AND LINDA   BORN BETWEEN 1943–1960

"God knows many of them are fools,
and most of them will be sellouts,
but they're a better generation than we were."

—LILLIAN HELLMAN

The Baby Boom was more than just a postwar—"Welcome home, sailor!"—diapers-on-parade, nine-months-after-the-party phenomenon. It was much more. It was the beginning of a dramatic reversal of an American population trend that had begun in the mid-1700s. It was the beginning of the end of the country's rural, agrarian lifestyle. It was the tumultuous and noisy dawn of a promising new day that had carried the Veterans through blackouts, rationing, and the anxiety of separation. It was the beginning of a new world that hundreds of thousands had died to make possible in the annealing fires of the greatest, fiercest war ever fought.

For nearly two hundred years the American population had been declining in size. The rigors of settling a raw wilderness, a tumultuous civil war, and a decade of economic depression had eroded the population of America faster than immigration and birth rate combined could replace the fallen. Then, in 1946, almost precisely nine months after VJ day, a tsunami of babies broke across the fruited plain and changed its physical and psychological geography forever. Not only were more babies being born every minute—one every seventeen minutes for nineteen years—but thanks to the miracles of postwar medicine, more of them were surviving birth and babyhood, formerly the highest mortality segment of life span on the planet.

Healthier. More wanted. Doted on and attended to. The first generation in which child rearing was a hobby and a pleasure and not an economic necessity and a biological inevitability. The Boom Babies were cherished by parents who had sacrificed and fought a war for the right to bear them, raise them, indulge them, and dream of a new Eden for them to live out their days in.

By 1964, more than seventy-six million of these cherished, loved, coddled, hoped for, and doted on Boomers were walking, talking, crawling, toddling, and spitting up—adorably—on the face of the planet. And they were learning to flex their physical and psychological legacy and to manifest their destiny.

Technically, physically, and temporally, the Boom Birth period began in 1946 and ended in 1964. But a generational cohort is defined as much by shared values, experiences, and world views as it is by zodiacal accident. A generation is defined by what it thinks, feels, and experiences together and not just by dates of birth. So it is as, or more, accurate to define Baby Boomers as those born between 1943 and 1960. Those in that added group, born in the three years preceding the official "go" date, often referred to as the Sandwich Generation, are more like Boomers than Veterans in a number of ways and for many of the same reasons that Boomers are Boomers. Many of them started the trends "true" Boomers turned into generational milestones and Boomer icons. Without a Barbra Streisand would there be a Bette Midler? Without the Beach Boys would there be the Stones?

And without Boomers would the Sandwich slice—those born just prior to and during World War II—have an identity at all? Think of them as the Lewises and Clarkses of the Baby Boom era. And the subtracted group—those born in the early 1960s—feel more affinity with the next generation, the Xers, who neither supported nor protested the Vietnam War and who don't remember the day of the assassination of a young president in a Dallas motorcade.

Their Generational Personality

The children of the 1940s and 1950s grew up in optimistic, positive times. For the United States, it was a time of expansion. The fertility boom coincided with the greatest economic expansion this country had ever experienced. The country was on a straight-up growth curve. With the only stable economy left after the destruction of World War II, the only imaginable obstacle to infinite expansion of American industry was imagination itself.

THE BABY BOOMERS

Seminal Events

1954	McCarthy HCUAA hearings begin
1955	Salk Vaccine tested on the public
1955	Rosa Parks refuses to move to the back of the bus in Montgomery, Alabama
1957	First nuclear power plant
1957	Congress passes the Civil Rights Act
1960	Birth control pills introduced
1960	Kennedy elected
1961	Kennedy establishes Peace Corps
1962	Cuban Missile Crisis
1962	John Glenn circles the earth
1963	Martin Luther King leads march on Washington, D.C.
1963	President John Kennedy assassinated
1965	United States sends ground combat troops to Vietnam
1966	National Organization for Women founded
1966	Cultural Revolution in China
1967	American Indian Movement founded
1968	Martin Luther King and Robert F. Kennedy assassinated
1969	First lunar landing
1969	Woodstock
1970	Kent State University shootings

- *They believe in growth and expansion.* Americans of the era were fascinated by the lore and mythology of their last great frontier. The mythical, mystical Wild West was glorified on television and in Saturday movie matinees. Think "Hopalong Cassidy," Daniel Boone, Davy Crockett, "Gunsmoke," Roy Rogers, Dale Evans, and "Wagon Train." According to the Boomer Institute, $75 million was spent each year of the 1950s on cowboy outfits for little Boomers.[1] At the same time, they became broadly fascinated by the new frontier of space: "to boldly go where none had gone before." Think Buck Rogers, Tom Corbit, Captain Video, and all those things that "came from outer space!" Perhaps it was the lure of both simpler and possibly idyllic future times.

- *They think of themselves as stars of the show.* They lived in nuclear families with a working dad and a stay-at-home mom. Children were, for the first time in history, in the spotlight, representing as they did to the Veterans, the symbol and fruit of their victories and the hopes for the future they fought to preserve. The American infrastructure was forced to expand rapidly to accommodate the needs of the Baby Boomers. New hospitals, elementary schools, and high schools. Health care and education became industrialized endeavors. Expectations for this new generation were so high that, in 1967, *Time* magazine actually gave its coveted Man of the Year award to the Baby Boom Generation, proclaiming them the generation that would clean up our cities, end racial inequality, and find a cure for the common cold.

It was a heady, tumultuous time. But it was not a Golden Age, as some would have us believe. Domestic violence was as prevalent then as now, but it went unreported. People with problems had few places to turn. Unhappiness was kept secret. Racist and sexist jokes were the norm, the handicapped were sometimes treated maliciously, and the retarded were often warehoused. The few gays who chose to come out of the closet became targets of derision and violence.

THE BABY BOOMERS

Heroes

- Gandhi
- Martin Luther King
- John and Jacqueline Kennedy
- John Glenn

- *They tend to be optimistic.* But... feeling of optimism and promise they were rais... or granted, to see as their birthright, had a tremen... t on the developing psyches of the Baby Boomer... ue today to look at the world in terms of its ...ities, something to be shaped and played wit... ...t passively, as a spectator might. The planet... to shape; an attitude as clear in the ways of ... as it is in the means of Boomer Developers.

- *In school and at home, the Boomers learned abou...* There were so many of them, like puppies in a pil... had to collaborate and cooperate, sharing texts an... times desks. They were the first generation to be gra... their report cards for "shares materials with classmates... "works with others." And everything they did was in t... spotlight, understanding tacitly, perhaps simply assuming... that the purpose of the world they lived in was to actively serve their needs, wants, and whims, a feeling they carried into adolescence and adulthood. They continue to be caught up in their own interests and priorities; some would say self-absorbed and perpetually spotlight conscious.

- *They have pursued their own personal gratification, uncompromisingly, and often at a high price to themselves and others.* If the marriage wasn't working out, they dumped it and looked for another. If they didn't like the job, they moved on. Caught in a shady deal? Apologize, shed a few tears, blame some circumstance and move on. They turned resurrection—and self-forgiveness—into a high public art. William Jefferson Clinton, the first Boomer President of the United States has turned public apology and the expectation of instant, soap-opera-like forgiveness into a political norm.

> **THE BABY BOOMERS**
>
> **Cultural Memorabilia**
>
> - "The Ed Sullivan Show"
> - Quonset huts
> - Fallout shelters
> - Poodle skirts and Pop Beads
> - Slinkies
> - TV Dinners
> - "The Laugh-In"
> - Hula Hoops
> - The Mod Squad
> - The peace sign

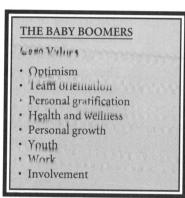

THE BABY BOOMERS

Core Values

- Optimism
- Team orientation
- Personal gratification
- Health and wellness
- Personal growth
- Youth
- Work
- Involvement

• *They have searched their souls—repeatedly, obsessively, and recreationally.* Surrounded as they were in childhood by the companion of material wealth and economic growth, perhaps it is no surprise that Boomers in their late adolescence felt compelled to pursue the flip side—spirituality, the inner world, and the meaning of life. Case in point: Boomers in the 1960s were attracted not so much by high-energy drugs like crack and cocaine, but to introspective drugs like marijuana and LSD, touted to take its users on a journey within. In the 1970s, if a given Boomer wasn't studying transcendental meditation, she was at a Ram Dass lecture or her yoga class. Today, Boomers devour books on any topic remotely concerned with spirituality. Nearly half the books on the nonfiction best-seller lists have spiritual themes. Deepak Chopra, who heads the Chopra Center for Well Being in La Jolla, California, and who has tapes, seminars, and seventeen books on the interaction among mind, body, and spirit has become a spiritual symbol, and a multigazillionaire.

Nor did the Boomers leave their fascination with spiritualism at home; they've invited and encouraged it in the workplace. A whole collection of books that link jobs and spirit—*Care of the Soul, The Road Less Traveled, The Heart Aroused,* are best-sellers among Boomer managers. Seminars, training programs, and retreats walk the fine line between church and work—dangerously, according to some theologians and executives. "But spirit has everything to do with work," one Boomer responds. "Work would be meaningless without it."

• *The Boomers have always been cool.* Ask one. In fact, they changed the sociology of coolness. Historically, trendsetters have been people in their late teens and early twenties. In the 1920s, two young book publishers ignited the crossword craze, and a fifteen-year-old from Baltimore started the flagpole-sitting trend that was copied from San Diego to

Philadelphia. But in the 1950s, little kids, by their simple presence, started the fads. The Boomers, when they were mere babies, took center stage and set the pace, passive though their participation was. For the first time ever, Madison Avenue recognized children as a market segment, and they pursued the Boom Kiddies directly via television. Commercials for cereals, snacks, and toys saturated the prime kiddy viewing hours for the first time; in fact, they defined kiddy viewing hours. Little Boomers could recognize the word "detergent" before they could read. Shortly thereafter, retailers found a new group of buyers: Baby Boom girls who were a little too big for children's sizes and a little too small for women's sizes. In response, clothing manufacturers invented "preteen" and "junior" sizes, and they sold like hotcakes. The Boomer Institute tells us, "they were the first teenage consumers to spend over $12 billion of their own money for such things as cosmetics, pimple creams, and hair products."[2]

Today the Boomers still think they're cool, "the continuously morphing" market everyone wants to click with. After all, they are the world; they are the children. And they'll never, never, grow up, grow old, or die.

The Legacy of Vietnam

There is no simple way to talk about what Vietnam meant, and means, to this generation. What we can say is that its effect has been profound and divisive. To begin with, the war was the primary cause of the generation gap between the Veterans and Boomers. The U.S. intervention in Southeast Asia caused many young Americans to question the integrity of our leaders as never before. Feelings about the war divided many a family, even close siblings. Perhaps even more disturbing is the effect the war had within the generation. It caused a schism that may never be bridged and that is rarely talked about, present as it is, like an unwelcome guest at a party.

The Boomers' reactions to the unpopular war were as complex as the war itself. Some Boomers signed up or were drafted, went to Southeast Asia, and became proud soldiers like their Veteran fathers in World War II. But they fought, died, were wounded, and returned home without ever understanding how their actions contributed to the long-term goal, or even what that goal was. Many returned and turned bitter and skeptical of authority, particularly governmental authority. Others served in Vietnam, but far less willingly. Some young soldiers participated in a military counterculture of sorts, tuning in, turning on, and dropping out, smoking pot, and listening to Jimi Hendrix. Many witnessed unspeakable horrors, which would haunt them for a lifetime. Yet, when they returned from the war, it was not to a hero's welcome like their fathers before them. Often wounded both physically and psychically, when they got off the airplane returning them to their hometowns, many were greeted by antiwar peers who spat at them and shouted epithets. They learned a bitter lesson: to be silent about the war and their experiences in it.

Neither were things simple for those who stayed home and never even entered the jungles and rice paddies of Vietnam. A small but vocal minority actively protested American involvement. Others wore the antiwar mantle inactively and silently; some simply because it was rather fashionable. Still others suffered in confusion, not knowing quite how to resolve issues of patriotism and loyalty, how to make sense of the headlines, and what to think of the decisions coming out of the Pentagon. Then there was a significant group of Boomers who took steps to keep themselves out of the war. Some joined the National Guard. Some signed up for college courses with professors who promised to give them As or Bs so they could keep their college deferments. Some filed

---

THE BABY BOOMERS

How Boomers Differ From Their Parents

Veterans	Boomers
• Followed traditional roles (male/female, ethnic)	• Redefined roles; promoted equality
• Were loyal (to their marriages and their companies)	• Left unfulfilling relationships to seek more fulfilling ones
• Were willing to be disciplined and patient, waiting for their rewards	• Sought immediate gratification
• Played by the rules	• Manipulated the rules to meet their own needs

as conscientious objectors and were able to serve in nonmilitary capacities. Some fled to Canada, Sweden, and other places. Some starved themselves to get below the acceptable weight for military service. Still others threw shovels through windows to prove they were not mentally fit to serve. Time does not, in fact, heal all wounds. The shadow of Vietnam and how it was viewed by whom will likely always loom over this generation.

First Half/Second Half: The Boomer Dichotomy

To add to the complexity of understanding Boomers, there's the issue of older Boomers and younger Boomers. Certainly within any generation, there is a great deal of diversity. We would expect important differences between those people of the same generation who grew up poor and those who grew up affluent, between rural and urban, between midwesterners and westerners, easterners and southerners. A "y'all come" Atlanta Boomer does seem different, on the surface, from a "hey yous guys" northeastern Boomer. And every member of the Baby Boom Generation can say that there are aspects of his or her generation's personality they don't see reflected in themselves and their lives. This is particularly true for those in the second half of the generation—those born in the mid- to late-1950s—many of whom find they simply "do not fit" the Boomer style as characterized in the popular press.

"Second-halfers" find "first-halfers" more idealistic, more likely to be workaholics, and more likely to have put career first, family second. In fact, demographers tell us that first-halfers, those born in the 1940s, make more money and own more homes than second-half Boomers, those born between 1950 and 1960. First-halfers' world view was more affected by the 1950s. They felt a more integral and active part of the 1960s "scene"—free love, drugs, sex, rock-n-roll, Vietnam, women's lib—if not as active participants, then at least as very aware observers. For second-halfers, the 1950s were mostly a vague memory and the 1960s "movements" more an observed than participated-in phenomenon, though individual exceptions do indeed abound.

But for all the qualifiers and exceptions, and Boomers are very firm about their sense of individuality and not being a part of a predictable, statistical group, Boomers are Boomers by virtue of one indelible fact: They experienced the same growing pains and forces, were preached to by the same geography-spanning media, and understood the impact these same said forces have had on others in their cohort group. To paraphrase Robert Heinlein, a literary hero for many Boomers, they "grok" one another. They may not—do not—agree with stands and opinions of every part of the cohort group or exhibit the same behavior in the same situations, but they do, in their hearts, understand one another.

First-Half Boomers: The Economic Achievers

Every generation has a cadre or cohort of "achievers" who change the world around them. Some achieve in commerce, others in literature, music, religion, engineering, science, philosophy, and the fine arts. Although all these areas of achievement set the tone and lead the way for a generation, it is commerce and the practical economics of the workplace that affect the most people. And every generation, indeed, has a subset of economic achievers, those who are more ambitious and more driven to succeed than most in their cohort. Concerned with raising fortunes rather than consciousness, achievers are always on the lookout for opportunities to get ahead, ways to increase their status and prestige, and chances to gain control and power. Goal and result oriented, they often "get along to get ahead." "Standing out" from the crowd has high value to Boomers, the generation that has refined "famous for being famous" to an art form.

Because Baby Boomers have a Pavlovian-like tendency to be driven anyway, the economic achievers among them are particularly remarkable; a real crème de la crème of ambition and accomplishment. The popular press has branded the achievement oriented as "Yuppies," and, although they really aren't typical of their generation as a whole, they are responsible for many of the stereotypes now commonly associated with the Baby Boom: ruthlessness, Rolex watches, BMWs, designer glasses, cellular phones, vacations in Bali, second homes in Aspen.

There is a love/hate relationship with the economic achievers. Modern versions of the old Horatio Alger story about the clerk whose personal drive and hard work took him all the way to the bank presidency are told with both admiration—and resentment. These economic achievers are the brunt of many a joke:

The Yuppie and his BMW were in a terrible wreck. "Oh, my Beemer, my Beemer," he whined. The first person to arrive shouted, "Ohmigod, he's lost his arm!" The Yuppie began to whine with renewed vigor, "Oh, my Rolex, my Rolex."

And few of us, regardless of our generational affiliation, want to admit that we might have "Yuppie" economic achiever tendencies ourselves. Put Donald Trump, Ted Turner, Michael Eisner, Steve Jobs, and Debbie Fields into this subset, and you can discern the pluses and minuses for yourself.

Linda: Achiever Par Excellence

It is 6:00 P.M., and the sun is setting across the San Andreas fault. It's been a long day. Linda is ready to leave her corner office with its sweeping view of the downtown skyline. Dressed in a bright, corporate-blue, Dior business suit, she is headed for the gym to meet with her personal trainer. A divorced career woman of fifty-five, Linda paid a high price for her "luxurious" lifestyle, putting in more than two decades of sixty-plus-hour weeks to the companies she has worked for. Child rearing, or even child having, went on permanent hold and was a great contributor to the demise of her marriage. She doesn't have much tolerance for people who don't work as many hours or who insist on a "personal life," whatever that is. She recently chewed out an employee at a staff meeting for taking a vacation without her cell phone. Today Linda is vice president of operations for a corporation that owns six hundred restaurants around the world.

In her company and in the food-service industry, Linda is well-respected. She started as a store-manager trainee right out of college and climbed her way to where she is, one rung at a time. She is known for her professionalism, quick wit, and personal warmth. People would tell you, however, that you don't want to get in her way. Linda knows what she wants and is accustomed to getting it. Politically wise, she knows the ropes and is demanding when she feels she needs to be. Though some have bluntly branded her "ruthless" behind closed doors, Linda would simply shrug and respond that her responsibility is to keep the corporation solvent, not soothe people's feelings.

The Late Boomers: Laid Back and Cynical

There were more than three million more babies born in the second decade of the Baby Boom than the first decade. Demographically, late Boomer 1950s babies are the largest single Boomer segment. They don't identify much with the 1960s; they were too young to feel the rush. Many of them were, and are, turned off by yuppie-ism. They see the BMW as the car for older, greedier, more materialistic Boomers; affluent younger Boomers tend to drive Accords. They say they were never as driven as their older counterparts, that they've always made decisions based on family—in the broadest sense. They take pride that fathering roles have shifted during the years that Boomers have been parenting and that the older Boomers, especially the fathers, tended to spend less time with their kids while the younger Boomers have shared parenting responsibilities more equally. They see their parenting obligation as not just financial but emotional and involving.

The late Boomers, or second-halfers, tend to feel different about work. They graduated from college and went to work during the Reagan era. They got the first taste of downsizing (large-scale layoffs) the country had experienced since the Great Depression. This has made them more cynical and less gung ho about management and the early Boomer mantra that "The business of America is business." They know that economics are as blind as justice; good work habits and positive mental attitude are not always rewarded, and often they are not enough to save a job, regardless of how well it has been done. When it comes to work attitude, they sometimes identify with Generation Xers who cite Dilbert as their cultural hero and workplace icon. "Oh, boy, here comes another consultant/fad/reform/reorganization/vision/plan. Same old dog food, different can. Duck! This too shall pass."

Tom: Boomer Marching to a Different Drummer

Tom is a forty-one-year-old employee of a major telecommunications corporation. A software designer, he has been in the industry for about ten years and has changed companies twice in that time. He is actually back with his original company, a change he made recently in order to take advantage of that corporation's policy of flexible hours. The father of three children under ten, Tom shares every bit of the responsibility at home equally with his wife, Tracy, who manages a small print shop in a mall near their home.

While attending college in the late 1970s, Tom worked construction in the summers to pay for tuition. Military service was never a concern for Tom. The Vietnam War and conscription ended before he got to college, though he remembers the angst and strife his older brother went through. Tom's main concerns have always been around career and lifestyle, particularly the balance between the two.

Today he is a self-described "fix it guy." Two years ago, he and Tracy designed a comfortable, functional house, the kind of home they wanted to raise their children in. They bought three acres of land on the outskirts of the city, did most of the construction themselves, and, finally, last summer, moved the family into their new home. Tom likes his job and works hard, but he is also devoted to his family, spending four nights a week escorting kids to soccer games, music lessons, and dental appointments.

His admirers, and there are plenty, refer to Tom as a caring, sensitive, modern man. Others in his peer group, the more driven, career-oriented, upwardly mobile types, think of him as the worst sort of Alan Alda clone. But Tom, no less than Linda, sees himself as pressed for time and struggling to keep everything together. In his case, keeping the important things in his life—family and career—together.

Tom and Linda in the Workplace

Linda and Tom represent and embody themes of their generational co-hort, the desires, aspirations, and values that make them unique among the family of generations who now live and work together, or at least side by side, in the transgenerational workplace.

Linda and Tom, though different from one another, are much alike in that they are both a part of the cadre of other sons and daughters of the optimistic post-World War II era, who prayed in school, gathered around the first television in the neighborhood to watch the "Mickey Mouse Club," and ate TV dinners. They watched the iron curtain descend, marched on Washington, and watched on prime time Neil Armstrong's first steps on the moon. They joined the Peace Corps and fought in Vietnam—or didn't. They benefited from a prosperous economy, tremendous medical advances, an explosion of scientific research, and a school system that was overcrowded but in fine fettle.

Today they comprise a full one-third of all Americans. Their impact on the workplace, where they account for 53 percent of all workers, is unmistakably huge. And as the oldest of their wave turn fifty, they are more determined than ever to think of themselves as forever and ever young. "Don't trust anyone over thirty" has become "Age is a state of mind. You are only as old as you think."

Working with Tom and Linda is different—different from working with the Veterans, the Xers, and the Nexters, and even from each other. To better understand Tom and Linda and to work successfully with the mishmash and milieu of the transgenerational workplace, we need to understand who they are, what influenced them, what motivates them now, and how they relate to others in the workplace.

THE BABY BOOMERS

On The Job

Assets
- Service oriented
- Driven
- Willing to "go the extra mile"
- Good at relationship
- Want to please
- Good team players

Liabilities
- Not naturally "budget minded"
- Uncomfortable with conflict
- Reluctant to go against peers
- May put process ahead of result
- Overly sensitive to feedback
- Judgmental of those who see things differently
- Self-centered

> ## THE BABY BOOMERS
> ### Messages That Motivate
> - "You're important to our success."
> - "You're valued here."
> - "Your contribution is unique and important."
> - "We need you."
> - "I approve of you."
> - "You're worthy."

The Boomers, especially the first wave, those born in the midst and just after World War II was ending, grew up wanting and needing desperately to prove themselves. Veteran dads and moms reminded them that theirs was a great destiny, paid for by unprecedented sacrifice. Grandparents warned of the ills of the depression and the chaos of despair that followed. These Boomers know well the land mine of possibilities that accompanies the prosperity dream. Therefore, work has held a singular importance in their lives. Their fathers had proved themselves worthy in World War II—"tempered by war, disciplined by a hard and bitter peace." The Baby Boomers—most of them—would have to be tested on the job. Business would be their war, the competitor their enemy. They would win or lose their personal battles on the warship called "work." They've tended to define themselves through their jobs and to achieve their identity by the work they perform. For this generation, "work ethic" and "worth ethic" are synonyms.

The drive to prove their worthiness has created a work ethic that has surprised many observers. These pundits remember the youthful activists of the 1960s who had challenged the establishment and promised never to "sell out" to the corporation. Many of those observers assumed the Boomers would be slackers. But the activist Boomer had never been anti-hard work. And work hard they have in the corporate world. Driven and dedicated, they still labor to prove they were worthy of the expectations that had been placed on them practically since birth. While the futurists were promising thirty-hour workweeks, Boomers were regularly punching in for fifty or sixty hours. Many were loving it, feeling fulfilled in their need to be needed and worthy.

Where They Work

Boomers have been drawn to all types of industries and organizations, from small nonprofit associations to multinational corporations. The key factor in their job choices has been opportunity, not glitz, glamour, and security, though they are not averse to these secondary attributes and see them as great perks when they are part of the package. And don't forget, these are lads and lasses who have made reading books on business a craze and made business writers and entrepreneurs national heroes. They can find romance, drama, challenge, glamour, and personal fulfillment in bagel baking and widget winding. By and large, they liked school when they were kids, and they've never given it up. Training as an industry has burgeoned under their tutelage. Not only do they pursue learning at work, but swarms of them sign up for evening and weekend classes. The National Center for Educational Statistics reports that 40 percent of Americans enrolled in adult education classes last year, up from only about 10 percent when the Veterans were middle aged, and the bulk of these participants are Boomers.[3]

Half are in technical and production jobs today. Nearly a quarter of them are in management, from the front lines to the executive suites. In the last five years, they've become the majority in the highest-paying categories: doctors, lawyers, and accountants. Others work in sales and clerical roles. In most aspects, they differ little from any other generation in that they're sprinkled throughout a variety of industries. Of course, the most visible Boomers are on Wall Street, clad in Gucci and Armani, buying and selling companies.

A large segment expresses a preference for work environments that are democratic, humane, and casual. They've carried their value for affiliation with them into the workplace, where they've advocated teams and team building, consensus, quality circles, and participative management. They prefer a workplace where there is a lot of room for relationships. They are not, however, as good at sharing as they'd like to be thought of. The slogan "all for one and one is me" isn't foreign to a sizable number. Some cynics suggest that teamwork and participation have only become fashionable as Boomers have figured out that the road to the top of their trade, craft, or corporation is already fully occupied. So, in typical fashion, if they can't reach the goal, they change it. If being number one is out of reach, they reach instead for the new leaderless work designs, where everyone is equal and being number one, individually, is frowned on (until the next chance to be "the star" emerges, of course).

In the service industries, we see Baby Boomers flourishing, as well. Perhaps because of their strong need to prove themselves, Boomers tend to be very good at delivering service. They want to be liked—one on one. They've learned to read people; they've had to. They're great rapport builders. They'll do what it takes to make the customer happy, as long as it puts them in a good light with someone—anyone.

Given their choice, they prefer to work for a manager (if they can't *be* the manager) who knows and cares for them personally. They tend to perform best for managers who treat their employees as equals, managers who let them feel they are in charge of something or at least empowered to dabble in everything.

Their Leadership Style

When they are in leadership roles, their tendency is toward a collegial, consensual, sometimes benignly despotic style. They are the ones who advocated turning the traditional corporate hierarchy upside down. Their motivations for their advocacy aside, they are genuinely passionate and concerned about participation and spirit in the workplace, about bringing heart and humanity to the office, and about creating a fair and level playing field for all. The Civil Rights movement of the 1960s had a profound impact on their generational personality; and fair treatment, whether it be persons of color, gays, or those with disabilities, is something they're willing to take to the soapbox and speak out for. It is the Boomers, particularly the early Boomers, who have bought millions of copies of "soft leadership skills" books with titles like *Steward Leadership, Managing from the Heart,* and *Leadership Is an Art.*

But those who report to them have found all this to be rather deceiving, a little disingenuous, and a bit bewildering. The Boomers grew up, for the most part, with conservative parents and worked in their early careers for command-and-control-style supervisors. Boomer managers sometimes have a hard time actually practicing, day in and day out, the management style they profess. Many, for instance, truly believe they are managing participatively, when, in fact, they're just giving it lip service. Participative management requires great skill in understanding, listening, communicating, motivating, and delegating. Many Boomer managers are lacking in these areas and are in need of development in order to become the leader with the style to which they aspire. Many who are lacking these skills are not even aware of their ineffectiveness. When Scott Adams created Dilbert's pointy-haired, cliché-spouting boss, he was modeling and mocking a dark and very, very real side of Boomer leadership—management by buzzword.

As Team Member

Linda and Tom tend to be good team members. They've been taught team work skills since childhood, and they enjoy being on work teams. But, at times, Linda's need to prove herself overrides her commitment to do what's best for the team. The eight-year-old who had to jump up and down in class screeching "Me! Me! Me!, Miss Smith. Ask me. Ask me!" lurks just below the adult veneer of many a Boomer and, sometimes, when the stakes are right, makes a guest appearance in conference room B.[4]

Boomers can be very political animals, especially when their turf is threatened. At times like these, those well-honed rapport skills are used to sell a plan for self-protection, territorial improvement, or self-betterment masked as concern, the best interest of the common good, or helping someone overburdened or with too much to do already. The net result is frequently confusion, frustration, and misunderstanding on the team. Of course, most Boomers read each other's machinations well and clearly. They recognize blind ambition and self-promotion for what it is, though they often haven't a clue for actually dealing with the "slick Willie" moves of their colleagues. For most Boomers, the playground taught that there are but two responses, two "models" of conflict resolution: knuckling under or duking it out—flight or fight. By the age of twelve, most had sorted out the approach that worked for them. They learned again in their initial forays into the work place whether they were pushers or pushees.

Midcourse, however, the rules changed. Perhaps it was the Civil Rights, women's lib, and equal employment opportunity movements. Perhaps it was Vietnam. Perhaps, as some feminists contend, it was the arrival of large numbers of women into the workplace, in professional and managerial positions. Whatever the cause, the natural selection system of schoolyard and workplace was turned on its head and a "play nice" ethic has been grafted to the Boomer adult psyche. Work rules, company policies, and mandatory consciousness-raising seminars have told Boomers without exception that aggressiveness—duking it out—is unacceptable, and assertiveness—stating and restating your "needs" until you get what you want—is in favor. Bottom line for the Boomer: They are, many of them, not very good at calling out conflict or dealing with it directly. There is a sizable subset of people with ulcers, high blood pressure, and tension headaches unable to express their fight-or-flight reaction—nature's way of saying, "You need to speak up!"—in an acceptable, authentic, or stress-relieving way.

Managing the Baby Boomer

Whether Linda and Tom are team mates or subordinates, their talents and needs are unique and special. They are members of the first generation where the question, "How do you want to be managed?" is relevant. Where the question, "How do you maintain and motivate the best and the brightest?" is strategically and tactically important to business.

The thing about Boomers is they'll make life hell if, in their view, you're mismanaging them. They won't suffer in silence, but they won't necessarily confront their issues directly. Says generational expert, William Strauss, "The generation that was awful for productivity was Boomers. That's when it stagnated. Everybody was scratching their heads saying, 'Gee, technology is getting better; how come productivity isn't improving?' Well they had young Boomer workers arguing with everybody about what to do."[5] They are used to *sharing* with their peers. They will make sure everybody knows if they're not happy with "da boss," and make "boss" a real four-letter word.

So how do Boomers want to be managed? How can you retain and motivate the best and brightest members of this generation without simply handing them the keys and saying, "Okay, you drive, smart person." How can you get them on your side and make them positive about being on your team?

Some Key Principles

Recruiting

1. Let them know their experience will be valued. Boomers have put in their time, and they want to know they'll get credit, and respect, for their accomplishments.
2. Give them the change agent challenge: "You're going to come in here and really make a difference."
3. Stress that this is a warm, humane place to work, though still a dynamic environment.
4. Show them places where they can excel, what their track will be.
5. Show them how they can be a star.
6. Demonstrate that your company is not backwater; promote the leading-edge nature of your organization and your industry.

Orienting

1. Direct your discussion to the near future of the company. Boomers tend to be future oriented. Although the years remaining in their careers are beginning to shrink, they like to see themselves in a larger, worthwhile context: "Come with us, Tom, and we'll dominate the world of self-sealing gaskets."

2. Focus on challenges. Boomers want to solve problems and turn things around: "We really need your talent here, Linda."

Opportunities

1. As with any employee from any generation, get to know each of your people as individuals. What is true for one may not be so for another. This is especially important when managing Baby Boomers, who put a high value on personal relationship and unique, personalized treatment.

2. Assure a Boomer job candidate that the company is poised on the edge of greatness and just needs the candidate to make it happen.

3. Show them how they can use this opportunity to really make a difference.

4. Teach people the politics of information; give them the inside edge on your organization's know-how.

5. Stress that they'll learn a lot and improve the value of the organization tenfold.

Developing

1. Boomers often need development in strategic planning, budgeting, coaching skills, and all the "soft stuff."

2. Watch for the Boomer with an "I know all that" chip on the shoulder. Many do, in fact, know a lot—intellectually; in a textbookish way. The problem is they're not doing it. You may be forced to quote (anonymous) complaints from the people they manage in order to get their buy-in to changing something about their management style. Note

the popularity of 360-degree management feedback schemes in the high Boomer workplace.

3. Provide Boomers with developmental experiences, assignments where you help them through and develop their skills. Give them projects they can cite ("I brought in the Meyerson account"). Give them gold stars even if it was a team effort.

4. Look for lots of Meyerson accounts.

5. Encourage Boomer employees to read business books and listen to training tapes.

Motivating

In your leadership role, take time for conversation. Find opportunities to become better personally acquainted.

1. Try the personal approach ("I really need you to do this for me").

2. Give lots of public recognition.

3. Give them a chance to prove themselves and their worth.

4. Give them perks—a company car, an expense account for first-class travel.

5. Assist them in gaining name recognition throughout the company.

6. Get them quoted in an industry journal.

7   Get consensus. Boomers think they invented participative management, and they will be mightily offended if you don't involve them.

8. Reward their work ethic and long hours.

Mentoring

Boomers have always valued personal growth; they continue to be committed to lifelong learning and self-improvement. Even in their fifties they see themselves as "learners." Witness a president who reviewed a disastrous failed attempt at a health care plan by saying, "We learned a lot from that." Although Boomers can be defensive, coaching is their preferred style of development.

1. Coach tactfully.
2. If you're blaming, they're not listening.
3. Be nice. Be warm. Find opportunities for agreement and harmony.
4. Let them tell you how well the Meyerson account went. When they ask for input or you see an opportunity, coach for improved performance.
5. Ask questions to get to the issues.
6. Think of yourself as a friendly equal. Ask permission every step of the way ("Would it be okay if we talked about your performance on the Meyerson job?").
7. The toughest coaching situations are those in which you think their performance is substandard, and they don't. Assure them they're doing well, but you think they could be achieving more.
8. Respect them, but not the way you would a Veteran. Please don't call a Baby Boomer "sir," "ma'am," "Mr.," or even "Ms."—but for their experience. Ask them; don't tell them.

Current and Future Issues

Today's Boomers are just hitting their stride (just ask one). Sociologists tell us they are beginning their golden age in terms of position, productivity, and earnings, despite being at an age that previous generations have labeled "over the hill." A.C. Nielson reports that Boomers are the biggest buyers of everything from toothpaste to financial services. The next decade will see them with increased freedom to enjoy recreation and leisure. They are actively turning fiftysomething. Make no mistake about it, they intend to approach these next years entirely differently than their parents did, pushing back the frontiers on what it means to be elderly. They look at Cher and Mick Jagger and say to themselves, "If they can still shake it, why not me?" At fifty, most of them have twenty more good, solid years of health and productivity to look forward to. And, given their poor saving record, few can retire or think about early retirement anyway.

Simply by virtue of their numbers, but also based on their positions and earnings, they have become the most important segment of the labor force and will remain so for the next twenty years. They are ensconced in middle management and will have taken over the executive offices and the boardroom within the next decade. By that time, the Bureau of Labor Statistics tells us women will finally make up a full half of the American workforce.

In the last twenty years, Baby Boomers have instituted most of the policies, procedures, and structures that govern organizations today, though they do still reflect many Veteran sensibilities in general outline. They are far more likely to switch careers and start their own new businesses later in life than those in previous decades. It's not just the Michael Eisners and Tina Turners of the world who aren't going to give up the ship. There are many others, and for some very important reasons.

As they grow increasingly more influential in the workplace, the Boomers will simultaneously attempt to achieve a more balanced work life. In the 1970s, the term "workaholic" was coined to describe their work ethic. In the two decades since they joined the American workforce, the average time spent at work has increased one full month per year. As the Boomers approach their mature years, they have begun to question this grueling pace and to seek a more balanced life. One-third of Boomers say they would quit altogether if they could live comfortably without their salaries; the absolute fact is that most can't. At the same time, companies are finding that employees in their late forties and early fifties are interested in more free time, even at the risk of less pay. They are blocking the upward path for "youngers,"—and they don't care.

They certainly would have plenty of things to do with more free time. Many are wrangling with issues surrounding care of elderly parents. Those with children in the twentysomething age bracket are finding they are more actively involved in their grown children's lives than they had expected. Their young adult offspring continue to put demands on their time and energy, demands they never would have thought to make of their own parents. Many are getting a big charge out of being grandparents. Still other Boomers waited until later in life to have children. Busy attending PTA meetings, these experienced and savvy parents, close in age to the most experienced teachers, are determined their opinions about what should go on in school be heard. In their pursuit of perfect children, some people in this generation have made life miserable for the schools, insisting their kids get third, fourth, and fifth tries—their talents and performance be damned. Meanwhile, these parents are still striving to create a balance between child rearing, work, and personal lives. They are quickly finding that "Life is work and work is life" is no longer an effective motto, and many are reluctantly admitting that they just can't have it all.

Turning Fifty

Boomers have made an art form of turning the mundane and ordinary into trendy sources of soap-opera-style drama, and they continue that practice in the way they look at aging.

In 1997, members of the official Baby Boom began to turn fifty; the early Boomers—the scouts—started a bit early, around 1993. For the next ten years, says the National Council on the Aging in Washington, one of them will turn fifty every 7.5 seconds. But members of the true, main contingent of Boomers have reengineered the process. Forget the black balloons, over-the-hill banner, gray hair dye job, and potency jokes. The Boomers are making the fiftieth as trendy as cappuccino and personal trainers. And celebrating with tucks, lifts, colors, and pills. Viagra, infomercials, life-lengthening diets, exercise regimes, and herbal magics—such as glucosamine sulfate—all play to the Boomer desire to extend your life and stave off old age.

With a lengthened life expectancy borne of medical advances, healthier lifestyles, regular exercise, and low-fat diets, many Boomers can expect to live into their nineties (maybe even to one hundred), making their fiftieth birthday the midpoint on their life's journey, not a signal for the downhill coast. Thus, they are marking it off as a major positive life event.

Just the same, for many, it's the first time they've looked into the face of Old Man Death—up close and personal—facing the fact that, alas, they might actually get old and die. There's no avoiding it: On the continuum from birth to death, they have certainly begun the trek along the second half, continuing to lengthen the span from birth, and shortening up day by day the time remaining. While this glimpse of mortality is causing the Boomers to reexamine their priorities, it also gives them another opportunity to put a designer spin on yet another life phase.

> *"We must live below our means. I decided to try to simplify my own life, reduce my consumption of material goods, eat lower on the food chain, and work toward mitigating the damage I was causing the earth. This was a start. But I also realized that if Patagonia tried to be what it is not, if it tried to "have it all," it would die... the American Dream is to own your own business, grow it as quickly as you can until you can cash out, and retire to the golf courses of Leisure World. The business itself is the product. Long-term capital investments in employee training, on-site child care, pollution controls, and pleasant working facilities are all just negatives on the short-term ledger. When the company become the fatted calf, it's sold for a profit and its resources and holdings are often ravaged and broken apart, disrupting family ties and jeopardizing the long-term health of local economies. The notion of a business as a disposable entity carries over to all elements of society. As we at Patagonia strive to make a sustainable product (hoping to make a sustainable business for a sustainable planet) we find disposability to be our greatest nemesis."*
>
> —Yvonne Chouinard, Founder and CEO of Patagonia

A midlife reality check gives many Boomers very low grades for life beyond work. Thus, there is renewed interest in flexible scheduling, which Boomers are using to pursue personal, even spiritual, interests while clinging to the security of work. Some have recommitted to family and personal relationships. Although they're feeling professionally experienced and comfortably competent, many have discovered they are not nearly as ambitious as they were in previous decades.

Work is slowly slipping down their list of priorities; it is becoming less and less the focus of their lives. This reprioritizing will actually have a positive effect on the workplace, according to Columbia/HCA Healthcare, as aging Boomers cause it to become both more informal and more humane, encouraging casual dress and schedules that allow for things like personal meditation time. They will encourage and promote healthier relationships, a more leisurely regimen, and more job-related fun, as they wean themselves off of their type A behavior. Generation Xers may find this change refreshing, and, for once, the two generations will find they actually have something in common.

Meanwhile, the Boomers are determined to age like wine—slowly and with style. Marketing research shows they won't be giving up the Rolling Stones, or their pizza, any time soon. They intend to be fit, healthy, active, self-indulgent older people. Tina Turner has become the queen icon, setting the standard for personal power, beauty, and grace. She makes fifty look "fabulous, Darling, simply fabulous."

Boomer feminists are seeking to change perceptions of the older woman, reasserting her value and importance. In ancient times, elders held power and enjoyed status. Free from the responsibilities of child care and the rigors of work life, they were the healers, the wise ones, the spiritual guides. As one fiftysomething said, "I want to be fifty and sixty in a completely different way than my mother was. I'm proud of my age, my strength, and my experience. I've just begun to be the person I worked for five decades to become."

Slide over, Tina! They're going to make a chorus line out of your solo act.

Why Care?

Simple. For all their new approach to aging bravado, Boomer bosses and peers will be/are going through a sensitive "life passage." Walk carefully around them. Avoid the temptation to treat them as Veterans or even the "elder statespeople" of your organization. They will laugh with you at pointed age jokes, but beware your next performance appraisal.

The Future: "Hell, No, We Won't Go"

THE BABY BOOMERS	
Markings	Designer glasses, cellular phones, whatever's trendy, BMWs, designer suits, designer bodies, vintage wines
Spending style	Buy now, pay later— with plastic
What they read	*Business Week, People*
Their humor	*Doonesbury*

The workplace will be dominated by the Baby Boom generation until at least 2015. While the next two generations might like to move up the ladder, the Boomers are, for the most part, secure and securing themselves in their positions. Not only is their experience impressive, but they are well-connected with the decision makers in their companies and the industries of which they are a part. They have taken connecting to a fine art—internally and externally. We think of the "man in the gray flannel suit" as a networker, but he couldn't hold a candle to the Boomers. They took the adage, "It's not *what* you know but *who* you know" and made it, if not a science, a high art form.

As the new millennium progresses, more and more Boomers will begin to retire. And, once again, the American culture will find itself transformed by the needs—living arrangements, retirement funds, accessibility, and big print—of this giant generation. Former Colorado Governor Richard Lamm says, "When the Baby Boomers start to retire, it will be equal to any demographic event that has happened to this country...as big an impact as the settlement of the West."

Boomers have popularized every phase of life as they've passed through it. Today it's trendy for women to have hot flashes and kibitz about "the M word." Those not yet experiencing menopause are, many of them, attending premenopausal seminars and support group meetings, and it's not just husbands who are showing up! The Boomers will redefine retirement, of course, just as they have adjusted every other phase of life to meet their needs. A recent Del Webb Corporation survey showed that more than two-thirds plan to work after retiring.[6] Most plan to work part time, and a few will even pursue a new career full time.

They may have to work, and they know it! Financial records show the members of this generation have

---

THE BABY BOOMERS

What the Other Generations Think About Them

Veterans say . . .
- "They talk about things they ought to keep private...like the intimate details of their personal lives."
- "They are self-absorbed."

Gen Xers say . . .
- "They're self-righteous."
- "They're workaholics."
- "They're too political, always trying to figure out just what to say...to whom...and when."
- "They do a great job of talking the talk. But they don't walk the walk."
- "Get outta my face."
- "Lighten up; it's only a job."
- "What's the management fad this week?"
- "They're clueless."

Nexters Say . . .
- "They're cool. They 're up to date on the music we like."
- "They work too much."

THE BABY BOOMERS

Fact and Fiction

Myths:	Facts:
1. They're on their way out.	1. The Organization for Economic Cooperation & Development says average life expectancy for today's woman is 78.8 years; for men, 72. Boomers can expect longer, healthier work lives than any previous generation.
2. They'll grow up.	2. According to the Boomer Institute in Cleveland, Ohio, sales of Harley-Davidson motorcycles doubled in the early 1990s, and the majority of buyers were Boomers.
3. They've always had it easy; they're assured of a comfortable retirement.	3. Of all the generations, Boomers have the largest credit card debt. They have an average of twenty years remaining on their mortgages. "They are coming late to savings," says Ken Feltman, executive director of the Employers Council on Flexible Compensation. "The distinction between generations can be seen in worsening gaps between what workers should be saving each year to ensure a comfortable retirement. For Generation X, that gap is $2,825. For Boomers, it's $3,564.
4. They've quit learning.	4. A *USA Today* (3/2/98) article says Boomers are creating a "cottage industry" that caters to old dogs learning new tricks. The National Center for Education Statistics reports that enrollment in adult education programs, everything from tap dancing to sushi making to elementary economics, is up significantly.
5. Boomers are workaholics.	5. The Baby Boomers have tended to work grueling hours for the past thirty years, but today many of them are committed to a slower pace. Yankelovich Partners says they are "the most stressed generation in history" who are eager to find creative ways to simplify their lives. Boomers, especially those approaching fifty, are working fewer hours.

not saved adequately for their retirement. The Employers Council on Flexible Compensation joined recently with Colonial Life and Accident Insurance Company to study retirement planning.[7] They found that the difference between what people should be saving per year and what they actually save varies substantially from generation to generation.

For the Boomers, that gap is nearly $1,000 per year more than it is for the Generation Xers, who know if there are going to be retirement funds, it's up to them to stash the money away now. As much as the Boomers would like to think so, not many of them will really be golfing in Palm Springs. In fact, they would need to triple their rate of saving in order to avoid a dramatic decline in their standard of living when they retire. The Discovery Channel nature shows like to intone the natural cycle of birth, growth, and decline. But the "natural order" for a pride of lions or a herd of Cape buffalo doesn't have to account for the intellectual willfulness of a group like the Baby Boomers. Beware, younger generations: They will not go gently. Watch *Modern Maturity* for further details.

CHAPTER FOUR

THE GEN XERS:

Absence and Malice

DEVON AND LI   BORN BETWEEN 1960–1980

*"It's no wonder Xers are angst-ridden and rudderless.
They feel America's greatness has passed. They got
to the cocktail party twenty minutes too late,
and all that's left are those little wieners
and a half-empty bottle of Zima."*

—DENNIS MILLER
RANTS

Generation "X" might well have been called Generation "I" for "invisible" or "L" for "lost." It's a generation that no one ever really noticed, that didn't exactly register, until recently. That quasi-invisibility, born of living in the long shadow of "The Boom," was but the lull before the storm of identity building. As a generation, it has been defined, in many ways, by what it's not more than by what it is. Xers grew up in the shadow of the Boomers and, like the middle child, passively resisted anything the elder sibling embraced. And everyone, especially the media, decided these kids were not the rescuers of the nation that their predecessors seemed to be. Besides the media was—is—run by the Boomers.

Again defined by what it is not, the X generation consists of a lot fewer people than the generation before it. While Boomers were topping the population charts—the birth rate climbed above four million per year for most of the Boom's two-decade run—Xers were the inevitable birthing recession after the boom, with a low in 1976 when only 3.2 million babies were born. That's seventy-six million Boomers versus fifty-one million Xers. The country is only now realizing these lower birth rates translate into significantly fewer workers for the current, robust job market, and many employers are panicking. Xers grew up aware of the industrial age, but they became fully sentient in the beginning of Toffler's Information Age. Boomers' economic fortunes in their formative years were so stable as to be a nonissue, allowing them to turn on, tune in, and drop out. Summers of love, drugs, political protests, and rock concerts were Boomer economic luxuries the Xers would learn they could never afford.

Gen X's collective psyche was to be shaped by a survivor mentality and can be summed up by the question, "Just tell me, is this going to be on the test?" It's a more important question than it seems at first. Xer critics see that sentiment as a sign these kids don't have the right stuff, don't care about the larger picture, and are only concerned about themselves. It is an inaccurate or at least simplistic critique. This generation has developed an almost myopic concern with survival, both economic and psychological. The question really means, "What does this have to do with my survival?" They sensed early that no one was going to hand hold them, so they must take care of themselves. That single question signals a very different agenda to the teacher, parent, professor, or boss. Minimize it as a signifier of slacker ennui, and you miss the message and a critical part of this gen's heartbeat.

But don't let all these things Generation X "is not" cause you to dismiss them out-of-hand. Employers and marketers who ignore this group or write them off as cynical slackers unwilling to make a real contribution to the workforce will be buying a one-way ticket to business failure in the new millennium. Gen Xers are settling in and moving up! They're going to be an increasingly critical part of the workforce. Some of the more well-known members—Michael Dell at Dell Computer, Jeff Bezos at Amazon.com, David Lauren at *Swing* Magazine, Jerry Yang and David Filo at Yahoo!—are already heading up their own companies. They'll soon be followed by tens of thousands of others. For the next three decades, Boomers and Xers will work together, and not always with the Boomers in senior positions. The Xers' technological acuity and growing business savvy are already putting a disproportionate number of them on an even hierarchical and authority plane with members of earlier generations. In high-tech companies in particular, Gen Xers are managing the very Boomers who only a few years ago were questioning the work ethics and commitment of the Xers.

THE GEN XERS	
Seminal Events	
1970	Women's Liberation protests and demonstrations
1972	Arab terrorists at Munich Olympics
1973	Watergate scandal
1973	Energy crisis begins
1976	Tandy and Apple market PCs
1978	Mass suicide in Jonestown
1979	Three Mile Island nuclear reactor nears meltdown
1979	U.S. corporations begin massive layoffs
1979	Iran holds sixty-six Americans hostage
1980	John Lennon shot and killed
1980	Ronald Reagan inaugurated
1986	Challenger disaster
1987	Stock market plummets
1988	Terrorist bomb blows up flight 103 over Lockerbie
1989	Exxon Valdez oil tanker spill
1989	Fall of Berlin Wall
1991	Operation Desert Storm
1992	Rodney King beating videotaped, Los Angeles riots

"I Survived the 1970s"

Where did this survivor mentality come from? Try growing up in the wake of Vietnam, the only war the United States ever lost, and you'll get a hint. Then, as you're beginning to become politically aware, watch a President of the United States go down in flames.

Nixon's resignation, the first in U.S. history, was further exacerbated—in the hearts of the children of the 1990s—by his pardon from the acting president, whose name had never appeared on the ballot. This was followed by an oil embargo that, while it simply reminded the Veterans of World War II of rationing, signaled to Xers what seemed to be the advent of a world in which anyone with a grudge could kick sand in the face of this once-respected superpower and bring our standard of living to its knees. In the 1980s, when many twentysomethings joined the job market, the Japanese shadowboxed heavily over our economy, again leaving our industrial base ruined and precipitating storms of lay-offs that would have made Noah squeamish.

Generation X watched as America seemed to fail militarily, politically, diplomatically, and economically. When the Japanese talk about saving face, this group nods enthusiastically; they feel the pain. They grew up watching their country lose face often. All the young, impressionable Xers could do was hunker down and learn how to survive in a world where everything was *not* going to be all right, where the happy endings of the movies were just shadows on the wall, where the American Dream looked like a running joke or, at best, a memory.

It's no wonder that Hunter Thompson's *Fear and Loathing in Las Vegas*, subtitled *A Savage Journey to the Heart of the American Dream,*" was more popular with Gen X college students than it was with its original Boomer audience. It resonates with a generation that not only knows things will never be as good as they once were, meaning what they perceive as the "sweet and naive golden fifties and sixties," but have lived the reality of disappointment and diminution up close and personal.

> **THE GEN XERS**
>
> Heroes
>
> (None)

This cohort has resisted labels, even balking at the moniker "Generation X," the title of a book by one of its defining writers, Douglas Coupland. They've been called "Slackers," "Twentysomethings," "Baby Busters," "Post-Boomers," and "The Thirteenth Generation," the latter because they're—roughly—the thirteenth generation of Americans born since the Constitution was ratified. None of the labels are welcome to this generation because categorization is a tool of the media, with whom Xers have an uneasy relationship. It was the media that focused so heavily on the Boomers, placing them in the spotlight, then creating new categories for them about every five years: The "Beat Generation" became "Hippies" became "Yippies" became "Yuppies," and on and on. Now every time some clever reporter comes up with another cute name for whatever phase the Boomers seem to be going through, Xers sit back and roll their eyes. For Generation X to accept any label at all is to become a media object. The Boomers clung so willingly to whatever label the media painted them with that the Xers' knee-jerk reaction is total rejection of all labels.

Consequently, because it defines itself reactively, it is one of the more difficult generations to describe. Any description is necessarily rife with generalizations, and this group has a duck-and-cover mentality about categorization. Nonetheless, categorization is inevitable. By definition, the Xers are those born between 1960 and 1980. One of the best test questions to determine whether someone is an Xer or a late Boomer

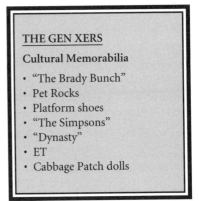

THE GEN XERS

Cultural Memorabilia

- "The Brady Bunch"
- Pet Rocks
- Platform shoes
- "The Simpsons"
- "Dynasty"
- ET
- Cabbage Patch dolls

is to ask them where they were when John F. Kennedy was shot. If they're not old enough to remember, they're probably part of Generation X. At the same time, there isn't a hard-and-fast dividing line between late Boomers and early Xers. Some people born in the early 1960s identify more with Boomers, whereas some who were born in the late 1950s, especially those who fared badly in the economic turmoil of the 1980s, empathize with the Xers like natives.

The Veterans were defined by a real war, where people killed and died for important principles. Boomers grew up during the cold war, where Armageddon was what they vicariously experienced when they crawled under their desks in school to practice "surviving a nuclear disaster." Generation X grew up during the economic wars of the 1970s and 1980s, where the battlefields lay in Flint, Michigan, and throughout the Rust Belt. It seemed, like the cold war, ongoing and endless. Although we know it now to be the opening round of industrial globalization, it seemed at the time as if our economy had been overthrown. But an economic war is a whole new animal, and the casualties show up every time some mega-corporation announces another 40,000 layoffs. Generation X grew up in this economic DMZ and it's shaped some very interesting characteristics.

Their Generational Personality

They formed their view of the world in the 1970s—the post-Vietnam-Watergate-John Travolta-Pet Rock-and-Lava Lamp era. It was a particularly unpopular time to be a child; they were some of the first babies

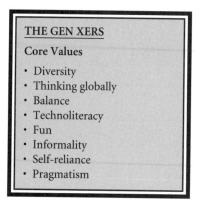

THE GEN XERS

Core Values

- Diversity
- Thinking globally
- Balance
- Technoliteracy
- Fun
- Informality
- Self-reliance
- Pragmatism

whose mothers took pills to prevent them. They came of age in an era of fallen heroes, a struggling economy, soaring divorce rates, and the phenomenon of the latchkey child—the first generation of living lifestyle accessories.[1] For their parents, it was what author Tom Wolfe called the "Me Decade," a time to focus on and develop themselves—at the health club, in self-help groups, at weekend "est" and Esalan retreats. For their children, it was another matter; it was parent-free childhood, a time to figure it out for yourself.

- *Gen Xers are self-reliant.* If the tabloids were to characterize this cohort, the headline might read, "Generation X: Raised by Wolves." They were the most attention-deprived, neglected group of kids in a long time. Parents were absent without leave for two reasons. First, nearly half of their parents' marriages ended in divorce. Generation X children lived and breathed in an environment of joint custody, visitation rights, and weekend fathers. While their parents' unraveling relationships devastated them, many of their assets as a generation—self-reliance, independence, and just plain old chutzpa—developed as a result of this absenteeism. Second, this was the first generation of kids within the bounds of the two-income family. Women were going to work in increasing numbers, and the economy was making it dramatically more difficult for a family to sustain a reasonable standard of living with only one wage earner. This one-two punch created a new sociological trend: latchkey kids. They became accustomed to being alone, yet feelings of abandonment shaped their psyches. They wanted more attention from their parents; at the same time, they were used to a certain freedom. They yearned for real attention, and the concept of quality time rang hollow with them: parents coming home late from work, pulling dinner together, and then spending the few minutes left "networking" with their children.

- *They are seeking a sense of family.* In the absence of parents, this generation has learned to create its own surrogate families by assembling a close circle of friends. Coupland's seminal book, *Generation X*, is primarily about how close friends, trying to survive a difficult economic climate amidst dysfunctional families, create their own nuclear family out of an assemblage of strangers. The popular TV sitcom "Friends" is based on the same premise. Dine out or see a movie on a Saturday night, and you will see twentysomethings in small groups, in sharp contrast with the one-on-one dating standard just a decade earlier. High-school principals report that, for the last eight or ten years, it's been far trendier for kids to go to the homecoming dance or the prom with a small group than with a date. On the job, managers tell us they see similar tight-knit groups of young workers who socialize both during work and after hours. Raised in the absence of tight-knit and supportive families, this generation still yearns for a sense of family, and they'll look for it on the job if they haven't found it elsewhere.

- *They want balance.* In the eyes of Generation X, their parents devoted their lives to the religion of work: spending evenings and weekends at the office, bringing projects home, and expending all of their energy and attention on work issues. It looked like workaholism to their kids, who couldn't help but notice that most adults decided their self-worth based on their success on the job. When family friends came over for dinner, the adults spent their time discussing their jobs; phone calls focused on problems with the boss; and kids regularly spent an extra hour or two in day care because a work deadline threatened. In the words of many an Xer, their parents "lived to work." Xers simply want to "work to live." Members of this cohort group are distressed by the high prices their parents paid for success: stress and health problems, divorce, drug and alcohol abuse. And it didn't look as if the companies to whom they had devoted all their time and energy appreciated their efforts. Layoffs were living proof. So it is that Generation X is committed to more balance in their own lives. They don't buy the Supermom and Superdad theory that you can have it all.

They won't try to juggle all those roles—parent, employee, spouse—or, if they do, it won't be with the same unrealistic expectations. They know something has to give. On the job, they expect to leave at 5:00 P.M., they don't intend to give up their weekends, and they will rarely volunteer to work overtime.

Says LanceW8850 on an electronic bulletin board, "Most of us don't have any particular problem with staying late; we just have a life outside of work. I've come in on weekends, stayed late, to get a project done. But I don't like to do it. Life wasn't meant to be spent at work; it was meant to be enjoyed with people you value. If we estimated the job correctly in the first place, there'd be no need to stay. Personally, I married my wife so that I could be with her; I'm not convinced that staying at work will bring me marital satisfaction."

- *They have a nontraditional orientation about time and space.* They don't think much of work hours. It won't be surprising if, within the next few years, a whole generation rediscovers management by objective (MBO). It strikes a chord with Generation X's philosophy of work, "As long as I get my work done, what does it matter how and when I get it done?" They show up late, leave early, and appear to be "slackers" because they are keeping their eye on what they think is the ball—getting the work done. If they do it at home, at odd hours, in the car on the cell phone, or while telecommuting, they think that's *their* business, not their supervisor's. They don't come close to understanding "line of sight" managing. Nor do they understand the idea of being carefully hired and matched to a job, then being policed like a jailed felon.

- *They like informality.* Having grown up in a serious world with a bunch of serious Boomers for parents and bosses, this younger generation of employees wants to see things lighten up. They take casual days very seriously. Being able to go to work in jeans and a T-shirt on Friday, many assert, isn't just a perk. They say it actually makes them work harder and get more done. Anything that makes work less "corporate" resonates well with a generation who feels betrayed by corporate interests, and some companies are beginning to recognize that the nature of the work doesn't really require the suit, tie, wing-tips, or nylons. Companies like Ben & Jerry's Ice Cream and Southwest Airlines, even though run by Boomers, are attractive places to work because the corporate cultures embrace having fun at work. Ben and Jerry's has a chief fun officer, known as the Grand Poobah.

- *Their approach to authority is casual.* Formal hierarchical relationships are lost on Gen Xers, who aren't so much against authority as simply unimpressed by it. They saw authority figures—Nixon, Reverends Bakker and Swaggart, and often even their own parents—step off the pillar and into the gutter. Their tendency, therefore, is to treat the company president just the way they would the front-desk receptionist. A Boston company recently hired a new company president. He was making his way around the building, meeting with each department. In one such meeting, a Gen X employee asked the new president where he lived. After the president responded, the young guy said, "Alright! I can get a ride to work with you." And that's what happened. Boomers and Veterans would not have asked the question; for them there's a certain aura around leadership that dictates what is appropriate and inappropriate to say and ask. Not so for this younger cohort, who would tell us we all put our Dockers on one leg at a time.

- *They are skeptical.* Gen Xers grew up with lip service—from advertisers and marketers, from their parents, from corporations and national leadership—that often didn't seem to be supported by action. Their whole class watched with great anticipation as Christa McAuliffe, the first school teacher in space, boarded the space shuttle Challenger. Within a few nanoseconds, the whole endeavor blew up and turned to dust right in front of their faces. They have learned not to place their faith in others, to be very careful with their loyalty and commitments, for fear of getting burned. One Nike ad says it this way, "Don't insult our intelligence. Tell us what it is. Tell us what it does. And don't play the national anthem while you do it." While the Boomers were told, "You can be anything you want—even President of the United States," Generation X was told, "Be careful out there. It's a dangerous world." And so they are careful and guarded in their personal and professional relationships, withholding their optimism and excitement for fear that things won't work out quite as planned.

- *They are attracted to the edge.* Where Boomers saw their careers as great melodramas and heroic endeavors that could consume their lives, to Xers, the job is "just a job." Their sense of risk and adventure is very much expressed outside the workplace. It's not uncommon for an Xer's Monday morning coffee chat to include matter-of-fact recountings of rock climbing, mountain biking, and parachute jumping exploits done with friends traveling in packs. After all, the X-Games were named in their honor and exemplify their spirit of eccentricity and physical derring-do.

- *They are technologically savvy.* (No kidding, Sherlock.) Xers learned to operate the microwave, program the VCR, and play video games when they were little tikes. Computer skills were every bit as fundamental in their elementary education as the three Rs were to generations before them. A cartoon in Howe and Strauss' book, *Thirteenth Gen,* shows two young soldiers in the Persian Gulf in a tank. One is reassuring the other, "Don't worry. I can drive this thing. I've done this at Chuck E. Cheese." There is that comfort with technology; this guy probably could indeed punch the buttons on the computer and make the tank run. Older generations may learn computer skills and become quite adept, but they will never have the natural affinity for technology that Gen Xers simply have "in their bones."

First-Half Generation X: "Please Sir, Can I Have Some More?"

The first group of Gen Xers to hit the workplace were the wretched refuse, the workers no one wanted. Not only did they join the labor marketplace in the wake of millions of Boomers, but they also arrived

---

THE GEN XERS

How Xers Differ From the Previous Generation

Boomers	Xers
• Fight against authority	• Aikido rebellion. Go around authority or turn it in your direction.
• Media darlings	• Avoid the media and the limelight and, above all, don't let them label you.
• Workaholics	• Get a life.
• Political	• Politics never solved anything, and usually they made it worse.
• Political at work	• Corporate politics wastes time we could spend doing something we enjoy.
• Nostalgia for the 1960s	• Oh, God, not again.

---

at a time when the U.S. economy was in the throes of globalization—getting our economic heart ripped out and handed to us on a sushi platter. "Downsizing" went from euphemism to anathema overnight, and college students who had been told that a liberal arts degree would be a ticket to a good job discovered they were the butt of an expensive joke.

"What did the art history major say to the engineering student?"

"Paper or plastic, Sir?"

So while the hippies were morphing into the winner-take-all Yuppies during the Reagan 1980s, the Xers, who were just entering the workplace, had some very cruel different lessons to learn. It wasn't uncommon for a college graduate to come out with a degree, owing $10,000 on the average in student loans, only to be handed the "opportunity" to work for minimum wage at a coffee shop or bookstore. To take a grim view of it—and they did—not only did the Boomers steal the nation's collective attention, they also took all the jobs with interesting wages.

When the layoff craze struck like a radioactive lizard in downtown Tokyo, things got even worse. The parents many Gen Xers moved in with after college were taking it on the chin, watching high-paying careers turn into corporate redundancy. Don't think this generation didn't notice. Their consequent resentment of corporate America has manifested itself in a variety of ways. The Boomers may not have trusted anyone over thirty, but the Xers didn't trust anyone in the Fortune 500.

Only companies like Starbucks seemed to understand that this workforce needed some of the same things other workers got, things like health care coverage (even for part timers) and a stake in the success of the company (stock options for all employees). That understanding stood them in good stead years later when the long predicted labor shortage finally came and other service industry leaders were scrambling to find workers in every nook and cranny. Says Howard Schultz, Starbucks Chairman and CEO, "But Starbucks gets back plenty for its investment. The most obvious effect is lower attrition. Nationwide, most retailers and fast-food chains have a turnover rate ranging from 150 percent to as high as 400 percent a year. At Starbucks, turnover at the barista level averages 60 percent to 65 percent. For store managers, our turnover is only about 25 percent, while at other retailers, it's about 50 percent."[2]

In any case, the first half of Generation X joined the workforce as the traditional "understood" job contract was being torn up and redrafted by corporations to fit the new "downsized," no stability employment model. The Veterans and Boomers chanted, "Whatever happened to loyalty?" during the layoffs of the 1980s, while corporations answered, "You're in charge of your own career. The company won't take care of you and never promised it would." Of course, since Gen X came of job-holding age during the age of downsizing, their predilection for survival clued them in: Everyone better look out for themselves. Thus was born a whole generation of corporate nomads, jumping from one entry level job to another. It has been a generation almost unique in its ability to persevere in the redefined environment. You'll never hear them gripe about company loyalty: it's as foreign to them as buggy whips are to Boomers.

The only ticket that got them anywhere in the new economy was their own skills, and the best way to develop those skills was through real experience in real jobs, not with college degrees or book smarts. The recent jump in internships—from 3 percent of all graduates participating in an internship ten years ago to a full third of graduating seniors now emerging from college with at least one internship under their belts—is only one indicator of this generation's lust for real, nontheoretical work experience.

Second Half: The Gold-Collar Workers

The second half of the Generation X workforce has begun to reveal it-self, and it's experiencing another major swing of the pendulum. The labor shortage finally hit full stride in 1997, and a significant proportion of the Gen X workforce has been positioned to cash in. With the explosion of information technology (IT) as a function of every company—in fact, an industry unto itself—anyone who knows anything about computer technology can negotiate some pretty impressive starting salaries. The truth is, most companies need qualified computer techni-cians and programmers, and they haven't come ready-made, fully formed from the ranks of Generation X in quite the way employers ex-pected. Consequently, companies are willing to settle for whatever they can get—anyone without a fear of computers—and train them, either formally or on the job. Say what you want about Gen Xers, people fre-quently do, but they're not afraid of technology. Companies are begin-ning to recognize that, if they can't get a qualified person for their IT needs, a confident person is the next best thing. Not only that, the rush to get a company up on the web has punched the ticket of many college students before they've even received a degree. Companies are hiring "web masters," anyone who has put up a web page as part of one of their classes.

A recent *Fortune* article called these new Gen X employees "gold-collar workers," a reissued term first coined by Robert Kelly in the 1980s, to describe highly desirable, technically trained college graduates because they are becoming increasingly rare and commanding some formidable starting salaries.[3] Most companies now offer a bounty or finder's fee of several thousand dollars to any employee who recruits an IT professional. Some of these workers are commanding signing bonuses as high as $40,000. How long before qualified computer tech-nicians learn to say, "Call my agent" before exiting an interview?

It's not just the money. These new workers are making a variety of unusual demands of their employers: being allowed to bring pets to work, working odd hours, working fewer hours, having fun at work, and dressing casually. They're requiring, and getting, these perks from employers desperate for their skills.

What once seemed madness now seems like eccentricity. That may be the central change in the mind-set of employers and recruiters—

most of them Boomers—around this generation. Ten years ago they were "whiners," "slackers," and "impatient nuisances" who couldn't seem to get it through their thick skulls that the workplace demands certain minimum behavior requirements: politeness, punctuality, teamwork, respect, proper business attire, and working within a hierarchy, never mind that it had been flattened. Now Generation X workers are the only game in town, and the downsizing pendulum is swinging the other way, at least in many industries, and absolutely for tech jobs. Not only has the labor shortage taken its toll, but some of the most adamant downsizers have begun to realize that they cut the workforce too much, that some of that dead weight was actually doing valuable work. Companies went through a contraction phase; now they are in an expansion period, mega-mergers excepted. The current jobless rate is at its lowest in twenty years, which is the traditional time period historians use to define a generation. Hello generation X.2, and welcome to the vault.

Whereas early Xers saw the workplace as glutted and underpaying, rife only with jobs as bag boys and baristas, those second-half Xers with advanced skills find themselves embraced by a labor market with between 100,000 and 400,000 unfilled technology positions. For the first time since the rush for engineers and MBAs in the 1980s, job seekers are in the driver's seat. The economics of the workplace for the second-half Xers are starkly different than those their earlier cohorts perceived to be their lot.

Devon: Generation X Economic Orphan

Devon graduated from a small eastern college in 1982 with a degree in psychology and a minor in anthropology. Graduation left him owing $40,000 in school loans, which prohibited him from going to graduate school. So he went looking for a job, hoping to land an entry-level position in a corporation and work his way up into a decent-paying job. He had dreams of his own apartment, a nice car, and an enjoyable nightlife with friends. After a nine-month search, however, he ended up with two part-time jobs: at a coffee shop in the mornings and at The Gap at night. These two jobs would cover his school loans but not much else. The dream of having his own apartment became dimmer, and it looked like living with his parents was going to be a long-term solution to his financial difficulties. He couldn't afford a car, so he biked to work. Any spare income seemed to get absorbed by printing up resumes and sending them, en masse, to hundreds of employers. He "forgot" to take any computer classes in college and regretted it every time he searched the want ads. In fact, it looked like he "forgot" to get any marketable skills, and he began to look for opportunities to acquire some kind of skill that a company would pay for.

He finally decided the only way to get those skills was to take a job with a nonprofit organization that would give him a chance to prove himself without "3 to 5 years of previous experience." A low-paying job in a homeless shelter actually paid off. It gave him work that he felt was meaningful, let him mix with others his age, and gave him some modest exposure to computer technology. The organization was open to all kinds of ideas, as long as the person attached to the idea was willing to do the work. Some of the other staff members were his age, and they often went out after work, forging a small circle of close friends. He even found a girlfriend. Best of all, the organization had a bunch of old computers people had donated. During quiet times, he began to experiment with them. He often ran into trouble because the software—sometimes donated, sometimes illegally copied—was much too sophisticated for the equipment. He therefore found himself digging in the guts of the computers, opening them up and fooling around with the hardware.

Today, Devon has finally been able to save a little money. Recently, his folks kicked in a thousand dollars, and he was able to buy himself a 1983 Accord while still handling his student loans. His dreams of having his own apartment still seem far off. When some coworkers recently proposed renting a three-bedroom place together he jumped at the chance. It meant a considerable financial strain, but he continues to hope for a better job. If he can just show some company what he knows, and, more importantly, if he can find one willing to teach him what they know, he may yet move into the labor mainstream. If not, he may yet be able to use his current job as a stepping stone to something better, although he isn't exactly sure what that "better" might be or how he will actually leverage himself from here to there.

Devon's liberal arts degree coupled with his 1980s entry into the workplace have added up to penny pinching, struggling to survive, and soul searching, a tough start to a slow-growth career. It has set a tone that has already colored his view of what is possible for him now and in the future, despite the employment—and unemployment—figures of the moment.

Li: Generation X Gold-Collar Employee

Li's is a happier story since it begins in the 1990s and includes a background in computer science. When Li was in college, the World Wide Web was just coming into common knowledge. What she knew about the Internet, which wasn't a lot, was about to change in dramatic ways, and she wanted to go along for the ride. She didn't buy into the line about how valuable a liberal arts education would be, so she added a computer science minor to her English major. Her final paper for her degree was a demonstration of how someone with access to the World Wide Web could assemble a graduate thesis on James Joyce's *Ulysses* by cutting and pasting from other work on the subject and, without plagiarizing, using only a standard, commercial search engine. She performed this feat live in front of three professors in fifteen minutes, earning looks of horror from the assembled academics and an "A" on the paper. After an extensive review of her previous papers, they gave her a diploma and wished her luck in her future endeavors. They needn't have bothered. Never have so few been wanted by so many.

Li had already made up her mind which job offer to accept. Although she was a below-average programmer, she understood computer networks like nobody's business. The job offers from two prestigious consulting firms during her junior year certainly were flattering, but unless they could guarantee she would get SAP training at the academy in Waldorf, Germany, she wasn't biting. They, for their part, were offended by her brazenness, but they kept her resume in their "active recruitment" file.

Until near the end of her senior year, she was undecided if she wanted to go to work in Seattle or Silicon Valley, or try to rustle up some venture capital with a friend who had a great idea for some software and strike out on her own. Trouble was, she didn't know anything about venture capital and had heard her share of horror stories. She wasn't interested enough in the world of high finance to learn what she needed to know, so she took a job at a small Seattle company that was working on networking three-dimensional computer animation. The money wasn't great, but the stock options could prove to be lucrative enough for her to set up her own company in a few years. As part of the deal, she didn't actually have to move to Seattle. She could set up her office anywhere, as long as she flew into headquarters once a month for some face time with the execs, mostly Generation Xers themselves.

So she rented a loft in the warehouse district and spent her small signing bonus outfitting her office with an espresso machine, refrigerator, pool table, two old couches, and a very fast Internet connection. Her friends come to the office all the time to see her, and she works whatever hours she pleases. She has no real plans for a husband or family right now, but she is dating a couple of different people. Her personal and office lives have completely merged, and she doesn't spend much time at her apartment anymore. That's not to say she works fourteen hours a day, however. In fact, it's hard to know when she's working and when she's goofing off. To afford her extravagant lifestyle, she does a little network consulting on the side. She doesn't really think of her job with the animation company as full time, so the consulting works to fill in the gaps when she is idle. She and the friend with the great software idea have hired an MBA intern to help them rustle up some venture capital, so she might be expanding her offices soon. She gets so many headhunter calls now, she always lets the machine answer the phone. She communicates with friends via e-mail and takes a nice leisurely trip to Seattle once a month to talk to her bosses and meet with some of the more cutting-edge people in her field.

Devon and Li in the Workplace

Although it's true that Devon and Li have different skill sets and income levels, their primary difference is history. Li came to the workplace with high expectations that came to fruition. Devon barely survived his bap-

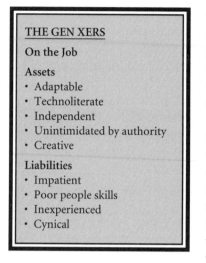

THE GEN XERS

On the Job

Assets
• Adaptable
• Technoliterate
• Independent
• Unintimidated by authority
• Creative

Liabilities
• Impatient
• Poor people skills
• Inexperienced
• Cynical

tism by fire—learning bitter lessons about promises, hope, and disappointment. If the economy should take a downturn and job demand dry up, Li could be in for some of the same bitter lessons.

Nevertheless, there aren't a lot of starry-eyed second-half gold-collar workers. Like their orphaned predecessors, they know that their economic mistresses, so pleased with them now, could grow bored and fickle, and send them packing to live with their parents. Because their work is rewarding in many ways, they are a bit more willing than their older peers to work long hours and devote more free time to their jobs. Devon and his peers will probably never make that commitment. It smacks too much of the Boomers who manage them, and it's an example they won't emulate. Devon knows there will always be too much work, and "having a life" has become gospel to him and his friends.

But Li and Devon still want many of the same things: atypical corporations where hours are flexible; independence is encouraged; fun and humor are incorporated into the work; and casual dress is an everyday standard, not just a Friday treat.

They also, for the most part, share their disdain for Boomer bosses. Like many younger generations observing the absurdities of those older in charge, this generation sees most of what the Boomers have done as wrong-headed, atavistic, and chock full of arrogant self-importance. When Xers ask themselves that "Is this going to be on the test?" question, they see most of the Boomer work behavior as beside the point. There is a natural enmity between these two groups, one born of years of coexistence that was neither peaceful nor equal. And nothing raises the ire of Xers more than technophobic Boomers. That many Boomers are both clueless and in charge rankles like nothing else.

So do the workplace fads they've seen come and go—the quality circles that turned into a search for excellence that became a call for empowerment that turned into TQM, reengineering, and the habits of seven highly obnoxious people. The new age sensibilities of the

Boomers are giving way to calls for "bringing the whole self to work" from the Xers, even when that includes your pet ferret.[4] Gen Xers don't want to get spiritually in touch with their jobs; they just want to be comfortable at work, be able to avoid some of the corporate politics, and just act like themselves. If Xers do embrace any management trend, it would have to be technology, particularly computer networks. That to them looks like salvation, a way to become more productive, less geographically limited, and, frankly, different from the generation before. Generation X has pinned its hopes for making its mark in the workplace, and in society itself, on computer technology. So far, it hasn't been a bad bet, although possibly an overstated one, eventually.

Their Work Ethic

Generation X didn't get labeled "slackers" for nothing. One of the older generations' chief complaints against this group is their work ethic, or lack thereof. One could argue, using PC jargon, that they are "differently oriented toward work." Let's face it, these younger workers have an attitude toward work that is as different from that of previous generations as anything we've seen before. Previous generations, maybe back to the beginning of history, have equated work with survival. The Boomers put a new spin on that, turning it into "work equals self-fulfillment." But Generation X learned that work is no guarantee of survival, that corporations can throw you out of your job without warning, logic, or even an apology, and that entry-level work is often mindless, dull, and exhausting.

They're not likely to change their perception. Just as a child's early years determine his or her personality, early work experiences permanently shape workers' attitudes about corporate culture. The sudden courtship of Generation X by companies who need somebody, anybody, to wait on customers, deliver their products, and fix their computers, will not likely redeem corporate America in the eyes of young workers. The prevailing attitude that all work is "just a job" is unlikely to change.

But Generation X workers can be motivated to do work—good work. Flexible hours, an informal work environment, and just the right amount of supervision are great places to start. It also helps to understand how their brains work. There are researchers who claim that the different media a child is exposed to actually physically change the brain's neural networks. For example, since the introduction of photography, television, and movies in the last 130 years, the average IQ has increased. A person taking an IQ test thirty years ago would score twenty points higher than they would on the test designed for today's audience. In fact, test designers have been forced to make the test harder over time, because it appears that people are getting smarter, and, with the advent of computers, video games, and the like, scores in visual acuity are rising even faster. That bespeaks a change in our brains, especially among children who have grown up with intense visual images.

One result researchers claim to see in the Generation X workforce is "multitasking." This generation, often accused of having little-to-no attention span, actually processes work in a very different way. Says Marc Prensky, vice president of Bankers Trust, "This under-30 generation thinks and sees the world in ways entirely different from their parents... largely because technology has created and reinforced certain cognitive changes in the ways they receive and process information."[5] William Strauss calls it "parallel processing," a computer term meaning the machine is doing many different calculations simultaneously. That's what this group does best: handle a lot of diverse information at the same time. Here's a scenario that illustrates this point. Bob sits at his desk while Ann, a Veteran coworker, explains the details of a very important project. Bob turns away to type some e-mail, glancing up from the screen occasionally to make eye contact with Ann. Soon, though, she stalks off in anger, saying, "I'll tell you about this later. It's clear this isn't important to you." Pow, Bob is whacked on the side of the head with a generational difference.

Ann's interpretation of his behavior was that he didn't care about her or what she was saying because he wasn't looking at her, facing her directly, nodding his understanding. And who can blame her? But to him, listening intently to Ann could be done easily while typing some unimportant e-mail. He was "parallel processing," which he says is the best way for him to concentrate. As he sees it, he is occupying his surface consciousness with trivial information so he can focus his deeper consciousness on more complex tasks.

If you're searching for the Generation X work ethic, don't look through the traditional lens. You won't find it. If you want to tap into it, give them a lot to do and some freedom regarding how the work gets done. You'll probably be surprised how much these "slackers" can accomplish and still walk out the door at 5:00 P.M.

Where They Work

It's true that many members of Generation X have gone into technology—inside of nontechnology and in the technology industry itself. And while it's true that Microsoft is populated primarily by Xers and Silicon Valley is a bastion for them, the truth is, Generation X hasn't produced more than its share of computer scientists and engineers. In fact, many statistics show this generation hasn't kept up with previous generations in its production of academically trained computer scientists. What surveys and research don't uncover is that most Xers learned computer "science" via trial and error. If a kid struggles for ten hours trying to get Doom to work on his network so he and three others can play death matches late into the night, he tends to learn some things of transferable value along the way, just like Veteran car mechanics did. In actuality, there are Xers in all areas of almost every company. The most visible ones work in the IT departments, helping Boomers and Veterans figure out why their computers are frozen up. In fact, even outside the IT group, if you see an Xer prairie-dogging over the cube walls, it's probably to answer some computer question from a fellow employee.

All the talk of labor shortages and gold-collar workers tends to bury the fact that there are still a lot of minimum-wage Xers out there. The service sector is still rife with them, in bookstores, coffee shops, and strip malls. Many of the first wave of Xers, if they're still in retail, have now advanced into management positions. Still, many are looking for a way out because they don't see retail positions as "real jobs." A real job, in their view, is one where they can work eight to five, have their weekends free, and actually get some health care coverage. And more than minimum wage.

There's also a strain of Generation X workers who have gone into a very special sector of the economy: their own. A lot of Xers opted so far out of the corporate milieu that they decided to start

> **THE GEN XERS**
>
> **Messages That Motivate**
>
> - "Do it your way."
> - "We've got the newest hardware and software."
> - "There aren't a lot of rules here."
> - "We're not very corporate."

their own businesses. Eighty percent of all new businesses started in the last three years belong to Xers, according to Scott West, director of National Marketing for Van Kampen Funds. The Boomers did a lot of this too, but usually in the wake of a layoff or midlife crisis. Xer entrepreneurs tended to jump in right out of college, or after a few years in the corporate world. That strong sense of self-reliance developed during their formative years. "Having your own business means not worrying about what some head guy in Dallas thinks," says Sky Eacrett, a Redlands, California, tile store manager. "No matter how much money you make for them you are still just an X. And you can be X-ed off. With my own business, I could come in at 7 am, and leave at noon to play golf."[6] They usually don't, but the option is what's important.

Their Leadership Style

With steadily increasing global competition, few things in the workplace have changed more dramatically in the last decade than leadership. The old chain-of-command system has proven tremendously burdensome; it simply takes too long to get the paperwork, the decision, and the product through the hierarchy and bureaucracy. Even Boomers will admit that they often succeed *despite* or outside of "the bureaucracy." Sophisticated and demanding customers expect their needs to be met right now. The new leader, then, must be skilled at supporting and developing a responsive, competent team of people who can change direction, or projects, on a dime.

Generation X is uniquely qualified for the job. They've never really been "good soldiers." They had an egalitarian rather than a hierarchical relationship with their parents; they went to school in a system that encouraged diverse viewpoints; and, in their first jobs, they usually worked for Boomer bosses, who espoused participation and involvement, although they often didn't practice what they preached. They thrive on change; many learned as kids to adapt to a new bedroom, home, and neighborhood on weekends. They are used to challenging and being challenged. Whereas the little Boomers were graded for "works well with others," little Xers were graded for their ability to challenge others' thinking. They were encouraged to disagree with things they read, to debate classmates, and to "Never just do what an adult asks. Always ask, 'Why?'"

They tend to be drawn to leadership for more altruistic reasons than the generation before them. For the Boomers, there's a sort of juju about authority; although many of them distrust authority, they've lusted after leadership roles, seeking to prove their status, prestige, and general worthiness by climbing the ladder. Generation Xers don't equate magic and leadership. Those in leadership roles tend to choose them, and be chosen for them, because they are competent and have good leadership skills. It's a job, just a job.

It is said that information equals power. Insomuch as this is true, Xers should be wielding more and more power because they're far more adept than the Boomers or Veterans at accessing information—on the Internet, via e-mail, and through the company's information system.

Generation X managers tend to be fair, competent, straightforward leaders. Their inclination is to create a conglomeration of circles of people into "campus cultures," complete with recreational opportunities. If there's one area where Xer leaders are not as strong as their Boomer counterparts, it's in the people skills arena. Xers tend to be honest, sometimes brutally so, and this can be devastating to a young employee in the midst of his or her first performance appraisal. A certain amount of tact on the part of the leader can go a long way toward employee retention.

The Boomers would tell you that they, themselves, are also better at corporate politics—knowing just how to say exactly the right thing to the penultimate person at precisely the right time. Xers would say they're not interested in that "political stuff." They see the 20 percent of their generation who are politically adept as corporate stooges.

As Team Members

There may be a serious backlash against the concept of teamwork before long, simply because Boomers are so team happy, and Xers tend to reject Boomer metaphors and baggage. Of course, Generation X workers are on all kinds of teams right now, and their quest for a sense of family draws them to teams, although they prefer team members of their own choosing. In their personal lives the "Friends" ethic is cherished—a group of friends hanging together working and playing as a unit. A "team" but without the explicit Boomer rules or the Veteran sense of duty.

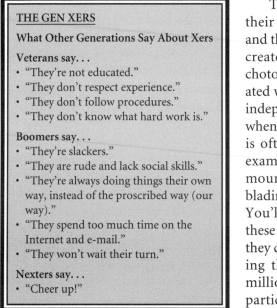

THE GEN XERS

What Other Generations Say About Xers

Veterans say. . .
- "They're not educated."
- "They don't respect experience."
- "They don't follow procedures."
- "They don't know what hard work is."

Boomers say. . .
- "They're slackers."
- "They are rude and lack social skills."
- "They're always doing things their own way, instead of the proscribed way (our way)."
- "They spend too much time on the Internet and e-mail."
- "They won't wait their turn."

Nexters say. . .
- "Cheer up!"

This collision between their independent nature and their yearning for family creates an interesting dichotomy. The sports associated with this generation are independent activities, even when done in groups, which is often the case. Take, for example, snowboarding, mountain biking, rollerblading, and rock climbing. You'll often see Xers doing these activities in groups, but they could just as well be doing them alone. There are millions of young people participating in all manner of team sports like football, hockey, soccer, and basketball, but when you think of sports "invented" by Xers, they tend to be individual efforts.

If you want an interesting view of Xer teamwork, take a look at the way many Microsoft groups write code. This company's huge programming projects are often assembled by many teams of software developers, each piece taken by a separate team that must coordinate its programming to meet the goals of that distinct section of an application. But programming is, by its nature, a very solitary effort. One programmer's code can look very different than another's, even if they both are doing precisely the same thing. Each has a style, and we're told that a project manager can tell which piece of a program was written by which team member by the style alone. A team leader's ability to piece all of these individually conceived programs together into a working software is critical. Microsoft's system is a good match with the Gen X mind-set.

In contrast, if this kind of project were set up by Boomers, it would likely consist of the whole team working in a shared space with no walls, so they could converse, collaborate, and generally do the project like a "community team." At Microsoft, however, software developers each have their own office, complete with walls and doors, and they write code in solitude. They get together as a team from time to time to check on progress and work out particularly gnarly problems as a group, but most of their time is spent working alone, with only minor supervision. That model—virtual teamwork—is the norm in most software companies. Much of the communication among team members is handled by e-mail.

This new style of communication and collaboration still incorporates phone conversations, face-to-face meetings, and conferences; it just obviates some of these and extends the usefulness of others. Its main dynamic is its asynchronous nature. Not since the advent of newspapers has asynchronous work taken such leaps ahead. Take an example from an early e-mail discussion group called "The Well." During the Russian crisis when Gorbachev fell and Yeltsin faced off the tanks, one participant on The Well was talking to his daughter, who was in Red Square at the time, and he was reporting to others in the chat room what she was seeing. He was getting the news to them faster than CNN, which his wife was watching in the next room. He was way ahead of her. Not only could he get the facts, but he could ask questions of the "reporter" and get responses, something no other audience had ever been able to do. This was years before the World Wide Web came into common use.

This new form of asynchronous communication is faster than the other methods, is more grass roots, creates a permanent record that people can go back to, and is more interactive. We've only glimpsed what it can do. To see how Generation X is going to work and play together in the future, join a listserv, get an e-mail address, watch the chat rooms, and relearn the almost forgotten art of letter writing.

Managing Generation X

If you're ready to create a fun, flexible, educational, nonmicromanaged work atmosphere where Xers have a variety of projects to engage them, you'll have Generation X beating down the door to go to work for you.

Let's face it: Most jobs are a mixture of intrinsically motivating tasks and drudgery. There's no evidence that Xers expect work to be totally engaging and completely meaningful. They are not naive kids; they learned self-sufficiency early and never expected the world to be a bowl of cherries. As long as you don't pretend that some meaningless task is really important, they will respect you for your frankness and honesty.

Sometimes the things that are on the test aren't necessarily the most important matters. They get that.

Just the same, managers of Gen Xers, particularly those on the front lines, need to be clear in communicating that some repetitive tasks are simply part of the job and that quality outcomes require some checking. Even tasks requiring only modest skills have enough nuances that, to be done well, they can't necessarily be automated. They require real human judgment. That judgment is only acquired through experience, and experience means staying at those repetitive tasks. Many Gen Xers recognize that, in sports, you've got to practice, practice, practice to develop skill and experience; sometimes they don't make the translation of that lesson to work. Helping with that translation is critical to creating a productive, happy, Gen X coterie in your company.

Some Key Principles

Recruiting

1. Include the phrase "we want you to have a life," at least three times during the interview. Allison Ye, a Gen X tax analyst at JC Penney, says one of the reasons she has stayed with the company is her boss' attitude about balance. "He knows for me to be successful at work, I need to be successful at home. I don't have a husband or children, but I do need a successful home life—spending time with friends, at church, edifying myself by educational programs, or whatever."[7] To an Xer, twelve-hour days and seven-day weeks either means your company is too cheap to hire enough people to do the job, or you are an incompetent manager.

2. Convince them that, in your company, ideas are evaluated purely on merit, not by the person's years of experience.

3. Don't try the "change agent" routine on them. Xers have a sixth sense about business BS, and a lot of the jargon that gets tossed around in business qualifies, as far as they are concerned. Instead, tell them that your company and industry are going through a lot of change. Leave it at that.

To an Xer, change means opportunity, opportunities to move up or broaden the scope of their skills.

4. Warm and humane treatment—so important to Boomers—doesn't cut it with the next generation. Instead, make it a fun, relaxed place to work.

5. Stress that your company wants to be a technological innovator and needs workers who aren't afraid of technology to make that happen. If you want a presence on the web, tell them so.

6. Say the phrase "hands-off supervision" at least three times in the interview. Stress that you'll need them to manage a lot of projects at the same time, that you're looking for a good juggler.

7. Consider setting up a special customer service department for employees. Irving and Norma Edwards of All Metro Health Care, in Lynnbrook, New York, have done just that. Their associates, mostly low-wage workers, have special needs—transportation, child care, language skills—that, unmet, interfere with job performance. Now three employees assist with arranging for child care and for loans, filling out paperwork for food stamps, and handling immigration matters. Efforts like this, according to the Edwards, help keep annual turnover under 80 percent.[8]

Orienting

1. Show them your company's intranet and let them show themselves around a bit.

2. They're not afraid to ask questions, so make it easy for them by giving them a list of who to call for more information on a wide variety of subjects.

3. Include the phrase "we want you to have a life" at least three times during orientation.

4. Xers hate corporate politics and often fault their Boomer predecessors for engaging in too much of it. Let them know, as their boss, that you will "take point" on political maneuvers so the Xer can relax and concentrate on the job.

Opportunities

Companies come and companies go. Nothing is static. Everything changes, and keeping your eye on the ball, for Generation X, means looking out for number one. A lot of rah-rah about contributing to the organization and the greatness of team efforts and "all for one and one for all" rings hollow with this group. Yes, they like being treated as individuals and getting personal attention, but there's a fine line for them between good managing and micromanaging.

1. That's why it's best to err on the side of freedom. Plenty of elbow room will appeal to your Gen X workforce and give them a favorable impression of your workplace. Because they are self-reliant, it's important to be there when they need questions answered, but also know when to back off and let them figure it out themselves.

2. Stress the dramatic changes your company is going through, with an eye to helping them develop all kinds of new skills. These are the corporate nomads, so if you have a large enough organization, you can let them roam from tribe to tribe without ever really losing them. For this cohort, moving sideways often is just as good as moving up.

3. An important message to send to this group who is trying to build a broad range of diverse skills is that training is an important part of their duties. Let them know they will be going through training on a lot of different systems continuously, as well as some professional development at outside conferences.

Developing

Development is critically important to Gen Xers. A recent study released by the Gallup Organization says that training and development are significant attractors and retainers for Generation Xers, who value on-the-job education even more than Boomers and Veterans. Eighty percent said the availability of training was a major factor in choosing a new job. Of those who received no training, 70 percent were satisfied with their jobs; when employees received at least six days of training within the previous year, job satisfaction increased to 84 percent.[9]

The nice thing about Xers is they are virtually self-developing. Their early years gave them the ability to learn quickly and develop skills on their own. Whereas many employees won't pick up a self-study computer course on CD-ROM, this generation will. They may not go through it in the order you want them to, but they will learn the important material. That's the key to these young workers: give them lots of resources so they can learn how to do their job, and give it to them in a variety of media. Books, computer programs, sound, video, and even face-to-face instruction all have their appeal to these employees, so make as many of them available—not mandatory—as possible.

1. A new method of developing your workforce's skills is just beginning to take hold in some workplaces. It's called electronic performance support systems (EPSS) and has been popularized by Gloria Gery, president of Massachusetts-based Gery Associates. The gist of it is to build an advanced computer program that will answer an employee's questions right there when they need it. If someone needs to know how to process a weird claim, an EPSS will run through the procedure, teaching how to do it just as it's needed. If properly designed, it works for anyone, but EPSS is particularly attuned to Xer sensibilities. It's computer generated, so it's a medium they are comfortable with. It's right when they need it, and Xers are not notoriously patient about many things. It taps into their ability to multitask because they're learning to do the task at the same time they're actually doing it. At its best, it's the ultimate training resource for self-reliant people.

2. Gen Xers tend to read less than their older and younger cohorts.[10] Keep training materials brief and scannable. Use headlines, lists, graphics, and bullets to highlight important information.

3. At the end of each week—better yet, at the end of each day—encourage new employees to inventory what they learned that day. Businesses that promote learning put themselves into the "cool companies" category, according to Lynn Taylor of Robert Half International, Inc., a California-based staffing firm. "These are companies in which

employees leave at the end of the day knowing more than they did when they started." Those who have recently recruited on college campuses know that the ability to continue learning is at the top of the list of desirable job attributes for today's new recruits.

Motivating

1. Most Xers enjoy lots of simultaneous tasks and projects; work they can juggle. Giving them lots of projects, allowing them to prioritize them in their own way, gives workers the feeling they have more control over their work. Most employees like to have the feeling that they have control over their work. It shows up on job satisfaction surveys, employee morale charts, and incentive reports again and again. Give people more control of their work, or even the illusion of more control, and they will do better work, and more of it. Generation X is no exception, and perhaps an extreme of the desire.

2. Like everyone else, Generation X employees need constructive feedback to become more effective. Some have even suggested they need it more than other employees. Because Xers yearned for their absentee parents' attention, positive feedback, sincerely offered, can be the difference between keeping them and losing them to competitors.

3. A little freedom goes a long way to keeping these workers satisfied. Give them time to pursue other interests, even have fun, at work. One software company actually encourages its programmers to play games at work for about fifteen minutes in the morning and fifteen minutes in the afternoon—for fun and to learn about the latest and greatest software available.

4. The one job perk Xers appreciate a lot is leading-edge technology. Your CEO may swoon over an XJ7, but this generation knows having the best computer equipment in their cubicle is as good as a corner office with a window and door. Give them the latest computer technology. Internet access is

a given, and they will see that the company is willing to invest in their work. Give them an old beater computer that some executive discarded, and be ready to keep an open account with the local paper's classified department.

5. Review your overall employee motivation package. Xers may not be all that anxious to get perks, but they resent it when others get very visible, expensive recognition. It smacks of the worst kind of corporate politics, the old boy network gone haywire, and it's likely to send Xer employees running for the exits. Xers don't want to know that their Yuppie bosses are driving their Beemers into a paid-for parking spot in the underground lot across the street.

Mentoring

Mentors are very important to this group. A mentor can teach them about some of the organizational politics, which Xers hate, in a way that makes assimilating into the workplace easier.

1. Pitch office politics as a way to get around the rules; that's something Xers love.

2. Make them feel like insiders as quickly as possible. Boomers, in contrast, like mentors because they think it will put them on the promotional fast track. Xers like mentors because they are a kind of surrogate parent, someone who cares about them and will support them.

3. Coach young employees to take responsibility for their own issues by asking them questions like, "How do you plan to go about solving this?," and "How do you think you might best approach this topic in the next staff meeting?"

Current and Future Issues

Generation X is finally coming into its own in the workplace. There are a lot fewer bellboys and bookstore lackeys, and a lot more gold-collar professionals and newly minted Gen-X managers who are demanding, and getting, decent or better salaries. As a whole, the labor shortage is increasing salaries, and this generation is finally looking at what they consider a livable wage. They are already planning for a retirement without social security; their self-reliance radar tells them that a sizable retirement nest egg will be a necessity. Look for IRAs and 401(k) plans to swell with funds contributed by this group.

They're concerned about health care. The renegotiation of the benefits part of today's employment contract has left too many of them facing either health care insurance payments that rival their monthly rent or no health care coverage at all. Companies that provide some form of health care coverage even to part-time workers earn a lot of points with this group.

But, like any younger generation, the here and now is also very important.

Companies that are able to offer convenience benefits to the employment picture are getting high marks from Gen Xers. Comprehensive "concierge" services at companies like Riverside Hospital in Columbus, Ohio, Netscape, in Mountain View, California, and Andersen Consulting, in Minneapolis, Minnesota, are warmly received by time-pressed, convenience-oriented Gen Xers. At Andersen, a contact concierge will do anything from picking up a relative at the airport, to planning a weekend getaway, to dropping a pressed professional's watch off for a battery replacement.[11]

But the bigger issue, one that really gets Xers' attention, is what will be left over for them—in the economy, in the environment—once the Boomers have looted both. Whether or not "the Boomers got all the good jobs" is yet to be decided. A prolonged labor shortage could drive up Xer wages until they have no room to complain. According to economists, that will also cause a recession, but Gen X is pretty adept at weathering recessions, and they have a resilience that makes them confident they can handle whatever the economy dishes out.

If Boomers are just hitting their stride, Xers are just coming into their own. As such, some are finally ascending into management positions—and God help the Boomers who get caught with Xer bosses. It may not be pretty if those managers choose to take out two decades of frustration on their subordinates. Some may become tyrannical. Others may emulate the Veteran managers of yesteryear, following the hierarchy, giving orders. It's more likely, though, that they will design a new-fangled form of virtual management, managing people and teams through e-mail and groupware. The jury is out.

The Future: Hell No, Please Don't Go

As much as the Xers loathe the Boomers, they also don't want to see them leave. Recent legislation to increase the retirement age to seventy and increasingly longer life span averages are encouraging to Boomers and Xers both. Boomers like the idea of living longer, more productive lives. Xers love anything that will keep the glut of Boomers from going quietly into that good night—retirement. The longer the Boomers keep working, the more they will contribute to the Social Security system and the long-term economic survival of Gen X. The prospect of they, the few Xers, taking care of them, the seventy-six million Boomers, via Social Security and Medicare, frightens Generation X more than just about anything. So keeping Boomers working well into their geriatric years looks very good to Xers.

With the economic landscape beginning to change for Xers, there's more hope that they will actually have a future, that someday they'll be in charge of their economic lives.

That change has altered their retirement outlook significantly. In the recent past there was a kind of "live free or die" mentality among Xers, that they might as well live for the day and have as much fun as possible because there wasn't going to be much left once the Boomers were done. They anticipated inheriting a country that was flat broke and ecologically bankrupt, with millions of old people to take care of. Now, after one of the longest economic booms of the century, things are looking up. Xers are turning their attention to their own retirement. If it seems a bit premature, blame it on the prophesied demise of Social Security.

Xers' retirement will probably be another case of them relying solely on themselves. But they're good at that. No need to worry too much about them. Just ask 'em.

THE GEN XERS	
Markings	Nose rings, naval rings, functional clothing, tattoos, Japanese cars
Spending style	Cautious, conservative
What they read	*Spin*, *Wired*, chat room dialogue
Their humor	*Dilbert*

THE GEN XERS

Fact and Fiction

Myths:	Facts:
1. They're materialistic.	1. Many are struggling to make ends meet. Economists tell us this is the first U.S. generation that probably won't be able to replicate or improve on their parents' lifestyle. They worry they won't have enough money to pay for a home and their children's education. They want to get out of debt. So money is important to them, but material wealth and status items are scorned by this generation.
2. They're whiners.	2. Gen Xers face some rather daunting challenges—college loans, skyrocketing health care costs—yet most are philosophical about the problems they're inheriting.
3. They have a "you owe me" attitude.	3. No more so than any other generation.
4. They're not willing to work hard.	4. In interviews, Gen Xers consistently tell us they are willing to work very hard. They don't want to be taken advantage of, though. Many believe it's unfair to expect a seventy-hour week for forty hours of pay. And, as a generation, they're committed to having a life beyond work.
5. They're living on "easy street."	5. In the 1950s, young homeowners could make the monthly mortgage payment by using 14 percent of their income. Today it takes 40 percent. And today, folks older than sixty will get back about $200 for every $100 they put into Social Security. Gen Xers will lose more than $100 for every $450 they contribute.

Adapted from Claire Raines, *Beyond Generation X* (Menlo Park, CA: Crisp Publications, 1997), pp. 30, 50.

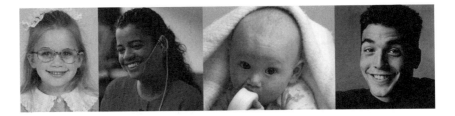

THE NEXTERS:

Chilling Out and Cheering Up

BRANDON AND CRYSTAL   BORN BETWEEN **1980–2000**

*"When summoned, these ordinary youths transform
themselves into thunderbolting evil fighters.
Whatever they do—from displaying martial
arts to piloting high-tech weaponry—they do
as a choreographed group...with strength in
cooperation, energy in conformity, virtue in
duty. Their missions are not chosen by
themselves, but by an incorporeal elder in
whose vision and wisdom they have total trust."*

—NEIL HOWE AND BILL STRAUSS
The Fourth Turning

Call them Generation Y—as in Y follows X—or the Internet Generation, Nintendo Generation, Millennials, Echo Boomers, or even Generation 2001, for the first graduating class of the new millennium. Author Dan Tapscott calls them the N-Gen (as in Internet Generation) in a recent book called, *Growing Up Digital.*[1] Whatever the tag, whoever they are, or whoever they will grow up to be, their origins and anticipations are clear. They will be the most carefully studied of all the cohort groups yet. Born between 1980 and 2000, Brandon and Crystal are the fawned-on spawn, the coddled and confident offspring of the most age-diverse group of parents ever—ranging from adolescents to midlifers, Xers to Boomers. One-third are born to single, unwed moms; hordes of others to Boomers who postponed having children until their forties, and now that they're parents, they're determined to do the right thing, going at child rearing with all the intensity and energy with which they've tackled everything else in their lives. Then, too, these Boomer parents have a history of getting what they want. If it's happy, well-educated, well-adjusted children they want, it's likely they'll get just that or drive the world crazy trying! Remember the jokes about the Yuppies who quibbled over which composer—Mozart or Bach—to pipe into their preborn's warm and watery environment? And how soon after their second birthdays to enroll their little darlings in their first LSAT cram course? Well, many of these are those kids coming of age, experiencing puberty, and starting their tours of college campuses, where recruiting directors say their parents demand statistics on campus crime rates, the academic environment, and a whole library of other information. If Generation X was "the lost generation," this is "the found generation," with parents not only escorting but advocating for them. Some are even beginning to report for their first job assignments—sometimes with a parent in tow, ready to explain little Johnny's special needs to you.

If ever there were an ominous chasm between generations, it's the one between the Nexters and the Boomers. TV virtually created the Baby Boom Generation. They were marked forever by the early black-and-white shows they watched after school; then, as young adults, they watched all their generational events on TV—JFK's funeral, Woodstock, Vietnam, civil rights demonstrations, the moon landing. The impact of the digital age on Generation Next will be immeasurably greater. For the first time in history, kids are the authority. They know far more than their parents about one of the basics. There aren't just three Rs anymore—as in, reading, writing and 'rithmetic—there's a fourth: the Internet. And it's as natural as breathing for Generation Next. So much so they don't even marvel at it much. Sure, in the past there have been things that kids were better at and knew more about than their parents, but not one so all-encompassing as digital technology. It is changing the basic dynamic of families. Today, as always, parents know more about most things; but today, as never before, kids actually know more about technology, and they're teaching and coaching their parents. Most Boomers can, and are, learning as fast as they can. But it's a little like learning a language. When you're a child, language acquisition is as easy as blinking. When you're an adult, it seems far less natural. It takes a lot more effort, so much effort that most adults choose simply not to add another language to their repertoire. The Boomers who make that choice with technology will find they're standing on the edge of a generation gap wider than their worst nightmares.

Type "F" to Go Forward

By the time all the Nexters have been born, there will be nearly as many, some say more, of them as there are Boomers. It looks like their generation will weigh in at about 72.9 million total, which is substantially larger than Generation X, but probably falling about 3 million short of the notch the Baby Boom left on the door frame. Primarily because of the lower birth rates in the 1960s and 1970s, this new generation will comprise nearly a third of the total U.S. population. So it is that marketers are hard at work trying to get a read on them. The huge number of Nexters will cause a tidal wave in trends, consumption, markets, and profits. Marketers who specialize in catering to teens love them, drooling after their large disposable incomes. "Allowance" is too modest a characterization of the discretionary dollars and purchasing influence these kids pack! Those with discretionary monies spent $141 billion in 1998—$94 apiece—says Teen Research Unlimited, and they influence family spending on everything from computers to vacations.[2] Many share in, and feel a part of, their parents' late 1990s affluence. Witness the growth of businesses like Learning Smith, a chain of educational stores

> **THE NEXTERS**
> **Seminal Events and Trends**
>
> - Child focus
> - Violence: Oklahoma City bombing, schoolyard shootings
> - Technology
> - Busy, overplanned lives
> - Stress
> - Clinton/Lewinsky
> - Columbine High School massacre

based in Cambridge, Massachusetts, targeted directly at affluent Boomer offspring.

By and large, their parents, two-thirds of them anyway—planned to have these kids, and these kids experience the confidence that comes from knowing you are wanted. In a 1995 national survey of preteens called KidsPeace, 93 percent of all surveyed ten- to thirteen-year-olds said they always feel loved by their parents.[3] Now they're experiencing that feeling of being wanted on the job market, the "Openings All Shifts" sign on the neighborhood McDonald's and at The Gap at the mall are not lost on them. Teen jobs are plentiful, and any Nexter who wants a job can find one. In fact, one-third of all teens work twenty hours a week, according to a recent article in *Brandweek*.[4] So far they tend to report for work with a long parental tether attached. Some employers report that Nexters' parents don't bat an eye at pulling their young one from work as easily and matter of factly as they pull them from school when a more "important" event, like a vacation or important family gathering, is on the parental calendar. "Beep. Hello, Mr. Smith. Johnny won't be at work today. His grandfather's seventy-fifth birthday is Saturday, and we, of course, need him to be there. Thank you. Beep." The same feeling of being wanted and needed holds true for the newest crop of college graduates. While basking on the beach at Ft. Lauderdale or Puerto Vallarta on spring break, college students are recruited to attend evening open houses, where big companies ply them with Corona and chips, hoping to entice them into the workplace with signing bonuses and attractive benefits packages.

The Nexters' parents are painfully aware of the mixed messages their parenting sends and the uncertain ends it could create. Joan Ryan, a *San Francisco Chronicle* columnist, puts it well:

> *We Mappies (Middle-Aged Professional Parents) have elevated child-rearing to a sacrament. We arrange our schedules around our children's soccer games, volunteer as much as we can in the classroom, hover over every science project and book report, and take our kids with us to restaurants and on outings with a frequency that makes our own parents snort and roll their eyes.*
>
> *We're told we will produce a generation of coddled, center-of-the-universe adults who will expect the world to be as delighted with them as we are. And even as we laugh at the knock-knock jokes*

and exclaim over the refrigerator drawings, we secretly fear the same thing.[5]

Their oldest members are still teenagers, a classification agreed by most to be a thing unto itself. From the very youngest to the oldest, they are all still a work in progress. We don't yet know what the generation's defining moment(s) will be. It is possible that some earth-shattering event will shape the way they see the world in some profound, yet unforeseen, way. Or from their ranks may emerge a hero, song, headline, trend, or motto that the Nexters will catalyze around and perhaps even name themselves after. It is highly likely.

Yet, they are teaching us about themselves as quickly as we can absorb the information. They are stepping into the spotlight the Boomers have occupied since the 1950s, becoming media darlings and a much-anticipated receptacle of hope for the future. The *Wall Street Journal,* Louis Harris Associates, Northwestern Mutual Life Insurance Company, McDonald's, and Hewlett-Packard have recently invested time and resources to begin to understand and serve this latest generation. Historians Bill Strauss and Neil Howe are writing a book just about them. We know for certain they will influence the twenty-first century every bit as much, and probably more, than the Boomers did the twentieth century. They just may become the most powerful U.S. generation yet. The size of their cohort, along with the size of their parents' generation, accounts for part of that power. The education system, which appears to be preparing them fairly well for the workforce, is another. Add in their technological sophistication, positive expectations, and their apparent bent for collective action and you probably have a formula for greatness.

THE NEXTERS

Cultural Memorabilia

- Barney
- Teenage Mutant Ninja Turtles
- Tomagotchi and other virtual pets
- Beanie Babies
- Pogs
- American Girl dolls
- Oprah and Rosie
- The Spice Girls
- The X Games

From Beanie Babies to Beepers

For the first time since the post–World War II era, it's "in" to be a child again. According to Landon Jones, author of *Great Expecta-*

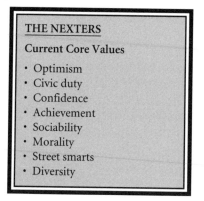

THE NEXTERS

Current Core Values

- Optimism
- Civic duty
- Confidence
- Achievement
- Sociability
- Morality
- Street smarts
- Diversity

tions, in the 1950s and 1960s, "Children were the whole point. Americans enshrined them. European visitors joked knowingly about how well American parents obeyed their children. American parents seemed to be making their kids their religion."[6] Then, in the 1970s, children lost popularity. The Gen X babies were some of the first whose parents had taken pills to prevent or at least to delay. As a matter of fact, the 1970s were actually the most antichild decade the country had known, say Neil Howe and Bill Strauss in their book, *13th Gen.*[7] But, in the 1980s, a "Baby on Board" sign in the station wagon's rear window signaled the return of a national concern for, and interest in, children.

Gen Xers complained that their two-career parents never had enough time for them, and they swore that, when they became parents themselves, they would find more time for their own kids. Those Xer parents seem to be doing just that, and they are joined by a whole cadre of Boomer parents who witnessed the result of their generation's benign neglect of Gen X children. The concept of "quality time" is obsolete— it didn't work—and parents are recommitting to their families. Then, too, a fifty-year trend to exert less and less control over children's lives has recently made a U-turn. In their book *Generations,* Howe and Strauss say, "Not since the early 1900s have older generations moved so quickly to assert greater adult dominion over the world of childhood— and to implant civic virtue in a new crop of youngsters."[8]

So kids are all the rage. Las Vegas has gone "family." Donna Karan, Nicole Miller, Abercrombie & Fitch, and The Gap have recently introduced new lines of clothing especially for wee ones. For $1,000 per month, a child-care center in Denver cradles kids in amenities and tutors them in "arts, sciences, math, music and more. Reading lessons begin at eleven months. By age two, some... speak Spanish and French."[9] Club Med, flying in the face of its sybaritic swinging singles' image of the 1970s, reports their family villages now account for nearly half of annual sales. A few years ago, there were three TV programs for kids under six: "Mr. Rogers," "Sesame Street," and "Captain Kangaroo." Today there are more than fifty. This new generation is already more literate than their predecessors, according to the *Official Guide to the Generations.*[10] Children are reading and being read to again; sales of children's books have quadrupled in the last ten years.[11]

And these are the busiest kids of all time. Not only did Bob Dole coin a new term in his 1996 presidential campaign, but "soccer mom" is a whole sociological phenomenon that describes the hectic lifestyle of moms and dads shuttling kids back and

THE NEXTERS
Heroes
• Michael Jordan
• Princess Diana
• Mark McGwire, Sammy Sosa
• Mother Teresa
• Bill Gates
• Kerri Strugg
• Mia Hamm
• Tiger Woods
• Christopher Reeves

forth from football practice to violin lessons to math tutoring to ballet to chess club to karate. Two and three decades ago, kids "hung out" and played with their buddies on the vacant lot on the corner, or they took off for parts unknown on their bicycles. Today there is no vacant lot, and, if there were, it probably wouldn't be deemed safe by Nexter parents. Riding your bike to parts unknown is simply not a good idea. "Commercial playgrounds" from Discovery Zone to Chuck E. Cheese to Dave & Buster's abound. Many infants are in day care by the time they're six weeks old, dropped off in the predawn hours by parents on their way to work. Kids live high-stress, fast-paced lives. Their amusements are far more dependent on their parents, primarily for transportation and funding, than for any generation before them. They know they have to be very careful and that the world is a dangerous place.

In the wake of the recent series of school shootings, in particular the Littleton, Colorado massacre, many adults find themselves asking, "What do these acts perpetrated by violent adolescents and pre-adolescents say about our young people?" Just as Ted Kaczynski isn't representative of Baby Boomers and Timothy McVeigh's actions say virtually nothing about Xers, so too do we get little insight into Gen Y from the Columbine High School shooters and others like them, the plethora of hand-wringing editorials and commentary that followed the Littleton incident notwithstanding. Certainly, the vast majority of young people—and their parents—are painfully aware of the danger surrounding them, and not just in the school library.

KidsPeace found that 54 percent of all preteens fear they will contract AIDS, and 45 percent worry they may be physically or sexually abused. Our own more informal survey found that the bombing of the federal building in Oklahoma City had a tremendous impact on the Millennials. In fact, the Oklahoma City bombing may become one of their defining moments. On a one-page survey we gave to three dozen children aged ten to sixteen years in Phoenix, Arizona, and Durango, Colorado, more than half listed it as one of the major events to occur in their lifetime.

A 1997 federal government assessment of the overall well-being of America's youth found that, "among all youths, the number who are victims of violent crime has increased from 79 per 1,000 in 1980 to 118 per 1,000 in 1994."[12] One eight-year-old Millennial recently asked his mother, "When will it be my turn to be mugged, Mommy?" Violence is all around them – on the Internet, on TV and videos, at the movies... . Many youngsters start their normal day by passing through the metal detectors on their way into school. The spate of schoolyard shootings beginning in 1997 had a tremendous impact on teens and preteens, and they're all too aware they've lost a number of their members and heroes, such as Tupak Shakur, Notorious BIG, Jon Benet Ramsey, and Ennis Cosby, to violent crime.

Perhaps the more important question is, "How will this spate (some say subculture) of violence affect the Nexters as a generation?" Our best and educated guess is that violence will become their cause celebre. The Veteran Generation united—and continues to unite—around World War II; Boomers splintered into factions that made a cause of Vietnam; Xers have been all too aware that they lack a cause around which to rally—save their fascination with technology and dislike of Boomers.

Nexters have the passion and personality to take on violence as a cause. Surveys indicate they "Possess an earnestness and willingness to grapple with questions of ethics and morality that link them to the idealism once harbored by their Baby Boomer parents."[13] Sociologists tell us they encounter a "new earnestness" and call to collective action among this cohort. A Roper-Starch poll found a "real sense of personal accountability among teens."[13] Combine their likely commitment to transforming our violent culture with their unmatched potential for communication via the Internet, and you could have a formula for seeking societal change equal to the passion that engulfed so many Boomers in the Woodstock/anti-Vietnam 1960s.

Kids today are growing up in families that, despite their child cen-teredness, have little in common with the Cleavers. In 1970, 80 percent of the nation's children lived in homes that included a dad; in the 1990s, it was 50 percent and going down. The two-income household was a real bone of contention to Xers when they were growing up. For the Nexters, it's a nonissue, a given. The U.S. Bureau of the Census projects that, by 2010, less than 30 percent of American children will live in homes that have two parents. The majority of Gen Nexters' moms have jobs away from home, and nearly a third of all births in the early 1990s were to unmarried women, according to the *Wall Street Journal*.[14] Therefore, this is the first generation of American children to grow up without expectations of a strong nuclear family. It just isn't on their radar screen. Yes, those apple-pie families on "Nick at Nite" do look ap-pealing, but the Nexters know that, if they're going to have those fami-lies themselves, they'll have to create them for themselves. So they es-tablish bonds with relatives, family friends, and neighbors as a means of finding security in an uncertain world.

By the way, they think Mom and/or Dad are cool. They think their parent(s) "get" their music or at least aren't hostile to it, and they think they even dress okay. Mom and daughter shop The Gap together, and father and son both go for blue jeans and t-shirts with someone else's name on them, though denim, the ubiquitous flag of youth for three decades, is on its way out say teen fashion experts. And, when their par-ents are Boomers, they share a whole slew of common experiences. Twinkies, Slinkies, and Pez are "in" again. And all the recent remakes of old Boomer favorites—"The Flintstones," "That Darned Cat," "Leave it to Beaver," "Lost in Space," "The Parent Trap," "The Mod Squad"—have created a common platform of entertainment experience between parents and kids.

While young Boomer women in the 1970s became involved in the women's movement, Nexter girls in the 1990s are actively involved in a new, more informal, but more far-reaching "girl's movement." When the Boomers were girls, one in twenty-seven participated in team sports in high school. Social pressure and the reality of "Title IX" has now made that number one in three according to the January/February 1998 issue of *American Enterprise,* perhaps encouraged, at least in part, by the deluge of Nike and other ads that urged coaches to "let girls play."[15] Take Our Daughters to Work Day grew increasingly popular in the 1990s, exposing hundreds of thousands of young women to career possibilities. For the first time, as many women as men are now graduating from college. A line of clothes for teenagers called "Girls Rule" is extremely popular, and Sears recently ran a new magazine ad for their "Mainframe Department" that is a takeoff on "Sugar and spice and everything nice." It says, "Nerves of steel...guts...and raw ambition (that's what little girls are made of.)"

Though they are, in many ways, far more dependent on their parents than Mom and Dad were on Grandma and Grandpa, today's young people are also very savvy...streetwise...sophisticated. By the time they're ten, they know about divorce, drugs, AIDS, anorexia, gangs, and guns. They are exposed to serious adult issues on daytime TV talk shows. Never before have sixth graders talked so openly with classmates, parents, and even their teachers about subjects like "oral sex" and "semen on the blue dress." Having learned in school about recycling, global warming, the destruction of the rainforests, and acid rain, this generation is, and will probably continue to be, the most concerned and actively involved group of advocates for the environment.

"What videos did you watch when you were a kid?," today's typical six-year-old asks her parent, taking for granted what may still seem like a bit of a miracle to the parent. Certainly technology played a huge role in the lives of the Xers, but Generation Next is the first to be born into homes that, by in large, already *have* computers. According to IDC/Link Resources Corporation, a market-research firm in New York, 60 percent of all households with kids seven and under have PCs. These beeper-wearing cyberjunkies consider microwaves, CD players, VCRs, and computers as basic to home furnishings as other generations did the kitchen table. "For them, technology is as natural as air," says Frank Gregorsky, social historian at the Discovery Institute, a Seattle think tank. They were weaned on video games, they're doing their term papers in full video, they troubleshoot the computer at home, and they teach their parents how to surf the Internet. Their connectedness has given them a new orientation in space and time. They have pen pals in Asia, and they see the world as global, connected, and round the clock. And, despite the doom and gloom we hear from lots of adults, it appears that Generation Next is flourishing under the tutelage of technology. A recent *Business Week* article cited every venerated institution from UCLA to Purdue to MIT to the *Journal of Applied Developmental Psychology* to support their argument that kids are learning advanced motor, spatial, and strategy skills via game technology.[16] "They can process huge amounts of visual information in parallel," the article says. And, the author contends, computer and video games cut into TV time, not reading. Prognosticators say Generation Next will make Generation X look like technological fuddy-duddies.

Unlike the Boomers who grew up in fairly homogeneous settings, the new crop of young people has much greater exposure to, and casual acceptance of, multiculturalism—a diversity of races, religions, and backgrounds. Thirty-seven percent of kindergartners in 1997 were non-white, according to an article in the *Wall Street Journal*.[17] Within the Nexters' lifetime, says the Census Bureau, ethnic "minorities" as an aggregate will become the majority. If they attend school in New York City, Los Angeles, or Chicago, kids may be exposed to more than one hundred languages among their schoolmates. Susan Mitchell, in an *American Demographics* report says, "The next baby boom will be the first generation to seriously question all traditional racial categories. The reason is that many of today's children and teens are of mixed races.... The larger share of minorities in the next baby boom means that there is far more interaction between people of different races than there was for most of the baby-boom generation."[18] Even in more affluent suburbs, schools include an increasingly more diverse population. All children today consider "ethnic foods" mainstream.

It makes sense, then, that a number of surveys have found the Millennials to be

---

THE NEXTERS

What Other Generations Say About Nexters

Veterans say . . .
- "They have good manners."
- "They're smart little critters."
- "They need to toughen up."
- "They watch too much TV... with crude language and violence."

Boomers say . . .
- "They're cute."
- "They need more discipline from their parents."
- "They can set the time on the VCR!"
- "They need to learn to entertain themselves; they need too much attention."
- "Can they do my web page for me?"

Gen Xers say . . .
- "Neo Boomers."
- "Here we go again . . . another self-absorbed generation of spoiled brats."
- "What do you mean, 'What's an album?'"

the most tolerant of all the generations. This, too, is part of their up-bringing. This generation has been reared without absolutes. It's per-fectly acceptable in elementary school classrooms for there to be more than one right answer to a question. And parents insist they are allow-ing their children to develop their own opinions. One young mother we know refuses even to divulge to her eleven- and twelve-year old chil-dren who she voted for in the last presidential election, seeking at all cost to avoid superimposing her political agenda on theirs. Nexters' par-ents tell us it's not only good, but it is great, for families to agree to dis-agree. And 64 percent of parents believe they're better at openly dis-cussing tough issues than their parents were. Others see Nexter parenting as overindulgent, overprotective, and value-free, a sure por-tent of a rudderless, amoral generational grouping. They point to the meaningless schoolyard violence cited previously as an early warning sign.

Handle With Care

But when you add it all up, Generation Next starts to look a lot like a modern, new-fangled version of their World War II grandparents and great-grandparents. In fact, in a recent study by Northwestern Mutual Life and the Harris organization of the attitudes and behaviors of 2,001 college students at 101 colleges, respondents seemed to feel little affinity with Gen Xers, apparently finding them rather dark and pessimistic. In skateboarding, snowboarding, surfboarding, roller-blading, clothes, and attitude they are "new school," not "old school." They don't just "hang out," they network. They don't ask, "Is this going to be on the test?," they ask, "What's the scoop on getting along with the teacher?"[19] The criteria most important to Millennials, "honesty" and "integrity," are barely on the radar screens of Xers, who wrote off such notions as naive and use-less early in their development. The Nexters feel a little better about the Boomers, but the generation they trust the most and feel most similar to is the Veterans, who ranked a full ten percentage points above the others on the survey. The popularity with Gen Next of the movies "Titanic" and "Saving Private Ryan" may have as much or more to do with the era they are set in than with Leonardo DiCaprio and Matt Damon.

Like their grandparents, the early Nexters seem eager to subscribe to a stricter moral code. Statistically, they're less sexually promiscuous than other generations, and so far they have a lower rate of teen pregnancy. Nexters were more offended than any other cohort group by the Clinton/Lewinsky scandal, which Bill Strauss predicts "will be a generation-marking event and will have a spot in the collective memory of this generation for sixty, seventy years."[20] Reacting to the excesses they perceive in their parenting generation, they will have a much stricter moral center. Youth Ethics Monitor, a 1994 study by Marian Salzman of TBWA-Chiat/Day ad agency in New York, concluded they are a "principled group," preferring love and respect to money. In a 1997 *Reader's Digest* survey, 93 percent of 1,022 teens said, "America is the best place to live," and the study concluded they are moral, optimistic, and hard working.[21] "This is a group of kids who want to fit into conventional society, rather than turn it over," says Harold Hodgkinson of the Institute for Educational Leadership.[22]

Manners seem to have been recently reborn in many of the Nexter's families. Many ritzy metropolitan hotels offer seminars on etiquette to the children of their well-heeled customers, and parents have been vigilant in insisting their offspring say, "please" and "thank-you," and sometimes even "Mr." and "Mrs." or "sir" and "ma'am." Just one more place where the Nexters match up with the Veterans.

Strauss and his colleague Neil Howe agree, "there's a social role available to Nexters because the Veteran generation is dying. That creates a yearning on the part of society for a return to what is missing...for someone to fill the vacuum." Strauss suggests, "since there's a dearth of heroes in our society right now"—on the KidsPeace survey 47 percent of preteens said they had no role model, and on our more informal survey, nearly half the respondents left the space under "heroes" blank— "this new generation will create new heroes within their cohort as well as anointing them in older generations."[23]

Crystal

It's dinnertime, and Crystal, 17, is doing her homework at the kitchen table while her dad cooks the two of them a pasta dinner, his specialty. Crystal's brother will eat when he gets home from football practice, and Mom will make her own salad when she gets home from her meeting. The family prefers to sit down to dinner together, but, at least during the school year, they're lucky if that happens twice a week—a casualty of all the activities the kids are involved in and work responsibilities both parents are juggling.

The family lives a fairly comfortable lifestyle—occasionally, they have to throw away their credit cards to get caught up with their expenditures—in a nice suburb of Phoenix. Crystal is an active girl and excellent student who pushes herself hard to succeed. She works weekends and holidays at a store in the nearby mall, plays soccer and basketball, and is learning to play the viola. She enjoys school and schoolwork. She thrives on math, in which she is taking an accelerated class. She decided years ago to go to Stanford—her grandfather's alma mater—and thinks maybe she would like to be an architect.

The family has had a computer for as long as she can remember, and Crystal finds herself depending on it more and more for getting her assignments done. She's looking forward to college where she'll have her own line, so she can spend more time on the Internet. She learned about recycling when she was in elementary school, and she's the "watchdog" at her house, making certain the family does all it can for a better environment.

Though she thinks life would be just fine without her brother in it, thank you very much, her parents are truly some of her favorite people. She enjoys spending time with them—watching TV, shopping, running errands, going to movies, and going out to eat. Though she has had a couple of casual boyfriends, she is not quite as "sophisticated" as some of her friends, one of whom had sex the first time when she was twelve. Crystal knows about safe sex, sexually transmitted diseases, and AIDS; and she's not in any real hurry to jump into that world. For the last few years she's had a group of friends, including a couple of boys—just friends—and she likes it that way.

Crystal's world seems fairly secure, but her parents know her security is not without peril. Crystal sometimes worries out loud that she is getting fat. Her parents are aware that she is at that vulnerable stage when young women can fall victim to eating disorders, peer pressure, drugs, and gangs. Although they've created a stable environment at home, what they read about in the morning paper and see going on around them sometimes makes them feel they're in the calm center of a potentially devastating social hurricane.

Brandon

It is dinnertime at Brandon's house, too. Thirteen years old, Brandon is a charmer. He's well-spoken, with a charismatic personality and a smile that can light up a room. Brandon's mom called from work a few minutes ago to see what he wants for dinner. Because they're both busy and she's not hungry, he asked her to stop by Wendy's or Taco Bell to grab a burger or burrito for him. He'll put his dinner on the coffee table in front of the TV while his mom gets the laundry going and checks on his two older brothers, who both work in the evenings.

The family lives in an apartment building near downtown Detroit. Tanesha has raised her boys pretty much single handedly, and she deserves a great deal of credit. Although she was on welfare for a few years, she has always used every penny judiciously, and she recently graduated from a program that taught her a wide range of practical administrative office skills. Now she works in an insurance company just a few miles from home. She enjoys the job, and she's hoping to save a little money in case Brandon might want to go to college. She is the backbone of her family, teaching her boys right from wrong, respect for their elders, and courtesy to everyone they meet.

Unfortunately, hers is an uphill battle. Both of the older boys have already had scrapes with the law, and she worries that one of them, who hangs around with a bunch of kids she doesn't approve of, has started using drugs. Brandon is her most promising child, and he started off doing pretty well in school, but he seems to be losing interest. His school is in poor repair, the teachers seem to range from bad to disinterested to mediocre, and the classrooms are overcrowded. Recently, a small grant from a local business provided the school with a few computers, but half of them aren't working now, and there's no budget to fix them. Brandon is on his own after school, and he usually spends an hour or so doing odd jobs for other tenants in the building. His mom has laid down the law about the hour that follows: He's to stay at home until his homework is complete. Recently, though, he tells her he doesn't have homework, and she finds him hanging out in the stairwell with an unruly group of other kids his age and older. She'd like him to get involved in some after-school activities, but the few that are available require money and transportation, two things she's not able to provide.

The Chasm

Crystal and Brandon represent a demographic phenomenon, the chasm between the "haves" and "have nots," which has grown larger with the arrival of Generation Next. According to Don Hernandez of the U.S. Census Bureau, "a significantly higher proportion of Nexters live in affluence than Boomers did." And while the middle has shrunk, those who live in poverty has grown. One of every four members of this generation is officially impoverished, living in a family of four with an income of less than $15,000. One of ten children living in low-income families reports there is not enough to eat. Nearly one-fourth "sometimes change what they do or where they go during school hours to avoid kids who physically threaten to hurt them."[24]

All children—those from the inner city and those from the suburbs, those in Kenosha and those in Singapore, those from New York and those from California—are experiencing more and more common, shared experiences via the Internet, computer technology, television, and newspapers. At the same time, children living in poverty are increasingly having an entirely separate experience, such that they develop a divergent group of values, a different set of filters, a contrasting view of the world, or at least an important addendum to life as this generation knows it. It becomes increasingly difficult to define and explain their generation without having an entirely separate section to speak of those growing up in poverty. Perhaps, as adults, Generation Next will take up this challenge as a group, addressing it with their optimism and collective energy. For now, it remains a troubling challenge.

But what will they be like at work?

Their Work Expectations

The Northwestern Mutual Life/Louis Harris research reveals quite a lot about the Nexters' wants and ambitions in the workplace. Almost half plan to enter the workforce right after college. The most popular career choices are education and teaching, medicine, business, computer-related fields, law, and psychology. They hope to work side by side with other idealistic, committed coworkers. Only one-third say salary is important, and only a quarter rate job prestige as important. They expect their salaries to start at about $38,000, though nearly half of them don't expect more than $30,000 when they begin their careers.[25]

David Krane, executive vice president of the Harris organization sums up their career aspirations by saying:

> *Much is said about the materialistic tendencies of younger generations. However, this survey does not paint a picture of students who are greedy, over-aggressive and willing to do whatever is necessary to get ahead. Rather, the research conveys an impression of a generation that some might say has idealistic and naive expectations of future career plans. Even though Generation 2001 students have not had to experience much of the real world on their own, they recognize that they need to work hard to achieve good things and work with like-minded creative and idealistic people. In return, they will be rewarded with the lifestyle that they grew up in. And yet, this will still require the need for a two-income household.[26]*

Nexters on the Job

This new wave of workers is both optimistic about the future and realistic about the present. They combine the teamwork ethic of the Boomers with the can-do attitude of the Veterans and the technological savvy of the Xers. At first glance, and even at second glance, Generation Next may be the ideal workforce—and ideal citizens—and generally the kind of kids you'd want dating your son or daughter. Harris's Krane writes, "If Gen2001 is going to change society, it will do so by working within the system. Where some might say these students are naive, others would say that what is most surprising is that this group seems particularly enlightened—and even mature—when it comes to certain aspects of their lives."

One of their strongest assets is their resilience. Perhaps it's because they've known such a different world from that of previous generations, but the things that really annoy or traumatize the other groups are rather taken for granted by Nexters. Whereas Generation Xers don't want to work more than forty hours a week, seeing no real point in it, Nexters expect to work more than forty hours a week to achieve the lifestyle they want. They believe—imagine this—that hard work and goal setting are sure tickets to achieving their dreams. Eighty-eight percent in the Gen2001 study had already established specific goals for the next five years and felt confident they would reach those goals. One might chalk this up to youthful exuberance, but had you looked at the same pool of Gen Xers ten years ago, you wouldn't have seen anything like that kind of optimistic, can-do spirit. Likewise, the Boomers' predilection for protesting and bucking authority draws a blank from this crowd. The Northwestern Mutual Life report suggests, "Generation 2001 is currently somewhat more optimistic toward the state of the union" than Boomers and Xers. They share a confidence in the establishment with the Veterans.[27]

It looks like, as workers, they'll resemble the Veterans in many ways: their belief in collective action, optimism about the future, trust in centralized authority, a will to get things done, and a heroic spirit in the face of overwhelming odds. Economists are predicting a dramatic increase in productivity with the arrival of the Nexters. It looks like they'll be hard working, dedicated, and ready to sacrifice personal pleasure for the collective good. Their ability to work in teams is unassailable; if you haven't recently visited an elementary school, you need to do so, if only to watch the way kids work together and accomplish results collectively under the influence of a strong central authority figure. The Nexters will be our best-educated generation ever, and they will probably continue their education well into adulthood to keep up with rapidly changing technology. Add to this formula their ability to use technology in unforeseen ways, and they seem uniquely poised to become the workforce everyone has been looking for.

Political pundits believe Generation Next will hit American cul-

> **THE NEXTERS**
>
> **On the Job**
>
> **Assets**
> - Collective action
> - Optimism
> - Tenacity
> - Heroic spirit
> - Multitasking capabilities
> - Technological savvy
>
> **Liabilities**
> - Need for supervision and structure
> - Inexperience, particularly with handling difficult people issues

> ### THE NEXTERS
>
> **Messages That Motivate**
>
> - "You'll be working with other bright, creative people."
> - "Your boss is in his (or her) sixties."
> - "You and your coworkers can help turn this company around."
> - "You can be a hero here."

ture like yet another socioeconomic tsunami. Here's why: Generation X has been uninvolved in legislation and politics, staying on the fringes and staying away from the polls. According to former President Jimmy Carter, voting and age correlate; approximately 60 percent of sixty-year-olds vote, 40 percent of forty-year-olds, 20 percent of twenty-year-olds, and so on. But political analysts believe this trend will turn with Generation Next, who, in school, have been actively involved in classroom political discussions, and virtually all of them have "voted" in their elementary school cafeterias across the nation. They will use their collective numbers to change legislation that affects the workplace—minimum wage, union issues, and workplace safety, for example. Their consensus on these sorts of topics is yet to be tested and determined and will surely be shaped by their early workplace experiences.

It is possible they will be a very demanding workforce. They have a bright, clear picture of the way work ought to be, and they're used to getting what they want. As more of them enter the workplace, conditions for young workers on the job are going to get a lot more media attention. When Generation X first went to work, they experienced the same benign neglect they had known in their families growing up. "No one cared how they did economically," says Neil Howe. Gen Next, though, stands behind the powerful advocacy of their parents, who will be there for them if their jobs and economic conditions turn out not to be all they're cracked up to be. "If the economy turns sour," Howe says, "I think there will be much more public activism on behalf of this generation not getting off to a good start in life than there ever was for Xers." Howe and Strauss predict the Nexters will demand pay equity among all workers, create fewer job definitions, reestablish the middle class, downgrade exorbitant CEO and executive salaries, create trade barriers, pass government regulation about labor standards, and even revitalize unions. "We're expecting Millennials to assert themselves politically," says Strauss, "and to fuel a new class-based politics and a new unionism."

Possible On-the-Job Liabilities

What we know of the Nexters' workplace skills suggests, if not some rough edges, at least unpolished facets. In food service and light retail, where the Nexters primarily work today, there is evidence that they are easily intimidated by difficult customers and likely to be stumped by customers less inclined to be their convivial, congenial "pals" than are their parents and teachers. And the "counselor for every kid" environment many experience and expect in the school environment doesn't exist in the workplace, which may come as a shock to many of them. Neil Howe suggests these new workers will need more supervision and structure than their Xer predecessors. "The younger new entrants to the workplace will be looking for more attention and structure from the authority figure."[28] Nexters will find themselves most comfortable in large organizations; if the trend toward smaller, entrepreneurial operations and independent home-based knowledge workers continue, they may find themselves needing discipline and skills that are not part of their current inclination.

Managing Nexters

American companies have, for years, given lip service to the concept of treating employees as customers. With the advent of this generation, that concept must move from pure dogma to literal, active practice. The culture of paying dues will become obsolete, even more than it already is. Those managers who believe all young workers need to experience what they themselves did in their own first five to ten working years—nearly abusive behavior from managers, seventy- and eighty-hour workweeks, no involvement in the running of the business—will find *themselves* out of jobs.

We'll be spending the next couple of decades learning how to recruit, motivate, and retain our newest generation. There is much to be learned. But here's a start on some basic principles to keep in mind:

1. Budget plenty of time for orienting. Create a clear picture of your work environment—what's good about it, what's not, your expectations and long-term goals. Simultaneously, learn about each new employee's personal goals and

develop a strategy for interleaving those goals with job performance.

2. When it comes to opportunities, throw away all preconceived notions about traditional gender roles, if you still have some. Nexters are known for "gender bending." In *The Official Guide to the Generations*, Susan Mitchell says gender roles will continue to "blur as men take on more household tasks and women...take on more traditional male tasks like home repair."[29]

3. In areas where you have lots of members of Generation Next, consider expanding the size of your teams, and appoint a strong team leader.

4. Be sensitive to the potential for conflict when Xers and Nexters work side by side. The gap between those two generations may end up making the one between the Boomers and Xers look tame.

5. Grow your training department. Nexters want to continue their education and develop their work skills.

6. Establish mentor programs. They work well with Nexter employees. They've likely been part of mentoring programs in the school. Consider matching young workers with your most seasoned people with whom they say they resonate.

Hewlett-Packard and Generation Next

In January 1995, Hewlett-Packard (HP) set up a mentoring program that matched HP employees with thousands of middle- and high-school students. This program is making a major positive impact on these students' lives. Unlike big brother/big sister-type programs, which encourage adults to find time in their already stretched-to-the-limit schedules to take their young counterparts bowling or to sit down and do their homework with them, the HP program operates on e-mail interactions. HP-ites "listen to," counsel, and encourage their youngsters, and sometimes they link them up with other network opportunities. One such connection we know of connected a NASA engineer with a young Nexter interested in becoming an astronomer. That's how she came to understand why fractions actually matter. "My mentor helped me understand what school is for," the young woman says in an article in *Fast Company*.[30]

The e-mail connection works well for such relationships by allowing frequent communication at both people's convenience. Typically they each spend no more than ten minutes a day and write to each other on the average of one to three messages each week. Because e-mail correspondents don't have to live in the same time zone, HP mentors from Hong Kong to Harrisburg are connecting with students in Colorado and Canada. HP mentors take ownership of the relationship, hanging in there when their proteges become discouraged or just plain bored.

The program has made such a difference in the young people's lives that HP has established the International Telementor Center in Fort Collins, Colorado. Director David Neils plans to get other companies involved and hopes to serve ten thousand students per year by 2003. "This has put a lot of gas in my tank," he says. "Mentoring is one of the best investments in the future that an adult can make."[31]

The Future

What kind of world will these social, savvy Nexters create? One possibility is that they will transport the spirit of for-profit management to the not-for-profit sector. Management guru and historian Peter Drucker recently pointed out that American job growth is increasingly in the public, charitable, religious, education, and nonprofit sectors. Neil Howe says not only are the Nexters themselves optimistic, but that society in general is optimistic about their future. "I think increasingly today people are looking for a new center of gravity for the country, both socially and culturally," he says. "The Millennials will be the generation in which people see that hope."[32]

Howe and Strauss believe that, between 2015 to 2020, we will see a national crisis akin to the American Revolution, the Civil War, and World War II. They say, "it will be a major turning point in American history and an adrenaline-filled moment of trial."[33] French physician and astrologer Nostradamus—who, in 1555, foretold many events that would occur in the following four centuries, including the date and manner of his own natural death—predicted a similar phenomenon soon after the turn of the millennium. In this time frame, the Boomers will be the elder leaders, Xers will comprise front-line leadership, and the Millennials will bear the brunt of the turmoil the country will go through. Howe and Strauss suggest this generation of young people will be equal to the task, whatever that task is.

THE NEXTERS	
Markings	Polyester, pagers, retro
Spending style	Spend your parents' money as fast as you can
What they read	Series: *Goosebumps, Baby Sitters' Club,* Matt Christopher, American Girls, Chat Room Conversation
Their humor	*Calvin and Hobbes*

Of course, without seeing how the first couple of decades of the new millennium unfold and watching the Nexters go through the vagaries of the job market and come nose to nose with the reality of the workplace, it's hard to know for sure what will happen. Just as early childhood experiences have dramatic effects on how each individual's personality is formed, so too do the early experiences of the workplace. If our newest generation runs into a job market that doesn't want them, doesn't value what they know, and can't afford to pay them a living wage, they could end up looking a lot like the every-man-and-woman-for-himself Xers before them. If, however, demographic and economic trends continue on their course, this generation could encounter a seller's job market where they will be welcomed with open arms and impressive paychecks.

The only thing we know for sure is, it's too early to tell. Nevertheless, if you own a business or manage a department, you may have a pleasant surprise in store for you when the next generation of workers arrives at your door. Welcome and nurture them, and you may prosper beyond your expectations.

THE NEXTERS

Fact and Fiction

Myths:	Facts:
1. The youth of this country are going to "hell in a handbasket."	1. Experts believe this is a fine new crop of young people who will make heroes of themselves.
2. Today's kids are getting a great education.	2. Not all of them. Gregory Schmid, of the Institute for the Future, Menlo Park, California, says, "Tomorrow's haves and have-nots are already diverging in today's third-grade classrooms as they either advance into the information age or fall behind for lack of reading and math skills or access to computers." (*Wall Street Journal*, 2/9/97)
3. Kids need to spend more time reading and less time watching TV and playing video games.	3. Kids *are* spending more time reading. *Business Week* reports that surveys show video games cut into TV, not reading, time. (4/19/97)

PART TWO

CASE STUDIES IN GENERATIONAL PEACE

CHAPTER SIX

WHERE MIXED GENERATIONS WORK WELL TOGETHER

Not all generationally mixed workplaces are awash with strife and tension. More than a few organizations are tapping into the positive potential of their generationally diverse workforces. They are harnessing the power in the convergence of diverse viewpoints, passions, and inspirations.

There are two keys to creating a successful intergenerational workforce: aggressive communication and difference deployment.

In *aggressive communication,* generational conflicts and potential conflicts are anticipated and surfaced. Generational differences are based primarily on unarticulated assumptions and unconscious criteria; therefore, surfacing them takes a giant step toward resolving them. The energy of behind-the-back complaining, passive-aggressive behavior, and open hostility is rechanneled to projects that can profit from different points of view, particularly the fresh perspectives of the young and the wisdom of experience. In the best and brightest intergenerational companies, overcommunication is the rule. These organizations are rife with ad hoc small group discussions, generationally integrated staff meetings, e-mail messages, and water cooler chats, conversation rich with talk about differing viewpoints and perspectives on vital issues of the day. And there's as much listening going on as there is talking. Unfortunately, many organizations continue to stagger along amidst the wreckage of intergenerational warfare with constant passive-aggressive verbal attacks and veiled accusations, just hoping the problems will somehow take care of themselves. But the companies profiled here have chosen to address generational issues head-on and to validate the differing points of view. They take the time to talk openly about what the different cohorts and the individuals within them are looking for on the job; what makes work rewarding...which environments are most productive...what types of work load, schedules, and policies contribute to a workplace that attracts and retains people of differing needs, viewpoints, and expectations of job and work.

Difference deployment is, simply, the tactical use of employees with different backgrounds, experiences, skills, and viewpoints to strengthen project teams, customer contact functions, and, at times, whole departments and units. In generationally "blind" organizations, managers and human resource departments labor mightily to homogenize employees; to fit them to a single template of the "good employee" (and to make employees as alike and easily predictable as possible). But as the head of employee selection research at a large mainframe computer manufacturer succinctly put the problem for us: "We spent years and millions learning to hire people just like the people who were already here. We never bothered to ask whether the people who could best fit in today would be able to help us survive tomorrow...until it was almost too late." It is an approach, a system, whose time is well past.

Generationally savvy organizations value the differences between people and look at differences as strengths. Generationally balanced workgroups—balanced not in the arithmetic but in a psychic sense—respect and learn from yesterday's experiences, understand today's pressures, dilemmas, and needs, and believe that tomorrow will be different still. They are comfortable with the relative rather than absolute nature of a situation, knowledge, skill, value, and, most of all, solutions to problems.

In generationally dysfunctional organizations, where generational uniqueness—as well as other important, individual differences—are subjugated by a desire to create one culture that requires individuals to "fit in," the result is pasteurization and placation. Although pasteurized organizations think of themselves as harmoniously diverse, they are paying a premium in stagnant thinking, lost creativity, and an absence of diverse opinions. Pasteurized organizations may look harmonious and productive in an outside-in snapshot, but the "glue" of that harmony is an expensive adhesive. It is based on strong adherence to peace and harmony over the outcome and the necessary innovative demands of the contemporary marketplace. Friction-free interpersonal relations are more immediately important than present and future productivity potential. Typically, younger workers are squirreled away in creative departments, new product and design groups, and the secretarial pool. Although on some level individuals feel they are cared for and "accepted," they are usually on the lookout for a workplace where they can fit in unconditionally and where their uniqueness will be seen as valid and acceptable, not simply as tolerable oddities.

The Way They See the World

	Veterans	Boomers	Xers	Nexters
Outlook	Practical	Optimistic	Skeptical	Hopeful
Work ethic	Dedicated	Driven	Balanced	Determined
View of authority	Respectful	Love/hate	Unimpressed	Polite
Leadership by	Hierarchy	Consensus	Competence	Pulling together
Relationships	Personal sacrifice	Personal gratification	Reluctant to commit	Inclusive
Turnoffs	Vulgarity	Political incorrectness	Cliché, hype	Promiscuity

The ACORN Imperatives

As we've gotten to know the companies featured in this chapter and other successful cross-generational friendly companies, we've been struck by five specific similarities or common approaches to making their environments generationally comfortable and focusing their people's energies on the business of the business. We've come to think of these as the ACORN imperatives, five potent precepts or operating ideas that these companies are using to grow oak-strong organizations.

As you peruse the profiles, be aware of why these organizations accommodate differences, build nontraditional workplaces, exhibit flexibility, emphasize respectful relations, and focus on retaining talented and gifted associates. More specifically, be on the lookout for the variety of ways these companies:

1. **A**ccommodate employee differences. With employee retention at or near the top of the list of corporate "must meet" measures, the most generationally friendly of companies are treating their employees as they do their customers. They are learning all they can about them, working to meet their specific needs, and serving them according to their unique preferences. They have painstakingly figured out what their employees' preferences are and have done everything they can to create a friendlier workplace in tangible and symbolic ways. There is real, not hypothetical, effort to accommodate personal scheduling needs, work-life balance issues, and nontraditional lifestyles. Each generation's icons, language, and precepts are acknowledged, and language is used that reflects generations other than those "at the top"; see, for example, West Group's Café.com as a smallish environmental accommodation and acknowledgment that nonetheless has meant much to the company's employees.

2. **C**reate workplace choices. The companies profiled here are a far cry from the stereotypical corporate environments of the 1950s and 1960s where everything was predictable and regimented from the executive boardroom to the way secretaries greeted executives in the morning to the standard memo format. Generationally friendly companies allow the workplace to shape itself around the work being done, the customers being served, and the people who work there. Dress policies tend to be casual. The height and width of the chain of command tend to be foreshortened, and decreased bureaucracy is taken on as a clear goal. "Change" is

not so much the name of a training seminar or a core value listed somewhere in the mission statement as it is an assumed way of living and working. All hands have a shared understanding of the temporary nature of "hot ideas" and the danger of emulating *Fast Company's* business of the month. They understand that leadership in an industry or a product area doesn't come with an insurance policy, nor does the accompanying organizational prosperity. In all these companies, the atmosphere could be described as relaxed and informal. There's an element of humor and playfulness about most of their endeavors.

3.   **O**perate from a sophisticated management style. You will notice the managers interviewed in the following profiles are a bit more polished than the norm; they operate with a certain finesse. They tend to be more direct. Generationally friendly managers don't have much time for circumlocution, "B.S.," as one put it to us, although they are tactful. They give those who report to them the big picture, specific goals and measures, then they turn their people loose – giving them feedback, reward and recognition as appropriate.

There are seven attributes that characterize their flexibility:

1. Their supervisory style is not fixed. How closely they monitor and manage, for instance, is a product of each individual's track record and personal preferences. Control and autonomy are a continuum, not solitary options.

2. Their leadership style is situationally varied. Some decisions are consensually made; others are made by the manager, but with input and consultation.

3. They depend less on positional than on personal power.

4. They know when and how to make personal policy exceptions, without causing a team riot.

5. They are thoughtful when matching individuals to a team or a team or individual to an assignment.

6. They balance concern for tasks and concern for people. They are neither slave drivers nor country club managers.

7. They understand the elements of trust and work to gain it from their employees. They are perceived as fair, inclusive, good communicators, and competent in their own right.

4. **R**espect competence and initiative. The old "manufacturing mode" of business was based on the precept that people are inherently "sliders" who are not all that interested in putting their best efforts forward without fairly close supervision and monitoring. The companies profiled here are very much a part of the knowledge and service economy. They assume the best of their people. They treat everyone, from the newest recruit to the most seasoned employee, as if they have great things to offer and are motivated to do their best. It is an attitude that has, in these companies, become a self-fulfilling prophecy. These companies hire carefully and do much to assure a good match between people and work. But they seem never to forget that they hired the best possible people for a reason—so that they will endeavor to do the best possible job.

5. **N**ourish retention. Many organizations are yet unaware there's a labor shortage, or at least they act that way. They expect employees to bend to the company's will and to adapt to meet the demands of the company culture. Then the executives complain about their high turnover, the difficulty of finding good people, and the skyrocketing costs of replacing those who've left. Generationally friendly companies are concerned and focused, on a daily basis, with retention, and on making their workplaces magnets for excellence—not employee-toxic. They know that keeping their people is every bit as important in today's economy as finding and retaining customers. Therefore, they offer lots of training, from one-on-one coaching opportunities to interactive computer-based training to an extensive and varied menu of classroom courses. Not only do

they encourage regular lateral movement within their organizations, but they have broadened assignments. No longer do insurance claims adjusters, for example, process only a small part of the claim. Today they take it from the initial call to the settlement check, which provides variety and challenge, and it allows employees to develop a range of skills.

You may notice something else unusual: these organizations market internally. In other words, they spend time learning how to become the employer of choice in their industry and region, and they continually "sell the benefits" to retain the best and brightest of their employees. Not a disingenuous internal public relations program, but a clear, conscious effort to remind employees of the good things the company offers.

Read any or all of the following profiles and see if these five principles don't shout their presence and importance to you.

FIVE THAT SUCCEED

Chevys Fresh Mex	TGI Friday's
Ben & Jerry's Homemade, Inc.	
West Group	Lucent Technologies

From Food Service to High Tech

Nowhere is the potential for generational conflict more obvious and prevalent—and more in need of positive management—than in the food service business. It is an industry highly dependent on the youth of America for both its labor force and its market. And it is, all too often, a business fraught with "kick the cat" employee and customer relations. When the manager has a bad day, be the genesis of that sour mood personal or professional, employees have a bad day. This, in turn, is passed right along to the customer with the salad and sandwich, at no extra charge. The net effect is a customer turned off and turned away, and an employee rethinking the option of a career in land mine removal. Increasingly, and especially in a tight labor market, it is a behavior pattern that is costing people in the food service industry the services of perfectly competent employees. A study by the Foodservice Research Forum found the factor that most often turns young people off to the food service industry was neither pay nor the kind of work involved. Rather, it was—and is—the behavior of managers toward employees, particularly employees like themselves.[1]

Making the mixed generational workplace work is imperative to both the operational and marketing success in the food service business. These businesses need employees from all generational groups, from Veterans to Nexters, to succeed. Turn off too many of these employees and labor costs go out of control. Keep on the payroll too many disaffected but options-limited employees who take their dissatisfaction out on customers, and those customers will abandon you for more pleasant environs.

The first two of our five profiles of companies with generationally friendly environments and successful accommodation efforts come from the chain restaurant business. The first is San Francisco-based Chevys Fresh Mex, a full-service restaurant chain with ninety locations and a straight-up growth curve. The second is the older, larger, and much more corporate TGI Friday's, a brand of Dallas-based Carlson restaurants. Both depend on youth and vigor to make their concepts work, and both have focused intensively on ways of making their workplaces cross-generationally friendly. The third profile, also in the food business—this time the food processing business—is a company of a very different stripe: Ben & Jerry's Homemade, Inc., is a company founded on different philosophies with a different vision. But like Chevys and Friday's, it is a mixed generational friendly company as well.

Tempted to dismiss Ben & Jerry's as a bit odd and "way out," and Friday's and Chevys as organizations that of necessity must cater to younger employees' expectations and demands? Okay. Not an unusual or unexpected reaction. But it is a bit harder to dismiss the cross-generational efforts and successes of West Group and Lucent Technologies, two companies in the mainstream of buttoned-down corporate America. Both of those organizations have indeed focused on, and succeeded at, creating effective mixed-generation workplaces, and they have done so for a very similar, very pragmatic reason: to bring the best of all their employees to bear on creating a high-performance workplace and highly competitive organizations. Both of these companies have made major efforts to be more generationally friendly and are seeing those effort pay off. If nothing else, they demonstrate the seriousness of the need.

In all of these real-world examples, you will notice something conspicuously absent: efforts to accommodate the Boomers and the Veterans aren't all that evident. Maybe you've already figured it out. But accommodating the generational preferences of these two groups falls under what we call the "status quo-efficient." That means that because the Boomers now dictate the corporate culture, and Veterans did so until very recently, very little adaptation to these cohorts' preferences needs to occur. They have created the status quo in their own image of the workplace. Like the new house on the block or the new building downtown, the companies in these profiles stick out from the structures around them. The rest of the buildings and houses around them may be perfectly constructed and even beautiful pieces of architecture, but we are accustomed to seeing them and they consequently don't attract our collective eye.

That said, there are aspects of some of these companies that are obvious products of a Boomer culture. Check out Thompson University at West Group, IdeaVerse at Lucent, and the whole culture at Ben & Jerry's if you want to see rampant Boomerism in action. In most cases, a Veteran vision of the workplace is part of a fading status quo-efficient. Companies trying to "embrace change" are discarding the old ways of working, whether they were effective or counterproductive, in favor of new organizations and remodeled corporations. You still see the Veteran's work preferences in many companies and, in some places, it's still the predominant way to work.

Nevertheless, the challenge for progressive companies, now and in the future, will be to keep enough of the "old ways" of working while cementing the new Boomer-centric status quo-efficient and accommodating Xer needs and expectations. Now more than ever, organizations will need to make older employees feel like they are part of the company's future. Wise companies will need to be more explicit about which parts of the work ethos they will never discard while changing their cultures to embrace the new corporate culture.

Boomers invented the concept of niche marketing, and they may be forced to turn that same lens on their own corporate culture. Maybe then this dominant generation can do an even better job of accommodating the various cohorts they must now manage.

Founded:	1986	
Headquarters:	San Francisco, California	
CEO:	Scott Bergren	
No. of stores:	100+ stores	
Sales (million):	$2–4 /store	
Distinctions:	Everything prepared fresh, every day	

When Kevin Bradley, director of training for Chevys Fresh Mex, was coming up through the ranks of the restaurant industry, there wasn't much talk about work-life balance. As little as a half dozen years ago, if you were a young restaurant manager, you worked nights. You worked weekends. You closed the restaurant, slept a few hours, and turned around to open it again the next morning. Fifteen-hour shifts were common if your store was short a manager. To get ahead you had to live, eat, and breathe your job. That's just the way it was.

Climbing your restaurant's corporate ladder, you could count on this: Every Mother's Day, you'd be seating happy families ready to enjoy a nice meal. New Year's Eve, Fourth of July, Christmas Eve, Easter—name a holiday and you, as a young manager, would certainly work it. As your children's school plays came and went unattended, as their soccer tournaments were fought and won uncheered, as your spouse waited not-so-patiently at home night after night, and as your friends enjoyed those long weekend vacations, you were helping servers out of the weeds—pitching in when they were overwhelmed by the sheer numbers of customers and orders—seating hungry diners, and doing spread sheets.

And throughout, you were thinking one thing: "When I'm general manager, I won't have to do this anymore. It will be someone else's turn to pay their dues."

Wrong. Welcome to the age of "Get a life!" The rules have changed.

There are big changes swirling around in the restaurant industry, driven by the juggernaut of Generation X servers and managers who make up much of that industry's growing employee base. Many restaurant companies, like the San Francisco-based Chevys Fresh Mex, are finding that the old ways just don't work with this new breed of worker.

It's about quality of life, and the unmitigated gall of Generation X restaurant employees to insist that they have some; and that when they are at work, they be treated with dignity and respect.

Chevys has had to make some major changes in its training and in its culture to come to terms with its Generation X employee base. It all started when Bradley began looking for new ways to attract, train, and retain good people. That troika—attract, train, retain—has motivated change in the restaurant industry, and at Chevys, as never before. Turnover in Chevys' segment of the industry average runs well over 100 percent a year; some insiders would argue 200 percent is a more truthful figure. Traditionally, getting good people wasn't a problem for Chevys. The opportunity of working on the ground floor of a fast-growing company was a great draw for talented servers and managers. As with most restaurant companies, keeping good employees was always the tricky part. And in today's lush economy, it has become even trickier. There is always something better, or at least different, on the other side of the fence, says Bradley, and good people were indeed being lured away by the competition.

"We just wanted to shut the back door," says Bradley. "We were even letting good managers leave. We had to stop that."

The migration was caused only partly by the economy, he says. It also was driven by the nature of this new breed of manager and server. "Our managers—and all the good managers in this industry these days—are getting cold called every day by headhunters and managers of other restaurants," he says. "We absolutely need to slam that back door shut and pay attention to what we weren't doing to keep these people." It boiled down to quality, he says. Quality of life and quality of work.

"We're fighting the restaurant reputation of eighty-hour, six-day workweeks," he says. "We needed to make changes or we were going to lose more good managers, not only to other restaurants, but to other industries that don't require such crazy schedules." (This, of course, addresses the *nourish retention* section of the ACORN imperatives outlined earlier.) Chevys is certainly on the front lines of the current labor shortage and understands the bottom line of heavy turnover combined with wage competition. This philosophy also is echoed in its approach to training its workers, as we will see later in this chapter.

In the restaurant industry as a whole, he says, people just aren't happy with the quality of their work life and the quality of their scant off-hours. This quality of work life can only be met through a flexible management style. Chevys was culturally ready to face the challenge.

Chevys decided they were going to change that. Now, instead of three or four managers per store, Chevys is striving to hire six, seven, or even eight. In addition, the company is now focusing on keeping enough hourly staff on hand so the managers working any given shift can actually manage, instead of filling in for the server who called in sick or helping out in the kitchen when the cook walked off the job. "One thing we found was that our managers were getting absolutely burned out by doing fill-in for short-staffed shifts," he says.

By hiring more managers and staff, Chevys is consciously trying to cut down on the hours its managers are expected to work, which is in direct response to the needs of Generation X managers.

"We really want to say we can guarantee every manager a five-day workweek," he says. "We're not quite there yet, but it's coming. Our managers have lives. Their jobs are not the most important thing in their lives. We have to recognize that and do something about it."

Training at Chevys also has taken a turn in the Gen X direction, says Bradley. "Our Generation X managers, they're all interested in what's in it for them. It has definitely changed the way I train our people. The old ways just don't work anymore." Formerly, says Bradley, "Managers would start out by chopping vegetables all day. Then when they had learned that, they'd go on to the P & L report." Now Bradley says he has to begin by training his Gen X managers on things like career development and other big-picture information that spells out, clearly, what exactly is in it for them if they choose to stay with the company. When the big picture is clear, then they can move into store operations.

Consultants who deal with restaurant companies see that as a smart course of action. They contend that Gen X management trainees, unlike their Boomer predecessors, place a high value on a predictable advancement path and potential. They do not equate hard work with job security. They've seen the fallacy in that claim and want the future spelled out for them before they put shoulder to grindstone.

That tentativeness to commit, Bradley has found, means the training and development of new managers from the new workforce must be different than the training Boomers went through and found acceptable. Because of those differences, Bradley says "Our Generation X employees just don't go in for the traditional industry training in which you learn and work every position in a restaurant before you manage it. They won't put up with that. We need to treat these managers differently, and make them feel that we really respect and value their intelligence and contributions or they'll just walk away."

In the training classroom, Bradley's style has changed as well. He's gone from telling to asking. He focuses on group interaction rather than "teacherspeak." They talk more about team building these days, and he asks trainees if they have better ways of doing whatever it is he's teaching them. "They question everything," he sighs.

But in dealing with Gen Xers, managers are finding it's not all bad. These new young workers have much more to bring to the table than simply a "what's in it for me" attitude. They have surprising technological savvy. And they are more independent and self-sufficient. A product, experts contend, of having to learn to fend for themselves growing up in a two-job, two-income family, they learned to adapt and improvise. A beneficial skill for the manager of an outpost in the far-flung empire of a food service company.

*   *   *   *   *

	Founded:	1965
	Headquarters:	Dallas, Texas
	CEO:	Curt Carlson
TGI	**No. of stores:**	500+ stores
Friday's	**1997 Sales**	
	(million):	$6,600 (Carlson Cos.)
	1997 Employees:	68,530 (Carlson Cos.)
	Distinctions:	Casual dining restaurant featuring a wide variety of trendy cuisine

TGI Friday's started life as a one-store wonder in 1965 on New York City's trendy Upper East Side. Created as a fun place for swinging-sixties singles to meet and mingle, there are today more than 500 TGI Friday's in 380 cities and 45 countries.

Friday's is arguably the oldest and definitely one of the largest casual dining chain restaurant companies in the world. On top of that, it is part of one of the largest, privately held, family-owned corporations in the world. On the surface, at least, a sure formula for organizational stodginess and rigidity, and a store-level culture where generational conflict could thrive. A clear potential. But not an inevitability, or at Friday's an actuality. Friday's is as new workforce friendly in the 1990s as it was "Summer of Love" fashionable in the 1960s.

How does it do it? By listening, and responding to, the needs of its employees with the same intensity it applies to listening and responding to customers.

Imagine you're a young person, given the opportunity to pick up stakes and travel around the country for six months without having to quit your job or give up your income. Imagine: Trying new cities on for size until you find one that hugs you like a chenille robe. Imagine: The freedom to go anywhere, anytime. Los Angeles this week. Seattle the next.

Unlike the hippies of the 1960s who prowled the corners of the world with nothing but a backpack and a belief in the kindness of strangers, you're doing it with the safety net of a regular paycheck. You've found that the open road is littered with cash machines.

It's funded exploration, and it's enough to make anyone with the solid, gnarled roots of spouses and children and mortgages and minivans yearn for the carefree, unfettered days of their youth. And it's one of the many things keeping younger employees happy at TGI Friday's. It also embraces two important factors of the ACORN imperatives: *create workplace choices* and *operate from a sophisticated management style.*

It's called the Passport Program, and it is part and parcel of the benefit package of Friday's. The program was designed with the wanderlust that is seemingly inbred in the immediate postcollege Xer mind today. Young people lucky enough to have the funds revel in getting a taste of the world before settling down into a serious job. By working for Friday's, even those without a silver spoon can take the grand tour, and the company doesn't lose its good employees in the process. (A great example of the *nourishing retention* ACORN imperative.) It's a win-win situation.

"Our employees love this program because it gives them the flexibility to stay with the organization while they're getting a taste of other cities," says Anne Varano, Friday's domestic vice president of human resources. "For us, it works because we don't want to lose good employees. And with this program, we don't."

Here's how it works: Whether you're a front-of-the house employee like a server or host, or a back-of-the-house worker like a cook or dishwasher, you can get a "passport" to travel around the country for six months and work at other Friday's restaurants along the way. Because the Dallas-based Carlson Restaurants currently operates, franchises, and licenses some 500 restaurants in more than 380 cities nationwide (including TGI Friday's, Friday's Front Row Sports Grill, and Friday's America Bar), employees can likely find a restaurant in every major city, wherever they go.

As a traveling employee, you relinquish your passport to the general manager of the store you're entering, along with a written address to which your paycheck will be mailed. At the end of your stay, whether it's a month, a week, or just a shift, the general manager signs, dates, and stamps your passport, gives it back to you, and you're on your way. You have a paycheck coming in a couple of weeks, tips in your pocket, and that long ribbon of highway ahead.

The fine print of the program looks like this: Passport holders stay on their home store's payroll logs and health plan. They are encouraged to arrange their itinerary well in advance by calling stores and setting up work schedules. They must keep in close touch with their home store by notifying them of their location every two weeks. The company does not provide travel expenses, nor does it arrange for accommodations. That's up to the traveler.

Not just any Friday's employees can get a passport. To qualify for the program, employees must work full time and have at least six months' tenure. They must be well trained and "validated" (Friday's term for certification of successful training) in all positions to be worked at other stores, and they must have no record of unsatisfactory performance. Tipped employees like servers must have been rated in the top third of their department staff for the previous three evaluation periods, and kitchen personnel must be validated in a minimum of two stations.

The Friday's passport serves as verification of who they are and where they've come from, signed and dated by the general manager in their home store. By carrying it, managers at other Friday's restaurants know the person appearing at the door asking for shifts is a legitimate, well-trained Friday's employee.

And that certainty is important, according to Troy Reding, another Friday's general manager. The thought of hiring a person off the street, with no interview process, would be a bit daunting to any manager and a bit appealing to anyone planning to criss-cross the country on the lam. But this program ensures the quality of the people who come through the door. This directly taps into the *respect competence and initiative* imperative. By giving a passport to employees it's an explicit declaration that the company trusts them, believes in their skills, and is unafraid to expose them to a variety of workplaces and work styles. This is a level of trust and confidence some people spend whole careers trying to achieve.

"I wouldn't send someone on the road that I wouldn't want working in my store," says Reding, who began his career thirteen years ago as a bartender. "So I don't have a problem giving shifts to anyone who has a passport. I know they're good employees."

Reding says that three to four passport-holding employees pass through his store each year. "They stay anywhere from a couple of shifts to a couple of months," he says. Reding's permanent employees tend to extend warm welcomes to the traveling passport holders, he says. It's exciting to work with someone new, even for a little while. It pumps a bit of vitality into the workday, and it breaks up the routine. As far as he's concerned, the program is a win-win situation with no risk on either side of the passport. His store gets the services of a verifiably great employee, and the employee gets the great benefit of traveling with the security of a paycheck.

Friday's Anne Varano echoes Reding's feelings about the program. It is a reward for an employee's loyalty and good work, she says, but the company is rewarded with a high level of employee retention as well.

Do the Passport Program and other benefits really increase the retention of employees? Varano says Friday's employees tend to stick with the company a long time. (Reding's thirteen years with the company is just one example.) That's unusual in an industry that seems to have a revolving-door philosophy of employee retention.

"Within our company, if you're not here five years, you're new," she says. "I have lots of people tell me that Friday's has been their one and only job."

The Passport Program, along with Friday's other benefits and thorough training process, does indeed account for the high level of employee loyalty, but it wasn't always that way. Varano has been working to increase the level of employee retention at Friday's. She began by analyzing at what point the company was losing their hourly employees. "It was ninety days," she says. "We were losing lots of new people. We found that most of the people we were losing just didn't like the restaurant industry, period. They didn't like the schedule or the hours, or working weekends. It's not that they didn't like Friday's."

So what keeps employees on the payroll? Varano says delving into what makes the new workforce tick has been a big piece of the puzzle. She found that the Friday's culture, as it was evolving, was moving directly toward the needs of Generation X workers. "I conducted research, asking both front- and back-of-the-house employees nationwide what they needed in a work environment," she says. The information she found isn't surprising or out of the realm of experience of other companies. "Generation X workers are definitely different than their predecessors," she says. "This group wants to be involved. They want a say in what goes on. They want to be asked their opinion. And they do not deal well with authority."

Varano found that Generation X workers at Friday's want their supervisors to look at them as individuals—as whole individuals with lives and families and problems and concerns—not simply as employees. They want a personal relationship with their supervisors, someone who will ask how their sick mother is coming along before assigning them a station for the day.

"These young people need a sense of belonging, they need to share parts of themselves that maybe their predecessors wouldn't have shared," she says.

In addition, Varano says training plays a large role in keeping young Friday's employees on the payroll. "We have a strong training program that we say provides our employees with competence so they can gain confidence," she says. "It's not negotiable; employees must go through the training before they're allowed to serve customers."

Young workers like that, she says. They want to feel confident and in command. They also want to know how they're doing. Friday's system of regular reviews and employee feedback matches your workers' need to hear progress reports early and often. Praise, rewards, or gentle guidance toward the right path. It's almost like parenting, a step or two removed, naturally.

* * * * *

	Founded:	1978
	Headquarters:	Burlington, Vermont
Ben & Jerry's	**CEO:**	Bob Holland
Homemade, Inc.	**1997 Sales (million):**	$174.2
	1997 Employees:	736
	Distinctions:	Unique ice cream flavors and public image as a company with a conscience

There may be no stranger, incorporated, stock-issuing company in the United States than Ben & Jerry's Homemade, Inc. Founded in 1977 in Burlington, Vermont, in a vacant gas station by two quasi-hippie childhood pals, this maker of quirky named (who hasn't heard of Cherry Garcia?), outrageously rich, exorbitantly expensive ice creams is a hotbed for gen spanning organizational experimentation. Today, their products are marketed through supermarkets and food service operations in all fifty states, as well as through licensed, franchised, or company-owned scoop shops. The company is currently extending its reach, with scoop shops in Canada, Israel, and the Netherlands.

You know you're working for a different sort of company when the corporate Joy Gang announces a "Corporate Dress-Up Day." It comes but once a year, the day when employees are encouraged to wear corporate attire like a suit and tie to work, just for the novelty of it. "Sometimes somebody wears a tie on a normal day," laughs Sean Greenwood, "and they're taunted unmercifully."

And then there's the matter of Greenwood's title. He is, officially, the Grand Poobah of Joy. Greenwood and his Joy Gang work at making fun. The schedule of events like Elvis Day, when everyone is the King, and the Dog Daze of Summer party, in which the company's employees at the corporate headquarters bring their dogs to work. "The Dog Daze of Summer has gotten a little out of hand," Greenwood laughs. "As we grew and moved into a new facility, we decided we didn't really want 170 dogs here. So we've had to change the party a bit."

It's almost an understatement to mention that Ben & Jerry's strives to *create workplace choices,* the second of the ACORN imperatives. In so many ways, this company has written the book on how to run a company by a whole new set of rules. Consequently, it will attract iconoclasts from all the generations. Your typical Xer will be drawn to it by it's very "uncorporateness," whereas Boomers will want to work here because it reminds them of the kind of company they may have hallucinated during the Summer of Love. Veterans who tended to buck authority will love this kind of corporate culture, and we can only wait and see how the next generation will react to this kind of company. In some ways, the business iconoclasm of Ben & Jerry's almost transcends the generational differences and brings together people whose common disdain for formal corporations transcends the tension that generational work preferences cause in other companies.

But there's method to all this madness. It adds up to happy, satisfied employees working together in a harmonious, fun environment. The generation gap? What's that? Greenwood reports that the company workforce is made up of Gen Xers and Baby Boomers, but the kinds of intergenerational problems that have plagued other companies haven't worked their way into the Ben & Jerry's corporate Eden. He's heard about such problems elsewhere, he says. They just don't exist here. What does exist is a rather smallish company filled with mostly long-time employees (not more than 750 nationwide, and 670 in the corporate headquarters), working hard to create a big measure of success. Doesn't sound so much like madness now, does it?

The Joy Gang officially began its mission of fun in 1988. "We were selling so much product that we literally couldn't keep up with the demand," Greenwood explains. "We were doing everything we could just to make ice cream. People were working twelve-hour shift after twelve-hour shift. It took its toll. We were putting great demands on people, and asking a lot of them." The company brought in massage therapists to help relieve the tension and bought pizzas for lunches, but it didn't feel like enough. "Jerry (Greenfield, one of the company's founders) decided we needed an official team that would infuse joy into the workplace," says Greenwood. He felt, "If it's not fun, why do it?"

A balance of hard work and rewards was important back then and still is, says Greenwood, who was with the company at the time. As the business grew, so did the demands it made on employees. There simply needed to be rewards for all the hard work; a payoff was essential if Ben & Jerry's was going to keep its good people.

So, Greenwood, who also plans special events and marketing, went to work. The Joy Gang is a team of representatives from departments throughout the company. They work with the rest of the staff to devise fun, entertaining diversions.

"It's important not to just foist obligatory fun on people," he says. "We don't just say: 'Okay at 3 P.M. today we'll be having ice cream in the lounge. Come and have fun.' Instead, we work with people and have them participate in the events somehow." Instead of a forced ice cream social, the Joy Gang might plan a potluck lunch, where someone from each department volunteers to bring a dish. That way, he says, people feel a part of the planning. They're helping. They're part of the fun.

Another now legendary Ben & Jerry's event began as a staff party after the company's annual stockholders meeting. Someone had the idea to hire a local band to play at the party. Over the years, this event has grown into an annual music festival featuring popular acts like Blues Traveller and Buddy Guy. Some fifty thousand people attended it last year. Everything at Ben & Jerry's closes down during the festival.

"When you're working seventy hours a week, you need to have fun doing it," Greenwood says. And he's not talking about the kind of fun that bonuses or hefty paychecks can buy. Ben & Jerry's pay scale, is, in fact, pretty low, says Greenwood. "When you look at what corporate America is paying people for jobs like ours, it's easy to see that most of us could be making more money working elsewhere, even here in Vermont," says Greenwood.

Let's see; long hours, hard work, low pay. Not exactly the formula that will bring reams of resumes to your door. But Greenwood disagrees. Even in this economy with, seemingly, more jobs than there are workers, people are literally lining up to work at Ben & Jerry's. "We recently opened a new manufacturing plant near our headquarters," he says with a laugh. "We had less than fifteen positions open. We got something like one thousand resumes."

Exactly what's in that ice cream, anyway? It's integrity, says Greenwood. It's walking the talk. Practicing what they preach. The ideas of the company—social responsibility, giving back to the community—are what attract people to Ben & Jerry's, he says. The reality of working there is what keeps them. The Joy Gang is only a small part of it.

Ben & Jerry's is known for both its creative ice cream flavors and mission statement and company philosophy. The mission avows that the company is dedicated to making the best products it can, profiting economically from these products, and doing so in a socially responsible way. Ben & Jerry's is committed to initiating innovative ways to improve the quality of life of a broad community outside its doors.

To that end, the company gives away 7.5 percent of its pretax earnings in three ways: the Ben & Jerry's Foundation, employee Community Action Teams at five Vermont sites, and corporate grants made by the director of social mission development. The company supports projects that are models for social change, projects that exhibit creative problem solving and hopefulness. The Foundation is managed by a nine-member employee board and considers proposals relating to children and families, disadvantaged groups, and the environment.

"People want to work for us because they believe in the company," says Greenwood. "They believe in the social responsibility."

But, he says, what keeps them (many Ben & Jerry's employees have been with the company for a decade or longer, and it's the only "real job" they've ever held) is the corporate culture and the atmosphere at work.

"One of the biggest pieces to this is the attitude of acceptance here," he says. "People are accepted for who they are. If they want to wear sandals and shorts to work, so be it. They're here because they're good at what they do. Period. We are a company in which people are going to have a good time at work," he continues. "If you come to our corporate headquarters, you'll hear people laughing." A great example of how they *accommodate employee differences.*

But, Greenwood is careful to stress an important point: Ben & Jerry's isn't a company filled with people wearing tie-dyed T-shirts listening to the Grateful Dead all day long, although some might get that impression with all this talk of fun and acceptance. It is a company of people working hard and succeeding in a competitive industry, he says.

"We're much smaller than our competition," he says. "Haagen-Daz is owned by a multibillion dollar conglomerate. We just can't spend the same kind of money they do. So we've had to be creative in order to be successful."

It's that same sense of creativity that makes the workplace fun, makes people want to work at Ben & Jerry's, and makes the company a success. In turn, it helps create happy, satisfied employees, a sense of acceptance for everyone, be they aging hippie Boomer or a what's-in-it-for-me Xer, and not a whisper of "My boss doesn't understand me." What a tidy circle. And so simple a formula when you think about it.

*　　*　　*　　*　　*

	Founded:	1872
	Headquarters:	St. Paul, Minnesota
West	**CEO:**	Brian Hall
Group	**1997 Sales (million):**	$1,383
	1997 Employees:	8,000
	Distinctions:	Leading supplier of legal information in the world

There may be no better example of a company's culture shifting and evolving in sync with its generations than West Group, the leading provider of legal information in the United States. Walk into any legal office in America and you see shelf upon shelf of leather-bound legal tomes, most of which come from West Group. As legal research turns more and more toward computers, West Group has gone "online," something they did before most people even knew what online meant, back when a fast modem collected data at 1,200 baud.

Although the company, then called West Publishing, kept its information delivery on the cutting edge, it was still firmly rooted in very traditional methods, emulating the environment of a law firm—albeit a very large law firm—more than anything else.

Founded in 1872 by John West to print and sell law treatises, legal dictionaries, and legal forms, West Publishing became *the* power in legal publishing by 1996 when it was acquired by The Thomson Corporation, a company with its own legal publishing business. Along the way, West Publishing created a notation system for cross-referencing legal opinions that is the heart of online legal research, and amassed a legal research capacity of 120,000 databases. The merger of the two companies precipitated a stunning culture change that today has West Group positioned as a legal publisher quickly evolving into a total legal information content provider with its fingers in some very cutting-edge technological pies.

But the technology isn't the story; it's just a factor in West Group's story, one that pushed it firmly onto the cross-generational radar screen. The real story is the successful transformation of a company from a Veteran management structure to a company run by Boomers. Down came the hierarchies. Down came the barriers between departments and functions. Down came the plush and unapproachable corner offices replete with wood and leather.

It was all replaced with a team-oriented, cross-functional, total quality, customer focused, participative management culture that has come to typify everything that Boomers have been implementing in companies across America. We've seen all of this before, in bits and pieces, but rarely do you get to see such a total and explicit transformation of a company's culture as you can see just by wandering around West Group's headquarters. You feel it in the air. You see it in the subtle changes going on in the halls and in the offices.

Patrick Sexton, public affairs officer for West Group, took us on a tour of the premises. As we walked past a vast array of beige cubicles, all in neat little rows, all precisely the same size, Sexton points to the small city and says one word that sums it all up: "Dilbertville." He explains that this particular suburb is a relic of the past and already on the schedule for renovation. Then we wander into a newly renovated section of the company. Again we see what could only be called cubicles, but in a variety of sizes, shapes, and colors. Some of the walls are higher, over there an arch decorates a passage, and generally you get the idea that someone with an eye for design went at the cubicle motif with a set of magic crayons. If Dilbertville was Kansas, the newly renovated sections looked more like Oz—fully in color and much more animated.

As we walked further, we comment that everyone looks pretty casual. Yes, says Sexton, they were trying out business casual during the summer months, but he is pretty sure it will stick. He can't imagine going back to business formal.

But Boomerism isn't the only thing happening at West Group. As it evolves its Boomer corporate culture, West Group is also reaching out to Generation Xers. Because more and more of the company's business is shifting toward technologically delivered information, young, high-tech workers are at a premium, not just to run the internal computer networks, but to actually deliver the product. Like everyone else, the scarcity of these techno-Xers is hitting the business hard and putting recruiting and retention issues on the front burner.

Enter Café.com and you won't wonder for very long whether West Group is serious about appealing to Generation X workers. A local chain of coffee shops, Caribou Coffee, has opened a retail store inside of the company's headquarters and is the centerpiece of Café.com. This may be the first time a retail store has established itself inside a company in a place where the general public really doesn't have access. But Café.com is more than just a bunch of tables situated around a fashionable coffee boutique. In fact, the coffee shop is only part of this central gathering place. As you examine it more closely you notice other oddities. In one corner, eight Internet workstations are open for general use. At about half the tables, you'll find outlets and modem jacks for people who want to drop their laptops down and get some work done outside of their cubicle. So much for being chained to your desk.

In another corner of Café.com, you find overstuffed chairs and couches organized into small lounge areas. Here too you'll find modem jacks and outlets, but these nooks look less like a place where you would perch behind your computer and more like a collaborative space where you could sit and mull things over with a few friends or coworkers. Chiat/Day, the Los Angeles-based ad agency, set up similar lounge areas so its most creative minds could have a place to relax and think literally and figuratively outside of the cube.

If Café.com is an Xer sanctuary, you don't have to wander too far to find a Boomer playground. Thompson University is the training function of West Group, and it's so much like stepping into your local Barnes and Noble that you might have to do a double-take. The place is floor-to-ceiling wooden shelves filled with the latest business best-sellers. The huge tables and check-out area will make you pine for your university library. There is an entire section of bookshelves dedicated to holistic thinking and self-actualization. Here you'll find everything from Steven Covey to Deepak Chopra, all clearly designed to help people become whole both at work and at home. Thompson U's main room is surrounded by a series of high-tech meeting rooms where they can hold traditional classes and video conferences.

Of course, you're never going to compare West Group to Ben & Jerry's in terms of the ACORN imperative to *create workplace choices.* But West Group is going in that direction. It's making the effort to reach out and accommodate employee differences, the first of our ACORN imperatives, and is thereby looking very different from the inside out. It will probably always "look" like a traditional corporation in many ways. After all, West Group is churning out legal information, not ice cream. But, from the inside, this company has come a long way in its efforts to create a nontraditional workplace, and that's what counts with the employees.

When you walk around and talk to people, they often refer to the "old West" and the "new West." Everyone is very aware of the dramatic changes that have occurred since the merger. The old West Publishing, as we've mentioned, was very hierarchical and dogmatic. Brian H. Hall, president and CEO of West Group and chief change-agent, is reshaping the culture. And true to Boomer methodology, his efforts started with a vision. Fortunately, unlike a lot of vision statements, this one is short, to the point, and easy to comprehend at a glance. "We support the system of justice in the U.S.," says Hall. No more. No less. Such a vision is vaguely reminiscent of NASA in the 1960s, where anyone could ask any employee—even the janitor—what his or her job was and the answer would always be, "I'm helping to send a man to the moon."

Likewise, supporting the system of justice in America is something most people can understand and rally behind. But there's more to it than just a good vision. Hall is trying to create a new culture from the two existing environments and the *C* word (Change) is a big part of that. "In the past, the culture tended to put a lot of value on the status quo and didn't value change all that much. We wanted to create a culture where change is embraced as a value, so we made available to everyone who worked here a change management program where they began to look at change a bit differently," says Hall.

Change is great, but if change doesn't lead to growth, people can feel like they're left spinning their wheels. That's why it's important to Hall that people look for growth both personally and professionally. "What people should do here is grow and develop as they are working for the West Group, so we set out to create that kind of culture, one where people could feel that there is opportunity, " says Hall. "We want to basically create a culture of collegiality and camaraderie where people feel good about the environment they are in." This philosophy manifests itself in a couple of ways.

Everyone wants to retain their employees these days, but this company embodies the *nourish retention* part of the ACORN imperatives better than most employers you will encounter.

One of West Group's more aggressive strategies is what Hall calls "the employer of choice." That may sound like a platitude or cliché until you start looking at what the company does to back up the talk. Creating an environment where people can feel like part of a team, where they can feel like they make a difference, is a good step in that direction, but it has its drawbacks. Hall says there are instances where employees feel comfortable enough to call him on the carpet when they don't like a particular policy or direction, asking him assertively, "Is this what an employer of choice would do?" If it's not, Hall is accountable to make the changes so that people want to stay. That accountability is what puts muscle in the "employer of choice" strategy. "It's good because people are starting to adopt that kind of thinking where they know they can point out to us where we are not exactly being the 'employer of choice,' when we haven't perhaps handled things the way we should. It's pretty potent," says Hall.

Of course being the employer of choice cuts both ways. It makes people want to work at West Group and stay there, but it also encourages other employers to actively recruit his people. "People want to work here," says Hall, "but other companies view us as a recruiting ground, which doesn't always make me feel real comfortable. But it makes me feel really good when I know our people have choices." By that, Hall means there's a lot of room for movement within the corporation, so if people need to move around a lot—particularly Generation X employees—they are encouraged to stay with the company while trying their hand at different jobs at West Group. The worst thing, says Hall, is if people feel trapped in their jobs. "When people don't have choices, then they become desperate and so they could potentially jump at any opportunity. That isn't good for the company, and sometimes isn't good for the individual. They think `If I don't take this opportunity today, I may never get another one.'" Hall compares it to shopping for a house: If you can only afford one house, then all the other houses you look at seem more appealing. "So I think the development of people through Thompson University—as well as the other things we do to develop people—provides them with a lot of choices, whether with us or someplace else. But I think if people have a choice, they can then make good conscious decisions as to where they want to spend their career," says Hall.

No one knows that better than Steve Buege, vice president of technical services for West Group. Buege, born in 1963, is an older member of Generation X and says he falls into the "young for my title" category. He's been with West Group twelve years, so he's seen the old and the new corporate culture and thrived in both. He says in the old West, it was a bit atypical to move around a lot, but his technological skills kept him jumping from cutting-edge project to cutting-edge project. He was doing online work before anyone knew what online meant, and then he moved to developing CD-ROMs, again before anyone knew what that medium was all about. Now, the new West is more dynamic, says Buege, and people move around laterally a lot.

Keeping people is particularly important to Ed Gilbert, vice president of human resources for the technology group and in charge of recruiting. And professional development is one of the key things he can offer. "We create a platform for you to grow your career. Our systems are such that if you want to try a wide variety of things, we'll help you do that," says Gilbert. And he says that's a very important message to his primary audience—Generation X. He says he runs into resistance from Boomers about moving horizontally through the organization, whereas Generation X loves it. If a Boomer is in the financial department, he tends to specialize in that and never really strays too far from the function, says Gilbert, a twenty-year veteran of Fortune 500 human resource departments. Xers, on the other hand, love to try lots of jobs, from operations to marketing to sales to accounting. "Generation X says 'Don't just tell me what it's like. I want to experience it myself,'" says Gilbert.

Recruiting Generation X high-tech employees consumes most of Gilbert's time. Although he's always worked in human resources, he sounds more like a marketer. "In today's communications-driven era, you've got to think radio, you've got to think alternative sites [for recruiting] where potential employees might be." He talks about venues for recruitment and establishing the company's brand. And his brand is: West Group is the employer of choice.

He's been targeting Xers by advertising on local alternative radio stations and sending the message that West Group is a great place to work. "Make your Mark" was a particularly effective ad campaign for recruiting these younger, highly sought, employees, says Gilbert, because being part of something important really appeals to them. In his ads, Gilbert says, "We moved away from the stodgy attorney on the screen with a bunch of law books. We don't show any law books whatsoever because we're not about that. We're about bringing in and attracting people with a wide variety of skills." The company's policies also help Gilbert recruit Generation X workers.

Hall explains that, after interviewing a high-tech worker for West Group, the company guarantees they will have an offer on the table for the potential employee within 24 hours if they decide to hire him or her. This fast turnaround is important, says Hall, because "With the Gen Xers—especially people in technology—we understand that we must move quickly because they move quickly. How you hire somebody is pretty indicative of the kind of company they're coming to work for." If his company can react nimbly and quickly, he knows that reflects the kind of environment a lot of Xers are looking for. Because many of these workers have plenty of offers and opportunities from other companies, being able to move quickly can be an important advantage. Of course, the ACORN imperative of *operating from a sophisticated management style* is directly reflected in West Group's fast turnaround time for new hires.

Gilbert agrees with the theory that the old West Publishing was very much a Veteran company that's just recently evolved into a Boomer-run business. Now it's reaching out in a big way to the Generation X workforce. He was recruited to come to work for West Group right after the merger and was a bit taken aback. When he saw the rows and rows of cubicles, he said to himself, "Holy cow, this is where Dilbert was born!" It's gotten a lot better since then, says Gilbert, but in terms of recruiting, he still sees room to grow West Group into a culture that really appeals to the high-tech Gen X worker. His strategy consists of paying more than competitors, having better benefits, and providing an enriching and rewarding environment where people can find opportunities to grow. "When I recruit people, I don't look at them for the job that we're hiring them for. I want to see if they have the capability to go two or three jobs beyond that," says Gilbert.

No one can tell us more about the difference between the old West and the new organization better than twelve-year veteran Buege. He calls the old West a private company with a capital *P*, a place where you weren't informed about the financials of the company and a bit afraid to make aggressive decisions. You never questioned the direction from above because it was assumed, often wrongly, that those making the decisions were more informed than you. "You did what you were told, you did it very well, you felt free to offer suggestions and add judgment along the way, but your job wasn't to set direction," explains Buege.

When Thompson merged with West Publishing, the culture turned upside down. Now most of the direction in the company is bottom-up, says Buege, "The analogy that I think fits well is: West Publishing was a kind of 'Ready, Aim, Shoot!' organization with a very organized, very methodical, very disciplined approach to almost everything. Thompson was a 'Ready, Shoot, Aim!' group with the attitude of 'Let's do something. If it's wrong, we'll fix it later. But damn it, do something and do it now.'"

Buege is also at the center of his own generational vortex, an Xer with a vice president title managing seven departments and almost four hundred employees. That means, of course, that he's managing people his own age, younger employees, and Boomers who are seven to ten years older than himself. It's been easier than it could have been, he says, because coworkers tended to give him the benefit of the doubt, at least initially. The Boomers he's worked with "don't tend to form an opinion of you right away. And that's all I ask for. Give me a month or three to prove myself. Judge me on what you see first hand. Don't judge me on what you may have heard about me. And I think for the most part that age group tends to do that," says Buege. "Sometimes you get a little bit of the attitude that 'you haven't paid your dues, you don't really deserve this, it fell in your lap and what are you going to do to demonstrate you're capable.' But to some extent, I think that's fair. If I were in their shoes, I'd be asking the same thing," he adds.

Downplaying his title and position has worked well for him, and it's a typical Xer sentiment that corporate politics and posturing is a waste of time. "I think you want to focus more on the people and the projects and less on the organization. The organization is an afterthought. It's a necessary evil, and they understand that. I think if you play it that way, then you're fine. But if you get into this *my position, your position* crap, they throw it back at you—as they should," says Buege.

Buege has a lot to say about managing people that is revealing of the "new West." It gives us a glimpse into what the Xer managers and leaders of the future might be like, the kinds of approaches to supervision that we could expect. Buege is on the cusp of the Boomers, a leading-edge Xer who nevertheless seems to embrace his predecessors' affection for consensus building. But primarily, this is a treatise on Xer management. Buege says, "In some ways I think being sort of in-between is an advantage. I'd like to think I could be seen as 'one of us' to each group I manage. I think that the older generation relied heavily on title and position to get respect and to get people to follow them. I don't think you can get away with that anymore."

"I think if you try, you're setting yourself up for failure. It's tempting, but you want to go out of your way to set that aside and attempt to talk to people as peers. Let them be the ones who factor in your title and position if they're going to. The minute you have to pull rank on somebody, you've lost. So I look at it as 'let's all put our labels aside, let's sit here and have a productive discussion, and let's tackle this problem.' And I think as you move around and your title changes, if you've operated that way, I think you'll carry respect into that position. If you've relied on your title, you're sort of hosed the day you lose it. That's worked for me."

And Buege on motivation? He says, "What I look for in people, in one word, is initiative. I think if you find initiative, then the job becomes about steering and directing and really just managing and not motivating. If I stay out of the motivating business, that's where I like to be. I don't like to be pushing people and kicking them in the butt all the time. I'd rather be pointing and steering and letting them run on their own."

What's happened at West Group over the past two to three years has been repeated and will continue to be repeated in companies across industries all over the United States. Gurus and pundits attribute it to the global economy, technology, and the rise of knowledge work, but it could be that the flattening of hierarchies, teamwork, participative management, total quality, and business reengineering are all symptoms of the generational changes taking place in workplaces across the nation. It sure seems that way at West Group. The Boomers have taken the reins of power there and are remaking it in their image of a workplace. And it's clear that Generation X is having its own effect, with places like Café.com and an increasing attitude toward employees that the company wants them to stay around for awhile. As Gilbert puts it, "it's not your traditional lock-them-at-their-desk environment anymore."

So it wouldn't be much of a surprise to see West Group gradually evolve toward a predominately Generation X work environment down the line. As it stands, the "new West" is firmly ensconced and an amazing case study in organizational change. If you put on your "generational" glasses and take a hard look at it, it makes a lot of sense. CEO Hall, talking about the environment he's trying to create, says it this way, "Anybody who earns a living puts a lot of time and energy into what they do every day, so part of the philosophy here is you need to have a good work experience. I want people to feel engaged. I want them to feel part of a community that this is a place where they can come in and feel fulfilled as a person. Their total life experience is a holistic event and this [environment] is part of it. We want to make it a good experience."

*   *   *   *   *

Lucent	**Founded:**	1996
Technologies	**Headquarters:**	Murray Hill, New Jersey
	CEO:	Richard McGinn
	1997 Sales (million):	$26,360
	1997 Employees:	134,000
	Distinctions:	Highly creative telecom manufacturer

Lucent Technologies is a brand-new, century-old manufacturer of telecommunications equipment and software, from telephones to business communication systems, switching and transmission equipment, and wireless networks. It was formed when AT&T decided to spin off its systems and technology business as an independent company. Lucent is the spiritual legate of Western Electric, the manufacturing arm of pre-divestiture AT&T and Bell Laboratories, the vaunted Ma Bell think tank. When Lucent "went public" in 1996, the initial public offering raised $3 billion, a very big birthing indeed. Lucent also inherited and took with it into its new life as a brand-new company the genetic inheritance of a make-no-waves, regulated public utility. The company's challenge, first under Henry Schacht and now under Richard McGinn, was, and is, to turn a company with a low tolerance for risk mentality and turn it into a creative, entrepreneurial organization capable of competing—and winning—in the heady high-tech atmosphere of the new millennium.

To turn a company with a history of respect for titles and seniority into an open incubator for new ideas and products that will routinely render all that has come before them obsolete is tricky business. Although the creative center of Lucent Technologies is still Bell Laboratories, inventor of the microchip, C++, and 101 other high-tech miracles, all of Lucent is today charged with making the company better, faster, and more competitive.

To make that a reality, Lucent has been breaking down the traditional barriers and formalities that limited the reach and responsibilities of employees and invited everyone to make as creative a contribution as they can. When you look at this mission in light of the ACORN imperative to *create workplace choices,* it can be a bit intimidating. A company like Lucent, with so much tradition and history behind it, has had a lot of success with what is now the status quo. On the other hand, with Bell Labs association, there was a lot of precedent for creatively pushing the envelope in terms of product development. This journey was daunting, but not insurmountable. But what happens when every person in the company, from John in accounting to Jill in sales, approaches everyday work from a creative perspective? In the best case scenario, you'd have a staff of experienced employees working with as much excitement and passion about their jobs as they did on day one. They're not only satisfied, they're energized. Nobody's wondering what's in it for them, nobody's counting the minutes until quitting time, nobody would rather be sailing. More importantly, nobody's calling competitors to inquire about job openings, and they're not answering when the competitors call them. Lucent is clearly demonstrating the *nourish retention* imperative.

In your dreams, right? Not necessarily. Lucent management believes it can create ways to infuse more creativity and passion into the cubicles of their employees, and they've convinced skeptical Boomers and scoffing Veterans to come along for the ride. Three years ago, Lucent employees Laurie Lamantia, Lari Washburn, Angela Just, and Chris Steinberg founded IdeaVerse, a creativity and innovation training center. That's right. Lucent has invested time, money, and other resources to help its employees to be more creative. You can almost hear the Veterans laughing at the sheer frivolity of it.

The concept behind IdeaVerse, Lamantia explains, was to give Lucent employees the space and time to be free with their thinking and to play with ideas without having to worry about the typical kinds of censure one often finds in the workplace. They wanted people to not only think outside the box, but to destroy it. Break down barriers to creative flow. Unleash the ideas and creativity within.

The result was a department within Lucent headquarters where the walls are purple, vice presidents color with Crayolas, and just about anything goes.

To Boomers who might be wondering how this will affect the company's bottom line (and their own quarterly bonuses) and to Veterans who scoff at its frivolous nature, IdeaVerse was a concept that took a bit of getting used to. Purple walls? Give me a break. Creativity? Forget it and get serious about the work. Creativity is for artists. It doesn't have much to do with daily life in a cubicle.

Doesn't happen, says Washburn. People use their creativity every day. And it doesn't mean you have to be composing a symphony to be doing something creative. "People have elevated creativity to something almost nonhuman," says Washburn. "But we're creating all the time." If you don't believe you're creating all the time, she says, think about a typical morning at your house. Does it involve getting the family up, dressed, ready for school, and out the door on time? Does it involve finding the quickest route to work and changing direction midstream to avoid heavy traffic? Does it involve juggling a million little things before you settle into your office? Follow yourself through a typical day, keeping one eye on creativity, says Washburn. You're being spontaneous and creative all the time, and you may not even realize it.

This isn't simply new-age, flower-power, I'm okay-you're okay stuff. Lamantia and Washburn can tie creativity directly to the company's bottom line. Through the success of IdeaVerse, they have demonstrated how employees can plug their creative juices directly into their jobs. That's bread and butter, solid enough to satisfy a company of skeptical Boomers and hesitant Veterans.

If employees are tackling their jobs with newfound creativity, exciting things can happen, says Lamantia. People look at old problems in new ways. John in accounting comes up with a great redesign of that same old tired spreadsheet. Jill in sales hits on a fresh angle that boosts her monthly sales. People are working with their eyes on high beam and their minds open. And that's not always the case in the average workplace, where people tend to perform their jobs on automatic pilot after a while.

"Accessing the whole, creative self hasn't been done in corporate America," says Washburn. But it should be, she says. Instead of focusing on only logic and rational thought in the workplace, people ought to draw from a deeper well. They'll get more from their jobs and be more on the job if they do, she says.

So, where does the average guy in accounting find the "deep well"? That's the job of Lamantia, Washburn, and their team at IdeaVerse. They act as the divining rod to help people find the deep well of creativity within. Lamantia is quick to explain that they're not teaching people to be creative at IdeaVerse. There's no need. People are naturally creative, she says. If you don't believe it, drift back in time to when a sunny afternoon, a cardboard box, and a couple of friends were all the fodder you needed to come up with hours of creative play. Everyone starts out creative, she says, but over the years it gets drummed out of one's conscious mind to make room for more serious pursuits like workplace norms, societal conventions, and the litany of rules and regulations Boomers live by.

Employees are encouraged to take IdeaVerse courses like "Tapping into Your Own Creative Power," "Wholeness in the Workplace," and "The Artist's Way" on company time, Lamantia says. And that's important to the success of the program. Employees, especially those who wonder about the seemingly frivolous nature of a course entitled "Life, Paint, and Passion," need the reassurance that this is something their employer actually wants them to do. It might feel like they're skipping school, but they're not. "We're making the statement that this is important, real work," Lamantia says.

But for Boomers like Lucent internal consultant Patrick Brown, viewing "Life, Paint, and Passion" as important, real work was a bit of a stretch. After all, sitting in a classroom for three days playing with paint and canvas doesn't have much to do with his everyday job. Or does it?

The course "Life, Paint, and Passion," requires participants to paint pictures for three days. It involves canvas and oils, but it is really about risk, says Washburn. It's about going out on a limb and discovering that the risk was worth taking, and heck, the fall wouldn't have been so bad after all.

To many Boomers and Veterans, the idea of sitting in a room alongside your colleagues, superiors, and underlings painting a winter scene on canvas brings, at best, embarrassment and at worst, nausea. Could you paint a group of kids ice skating on a frozen pond? Do your eyes tear up at the thought of your boss seeing the ridiculous-looking stick figures you'll surely produce?

That's self-censoring at work. That's what the course is designed to break. And when you get past the idea that your picture has to be a Da Vinci masterpiece to be of value, you're half-way there.

"This course helped me to go one step beyond the edge of my knowledge or safety zone," says Patrick Brown. "It showed me that I can go beyond the box into what might seem, at first, like uncomfortable territory." Brown says the course also taught him to rethink his notion of the concept "finished." There were many times when he felt he was finished with a painting, and the course facilitators pushed him to do more. At first, Brown didn't know quite what they meant. The painting was finished. That was it. Then facilitators asked him to think about the last element he would ever consider using in the picture. What would happen if it were included? Where would the picture go from there? By considering these things, Brown says he discovered that there is more beyond one's self-imposed boundaries. In pushing his limits, Brown says he unblocked the flow of spontaneous creative energy, a clear example of *respecting competence and initiative.*

He could go one step beyond. There was indeed more. "It was powerful to learn I could do it," he says.

Touchy-feely stuff. But look a bit deeper. Brown says he was able to bring the experience back into the workplace and translate it into better on-the-job performance. He says the idea of not stopping at a predictable place, but instead going out on a limb and discovering what's beyond the boundary has been helpful in his creative brainstorming with clients. When he's designing a project plan, for example, he now will find himself pushing his limits to get at the stuff that lies just beyond his self-imposed boundary.

Creative risk-taking is where all great ideas come from. Any new idea sounds a bit crazy at first, right? The whole point, says Washburn, is to help break down the self-censoring that can prevent new ideas from coming to light. When you're in a business like communications technology, which is the kind of business in which a crazy idea today might mean the next-generation Internet tomorrow, creative risk-taking needs to be "job one."

PART THREE

ADVICE-O-PLENTY

CHAPTER SEVEN

THE PLIGHT OF CHARLIE ROTH:

A Cross-Generational Workforce Case Study

Charlie Roth is having a bad day in the middle of a bad month in the midst of a crummy year in what looks like the wrong career choice altogether. Today the news came down that all midlevel managers and below will need to reapply for their jobs. Of course, they will change all the job titles and shuffle the responsibilities, but no one is fooled. The big guys found yet another way to downsize without the appearance of being a pack of corporate serial killers.

In earlier times, with better staff performance, this kind of hazing wouldn't have worried him in the least. Charlie always hits or exceeds his numbers as a source of pride and with an eye toward survival. He knows that, in corporate politics, if you can't razzle-dazzle your way up the ladder at Alpha-Beta Surety, Inc., great productivity and profitability numbers are the next best thing. It takes hard work to get them, but while some rest on their laurels, Charlie rests on his numbers.

But the numbers aren't working for him lately. Recent shakeouts in the insurance business have promoted him to what he fears is his level of incompetence. He is now in charge of a subrogation unit—the group that parses out who owes whom what in liability settlements—of one hundred people; ten teams of ten apiece.

And most of them are failing to make their goals.

By any measure, Charlie's department is in trouble. Productivity is down; claims paid are up; customers are angry; subrogation units from other insurance companies see his people as easy marks—they hardly ever fight a counterclaim; department morale is in the cellar; and turnover is high. Quotas are low, lower than ever, and they still don't hit their numbers. For the first time in his career, and maybe the last, nothing is working for Charlie. He is forty-eight years old, and, as of today, it looks like he is due for a career change.

He has a month to turn things around, and panic is the calmest feeling in his emotional spectrum. There isn't any point to scheduling meetings with all the teams until he figures out what the problem is, or at least the general neighborhood where it hangs out, so Charlie has been to see the resident organization development specialist. She suggested he make a list of what each team did well and find ways to encourage his people to do more of the same.

No way Charlie will have time for all that fluffy, touchy-feely analysis, and he certainly can't turn things around in thirty days without tackling problems instead of mouthing platitudes and playing with woo-woo panaceas. But he decides to do at least part of what she suggested: he will jot down the characteristics of both his best and his worst teams and see if the contrast will clear anything up in his own mind.

Team two is his gem. They do everything right and are a joy to deal with, so much so that many of them have become Charlie's personal friends over the years. Matter of fact, Linda, the team leader, named Charlie godfather to her son when he was born twelve years ago. The team members are mostly energetic and focused, and they know the value of friendly competition. They work together like the Chicago Bulls in their heyday. The team has its top performers, but no one has any illusions they could do as well alone as they do as a team. They are willing to work hard and put in extra hours when necessary. In fact, he sometimes worries they work too much, but with the lousy productivity of the other teams, he appreciates the extra effort. Politically this group is sharp. They know how to look good in front of upper management and how to make him look good, too. They network with other teams well, both inside and outside the department and they still can handle the competition. Most of them belong to the same downtown gym, and they often get together after workouts. If he could put this team on the copy machine, he would make nine copies, and his job would be saved.

On the other hand, every time Charlie looks at team nine, he is reminded of a cat fight. They are notorious for their knock-down drag-out fights, shouting over the cubicles like it's the trading floor at the stock exchange. It is worse when they are silent. That means they are beyond fighting and aren't even talking; they're pouting. That also means they aren't working, at least not productively. Everything team two does right team nine screws up. He can't take them out in public, and they don't play well with other teams.

Sometimes he thinks team nine's high turnover is a blessing, a way to get rid of the troublemakers, but it never seems to work out that way. There is always more than enough trouble on the team and enough troublemakers, and, with the burgeoning labor shortage, the pickings in the labor market are getting leaner.

On paper at least, most of team nine's members are salvageable. They are bright, enthusiastic workers he personally likes. They are constantly requesting transfers to another team, and, though he feels sorry for them, he can't justify the move.

Team nine's battles concern technology, interpersonal communication, hours, and work assignments. A couple of members are highly adept Internet users with no patience for the "dinosaurs." Of course, it doesn't help that the extreme technogeeks are the same ones who show up late for work, leave early, and won't work overtime. They are notorious for not following directions, which grates on the nerves of some members of the team more than others and sometimes on his nerves as well. Their team mates complain that the technogeeks don't listen, exhibiting such behavior as typing e-mail messages while another team mate is trying to have a heart-to-heart conversation with them.

The geeks have a point, especially about procedures. Some members of team nine are such sticklers for details and doing things by the book that it drives Charlie and the rest of the team nuts. These same folks are so enamored with face-to-face, or at least voice-to-voice, contact that they refuse to leave or return voice mail messages. The upshot, Charlie believes, is that they are missing a lot of opportunities to get things done efficiently. When it comes to the Internet, forget about it. The technophobes only do what they are told, and they rarely come up with new approaches. They see technology as a way of hiding from confrontation and favor taking on the enemy one to one, hot and heavy. Their touchstone seems to be, "We've always done it this way." The good news: They always show up on time and are willing to go the extra mile.

Then there is the rest of the team—the vocal majority. Generally good individual performers, they are extremely judgmental and intolerant of the other two, often warring, contingents—the technogeeks and the technophobes. Their complaints, brought directly to Charlie instead of to Devon, their team leader, echo Charlie's own frustrations. They are hardest on the newest members of the team. They accuse them of a poor work ethic, loathsome interpersonal skills, and an unjustified "What's in it for me?" attitude. Those in the vocal majority complain that the technogeeks want to change everything faster than anyone could adapt to and that the technophobes don't want to change at all. The vocal majority knows change has to occur, and they believe they know exactly how to accomplish it, if only the other two sides would just listen.

To get another spin on things, Charlie sets up a meeting with Linda and Devon, the leaders of teams two and nine, respectively. As he walks through his assessment of the two teams, Linda preens and gloats—subtly, of course. Devon erupts all over the room: "Of course those guys do it 'right' all the time. They're Boomers. You're a Boomer. It all fits. If I were a Boomer, I could be just like all of you, and everything would be great. But I'm not a Boomer, and I don't want to be, even if it means losing my job. You're all absorbed in yourselves and your work and your way of doing things. It sucks. I've got news for you. I'm not managing people *like* Linda's."

A 200-watt light bulb suddenly sears the inside of Charlie's head. It is true: Nearly all of the members of team two are in their forties. A few are older, but those folks are good soldiers who generally do what they are told and have been around Alpha-Beta for awhile.

On the other hand, team nine is a virtual menagerie of generations. By and large, the technophobes are the elders on the team, and, of course, the geeks are the young ones. Then there is the vocal majority—solidly Boomers, all five of them.

Team nine, Charlie realizes, may well be a microcosm of the problems on most of his other teams. Luckily, most of the others aren't as vociferous, contentious, and just plain obstreperous. If he can help Devon's team, he's sure he can turn the whole department around. But can he do it in time?

*   *   *   *   *

Your Mission—Should You Choose to Accept It

Okay, Dear Reader. You've got yourself a genuine, bona fide, concrete, grade AA case study here. Like most workplace situations, it is complex, ambiguous, and multifaceted. It's drawn from a real situation, though we've changed the names to protect the anonymity of our main character and his company. There's no one simple, obvious method for solving the case, so it offers insight by asking you to compare your solution with that of others.

Put yourself in Charlie's Birkenstocks. He has a meeting scheduled with Devon and his team in two days to scratch out a do-or-die improvement plan. He's toyed with a dozen ideas: rebuild the teams along generational lines—all the Boomers and Veterans in the deep end of the pool, and the Xers in the shallows; get the corporate shrinks and team builders on the floor and don't let 'em out until people start working on cases and stop working on each other; lay down the law to the whole lot of 'em—"Shape up or ship out"; or just put it on the team leaders' heads, back them up, and stand back.

What would you do if you were in Charlie's shoes? What do you see as the "big picture" issues at play? What internal and external forces are at work? How do generational differences play a role? Would you deal with the generational differences directly or simply factor them into your solution? How would you get things back on track and restore some harmony to the department?

As a result of analyzing the case yourself, you'll develop a better understanding of the generations and the types of problems that tend to rear their heads in the mixed-generation workplace. You'll see that the feelings, beliefs, and perspectives here are not logical, but they're important and must be considered.

Think it through for yourself. Then, once you've decided how you would handle Charlie's rather desperate situation, compare your ideas with those of some other experts. You will find responses from managers at Starbucks, McDonald's, Bath & Body Works, Custom Research Incorporated, and TCF National Bank, along with the thoughts of the author of another book on cross-generational issues, and an expert on mentoring and team work.

Ideas From the Experts

As we studied the responses from these seven experts, we were struck by a couple of things. One is that the approach of the one Gen X expert is subtly different in focus from the approaches of the Boomer experts—and in just the ways we might have expected—but judge that for yourself! We were also struck by three specific similarities or common approaches in all the respondents' advice.

They began their approach to Charlie's problems by defining the big picture. Most thought Charlie was up against "change" issues and the generational differences were primarily compounding the problems, not causing them.

They all saw Charlie's generational plight as centered around the broader issue of "diversity." All recommend he leverage the positive potential in the differences among his teams and team members rather than treating those differences as a continuing source of conflict.

All believe Charlie should shift the focus from his people's festering interpersonal issues to the results they need to produce.

As you peruse the responses to Charlie's situation, be aware of the manner in which each expert suggests Charlie implement these three remedies.

Bruce Tulgan's Response

Bruce Tulgan, author of Managing Generation X and Work This Way, and is founder of Rainmaker Thinking, Inc. in New Haven, Connecticut. He is a lawyer and a member of Generation X.

Charlie is facing the new diversity issue in the American workplace—age diversity. On one extreme, the workforce includes more older workers than ever before, not only because people are working longer, but also because the U.S. population at large is aging. On the other extreme, a new generation is starting their working lives in the midst of the most profound economic changes since the Industrial Revolution. Older workers experience these changes—globalization, technology, downsizing, restructuring, and reengineering—as revolutionary and discomfiting. For the Gen Xers, nothing is changing; it was like this when they got here, and most of them like it this way.

Reactions of the Boomer majority are divided. Some are digging in their heels and resisting change, while most are making the necessary adjustments to move forward. Although all three cohorts are working in the same environment, change looks different from each of their perspectives. Like any diversity issue, this one seems intractable only when the difference among team members is positioned as a source of conflict, rather than as a means of leveraging each person's uniqueness as sources of learning, productivity, and innovation.

Charlie needs to step back from the personal conflicts and focus on his core mission. He is not operating in the workplace of the past anymore. The future workplace is upon us. The only thing that matters is his employees' ability to create tangible results and generate the added value needed to sell in the marketplace. If some of his people want to go out together after they work out, fine, but that has nothing to do with getting the job done. To succeed, he must learn to manage the flexible, adaptable, technoliterate, information-savvy, independent, entrepreneurial Gen Xers on team nine, because they are the stars of the workforce of the future. They see themselves as sole proprietors of their skills and abilities, think of their employers as "clients," seek to move seamlessly from one opportunity to the next, often juggle several "clients" at once, and seek to cash out their career investments often so they can reassess and renegotiate. And although the trend is strongest among those of Gen X, more and more stars of all ages are looking at their working lives in a different light. Charlie will waste his time if he fights the trend. In today's high-tech, fast-paced, rapidly changing, knowledge-driven global economy, only the nimble will survive. Charlie must turn the age diversity "crisis" in the subrogation unit into a strategic opportunity to transform the unit into a fluid hub of value creation.

Charlie needs to rethink the problem. It is not about technology, interpersonal communication, hours, and work assignments. It is about productivity and customer satisfaction, tangible results, and added value. Charlie must stop managing time and process, and he must start managing goals and deadlines. Each person brings different skills and knowledge to the table, and each team has what it takes to succeed. The generational issues are merely a reflection of the business issue at play—transition to the workplace of the future. Charlie must get things back on track and restore harmony by getting people focused on mission instead of personality. Charlie needs to gather every person's input about mission, goals, and roles; promote ongoing dialogue; and seek buy-in. Those who are unable to focus on bringing the resources of the team to bear on mission, goals, and roles will not be able to continue as members of the team.

1. The leaders must clarify mission and goals. In fact, in my view, any evaluation of a generational issue in the workplace is incomplete if it doesn't take into account the fundamental big-picture business issues that are going on. For me the only reason to look at generational issues at all is because they have a direct impact on the bottom line. The only value of looking at them as generational issues is if looking at them through that lens helps business leaders and managers to get a better understanding of what's actually going on and how to solve the problem and move closer to an optimal position in terms of the organization's goals. What is the work that needs to be done by each team? What are all the projects, tasks, and responsibilities? What are the major goals and deadlines for each project? What are the key guidelines to observe—not just the old standard ones but those that are truly necessary? Which guidelines are negotiable? Which are not negotiable?

2. Leaders must get their teams focused on mission—communicating the clear mission, goals, deadlines, and guidelines. Once that information has been communicated, it is a good time to see who will continue as a member of the team and who will not. In fact, I do a lot of work with the armed forces, and those organizations focus on the end game, strictly keeping their attention on the mission in front of them. This resonates with Xers very clearly. That may be a point where the Schwartzkopf generation (Veterans) can find some common ground with Xers. Both groups understand the importance of getting the job done, though their paths to get to that result may be different.

Getting Xers and Veterans to focus on the task is easy. Selling it to Boomers may take more work. The way I sell it to the Baby Boomers is I show them where they are bleeding financially. I show them what recruiting is costing them, what training is costing them, what turnover is costing them, what less than optimal performance is costing them, what people who are looking at it as "just a job" is actually costing them when competitors are able to get people to innovate. Though they may not tell their managers, Xers tell me, "I'm much more likely to be into a task—to do a great job and be an innovator—if you just give me the target and let me hit it my own way." Focus on results instead of process. The Xers I talk to roll their eyes back in their head in frustration when they tell stories about managers who go on and on about how something should be done as opposed to what needs to get done. Another turnoff is when managers focus inordinately on what has happened as opposed to what needs to happen. Most Gen Xers want to get the job done and go home. When the boss starts going on and on about anything that doesn't have to do with "get the job done and go home" they tend to get a little bit bored—not even bored but sort of irritated. That's when they ask seemingly rude questions such as, "What are you talking about?" and "Why are you wasting my time?"

3. Team members who remain need to clear the air. I call the approach I recommend, "passing the stop watch." It means each person takes a turn holding a stopwatch and talking for, say, three minutes at a time. The process continues until the air is clear. One approach is to have several rounds. In round one, each person says something that she or he appreciates about each other person. In round two, each says something that could be improved about each other's performance. In round three, each says something that she or he is committed to improving about her or his own performance.

4. Team members, facilitated by the team leader, need to brainstorm in order to clarify roles and make a plan. How are we going to get the work done? How are we going to

achieve the mission, meet goals and deadlines, and stay within the guidelines? This may be a hard sell with Xers, because they like to take their own path to the end. But if they get to have a say in how things get done, you might get some buy-in. Who is going to do what? When? How? How will we measure performance and success? Who has the skills, knowledge, and experience best suited to which goals? That should be the determining factor for assigning ownership of goals and deadlines. Once team members start taking ownership of goals and deadlines, it is important to determine which goals need to be achieved and which do not. Remember that place and time are limiting factors that may be irrelevant to much of the work that needs to be accomplished.

5. Create an easy system for keeping team members in touch. Consider having each person generate a daily to-do list that can be shared with everybody else—or a weekly report of "what I did last week and what I'm going to do this week"–or a brief list of "what I need from each person this week." This kind of just-in-time communication keeps everybody in the loop and creates more opportunities for collaboration and natural synergy.

6. Make sure team leaders are playing the facilitative role necessary to keep a dynamic team performing, engaging in day-to-day coaching-style interactions with each team member. Make sure team leaders know how to stay in sync with the pace of each member's performance. Each will require different levels and different types of feedback, but all want frequent, accurate, specific, timely feedback. Give team members feedback for every significant input, and make sure to tell the whole story—balancing the positive with the negative. Don't just tell people exactly what they did wrong and exactly what they did right; tell them exactly what you want them to do next. That is what makes it coaching. And tell people right away, while they can still take action based on the feedback they receive.

7. Make training an obsession in your organization so that everybody is building the skills and knowledge they need to

keep performing at highest capacity. Put training resources at people's fingertips so they can access them as they need them. Send a clear message that everybody's work is knowledge work, and you expect them to be voracious learners. In some cases, training may be required to help people learn to honor and learn from each other's differences, manage their own goals and deadlines, and work together with other team members more effectively.

8. Reward team members for the performance you want them to deliver. If your rewards system is not tuned into goals and deadlines—clear performance benchmarks—realign them. Identify which rewards motivate which employees and offer them accordingly. The more control over their own rewards people have, the more they will operate those levers of control. Don't wait until the end of the year to reward people—give immediate rewards. And don't limit your repertoire of rewards to money; instead, mine the workplace for nonfinancial rewards—training opportunities, exposure to decision makers, increased responsibility, or more control over their own schedules.

9. Consider new approaches to retention—part time, flex time, overtime, flex place, and so on. Once you've invested in recruiting, training, and orienting, it just doesn't make sense to lose people. Why not keep part of them? At the very least, when good employees decide to leave, recruit them into your reserve army and use them for special projects.

10. Charlie must keep his finger on the pulse, talking with everybody, regularly surfacing issues in order to resolve them before they disrupt the team. Whenever it's necessary, he'll need to bring the team together to clear the air and refocus on the core mission.

I wish Charlie the best of luck. It's going to be fine. It might even be fun. When everybody starts focusing on results and working together, each person will be leveraging his or her uniqueness, and the differences among the group will become forces of collaboration and synergy. What that means is innovation, and, in the workplace of the future, innovation is what it's all about.

Gloria Regalbuto's Response

Gloria Regalbuto is director of human resource development at Bath & Body Works in Reynoldsburg, Ohio. She is a Baby Boomer.

I'm uncomfortable assuming that what's going on at Alpha-Beta Surety is "simply" a cross-generational problem. I would want to talk to more of Charlie's team members to determine what they perceive to be their "barriers to performance." If Charlie, as manager, really had his finger on the problem, he probably could have made more headway by now. Additionally, I would want to get down to specifics. What is the nature of the technological barrier that interferes with the technophobes' ability to work? Is this purely a social-emotional issue, or is it related to task performance? What, if anything, interferes with the technojunkies' ability to reach the expected level of productivity? To my mind, no solution can be formulated unless the detailed nature of the problem is laid out. If, in fact, Devon's team can be divided into the three subgroups described, a different solution may be needed to remedy each group's performance problems. This does not appear to be a "one size fits all" kind of issue.

I would also want to know the degree to which each member of the team understands and accepts the team's goals. Has Devon told the Xers that they need to perform to a specific standard? They may not need to live by the clock, but they certainly have productivity requirements tied to specific deadlines they must meet. Has Devon told the technophobes they need to learn to use the technology in order to meet the productivity requirements? If that is indeed the case, I still believe that, in some instances, the promise of increased productivity offered by technology is mythical, and that, John Henry-like, there are still some nontechnological solutions that can drive steel faster and better. Hmmmm, does that make me a technophobe?

I would absolutely factor generational differences into my solution. If Charlie chooses to begin by working with Devon's team, it would not take a lengthy analysis to interview individual members to determine the many factors that may be contributing to the problems. So I don't believe there's even the excuse of the need for expedience to justify that kind of decision making by sound-byte stereotyping.

This group is clearly in need of at least two things: alignment and leadership. I would recommend that Charlie make sure Devon really does have the wherewithal to set clear standards, monitor performance, and provide feedback. He appears to be a little too laissez-faire in waiting until someone asks for help in order to respond with support.

Once the goals and performance are made clear, I would engage the team in problem solving. They very much need to align around a mutual goal to help overcome their stylistic differences. Diversity is much easier to value, I believe, when you feel assured that your partners have mutual goals and core beliefs. They need to come to agreement on the causes contributing to their lack of productivity and to work together to develop solutions. They must take ownership of the need to solve the problems and mutually agree on approaches in order to succeed.

It also needs to be clear that their success, indeed, it seems, their very survival, depends on their ability to pull together and work toward a known goal. The present adversity can actually be seen as an opportunity to create unity. I've often heard Daryl Connor, a change management consultant, say that people change only when the consequences of continuing to pursue the current path becomes "scarier" than the unknown effects of change.

Let me be blatant about the assumptions and "biases" that underlie my advice to Charlie. They are a system of beliefs I've acquired over a long period of helping teams solve problems, so I think they're "good" biases:

- Most, if not all, problems have multiple causes and are the result of a fairly complex system of interactions.
- Most people fail in problem solving because they assume there's only one cause.
- Most "stakeholders" in problems have a pretty good understanding of what's wrong, although their view is necessarily limited.
- Putting together all of the stakeholder perspectives on a problem provides you with a pretty good set of mutually exclusive and exhaustive causes. It also helps to legitimize everybody's point of view and allows them to "come to the table" and be heard. I'm fond of telling groups, "I don't believe anybody. I believe everybody."
- Assuming that the manager of a team has the best view of the problem is usually a bad assumption. He or she is a stakeholder like the others and has the same limitations in view as the others.

- Most people tend to rely too much on easy, sound-byte di-
  agnosis of problems like "generational differences." I don't
  deny that differences exist, I just refuse to assume that that
  is the nature of the problem until I've gathered more data.
  In fact, the team itself may decide that this is an easy way to
  describe their problems. However, that "easy" description
  may be an excuse *not* to do the work it takes to figure the
  thing out in all its complexity.

Deidra Wager's Response

Deidra Wager is executive vice president of retail operations for Starbucks Coffee Company in Seattle, Washington. She is a Baby Boomer.

To help Charlie and his ten teams turn the corner and start down the path to success, I would find out what some of the team and individual successes have been to date. Then I'd recommend that Charlie put together trending reports on all of his teams to see where the relative strengths and weaknesses are. Charlie should gather a personal biography on each team member and learn as much as he can about all of them. I'd ask Charlie to consider having team members complete one of the standard personality profiling instruments such as the Myers Briggs Type Indicator, because these personality profiles spark a high level of introspection as well as great conversations that lead to better mutual understanding. I would factor generational differences into the solution. People typically want the same things at the end of the day, no matter what their age, race, or education; but generational differences, like personality, make the specifics of "the same things" idiosyncratic. They want to be heard, recognized, acknowledged, appreciated, and valued in a way that feels right for them.

Then, to help Charlie get things back on track and restore harmony, I'd recommend he gather his team for a session together, perhaps using an external facilitator. The session should start off with Charlie and the team leaders describing an end vision, being sure it speaks to the issues and concerns of the group: "My dream for this team is that each of you achieve X...and that the team achieves Y...and that all this be done in a way that brings joy, laughter, and a genuine feeling of caring to each of you. The power to do this rests with this team and each of the unique capabilities you bring to the party."

I would then spend a serious day getting them to really talk to each other, to listen, hear, and understand how to find value in each other. Get pragmatic about how the technogeeks can coexist with the technophobes and that it's the responsibility of all of them to make it work. Get tough on the concept that the success of the team and each individual rests in the conversations they have with each other, no matter what the medium. The future of the team lies in every action and word they speak from here on out. If the words or actions are negative, detrimental, or counterproductive, then who will be surprised when they end up with so much less than what is possible.

Charlie should require the team to put together a set of ground rules about how they intend to "be" together. Then he should schedule regular follow-up meetings to discuss progress. These meetings offer an opportunity to discuss the business as well as progress on team dynamics.

Pat Crull's Response

Pat Crull, a Boomer, is vice president and officer in charge of learning and development for McDonald's.

Charlie needs to speak to each of the team members regarding both problems and the actions they would recommend. I think he should deal directly with the generational issues—they are real and make a difference. They should be acknowledged. Charlie needs to seek input from those closest to the problems. Perhaps he should use an organization development specialist to facilitate a process for better understanding differences. He needs to find ways to accommodate his Gen Xer's needs—flex hours and development opportunities. He should model, train, and reward the Baby Boomers for improving their skills, technical and other. This course of action is based on these three assumptions:

1. There is a flip side to every characteristics of the generations that can be tapped into. For example, although Xers may seem arrogant, they are fiercely independent.

2. The generations can complement each other. Xers want feedback and Baby Boomers want respect as mentors.

3. Understanding generational differences is an important starting point.

Dr. Chip Bell's Response

Dr. Chip Bell is a Dallas, Texas, management consultant and author of Managers as Mentors (Berrett Koehler, 1996) and Dance Lessons (Berrett Koehler, 1998). Chip is a Sandwich Generation resident.

Charlie's problem is he's a wimp! The in-house organization development specialist should have recommended a personality transplant instead of a list! He's got a seriously burning platform and he seems to be the only one in the room smelling smoke. He has a superstar technophobe team feeling cocky and hoping everyone else crashes and burns. He has a rag-tag technogeek team that is crashing and burning and blaming everyone else. And, he has the vocal majority jeering in the peanut gallery instead of swinging in the batter's box.

Charlie needs to put his diversity concerns on the back burner and save this sinking ship.[1] It's probably been a coon's age since anyone has seen the veins on this neck stick out or witnessed the conference table bend under his slamming fist! He even lets a direct report say, "You're all absorbed in yourselves and your work and your way of doing things... it sucks," not only to his face, but to his face in front of another subordinate! They sound like a bunch of whining kids trying to make daddy punish a sibling.

I would recommend Charlie call a meeting of the entire subrogation unit... a stand-up meeting with required attendance! Give them the raw truth about low productivity, claims paid, angry customers, low quotas... the works... in living color. Let them know the entire unit has to work together or all their jobs (including his) are in serious jeopardy. He should be honest about his own fears and loud about his "go to the mat" passion for making the unit the pride of the company. He should acknowledge there are major work style differences within the unit, but those are low-priority issues that will be addressed after the bleeding has stopped. If they see this crisis as real and Charlie prepared to "go down in flames" turning it around, they may stop blaming and start aiming.

He needs to lead them in a series of problem-solving discussions. This is not a job of the organization development specialist. Charlie needs to demonstrate he can assertively lead an entire unit. He should arrange people in small, cross-unit, heterogeneous groups that enable them to gain appreciation for unit members who are different. Their first group task would be to focus on identifying the key barriers to greatness within the control of the entire unit. Given the identified barriers, their second task would be to brainstorm solutions for solving a particular barrier, recommend accountabilities within the unit, and agree on short-term deadlines. No bitching is allowed; no name-calling is tolerated. They are all a part of this problem... they need to be a part of its solution. Besides, people will care if they share.

Quickly following this session, I would direct team leaders to meet with each team—at least two team leaders per team. If the ten teams observe the team leaders working together, they will begin to model similar behavior. Charlie should be very active keeping a finger on the timely implementation of the plans crafted. He should offer support, provide encouragement, and, above all, exhibit focused rigor.

So part one of my advice is: Wake up Charlie. You're the leader, not the social director!

Part two comes after the dust has settled and things are looking a little better for the department.

We roll the camera forward and get Charlie through the next thirty-day crunch. What next?

Charlie still has Boomers booming, Upstarts upchucking, and the team as frustrated as a chicken trying to drink water from a pie pan.

Charlie needs to meet his diversity challenge with a clear focus on the mission of the unit and the key results that will achieve that mission. He needs to trade in his preoccupation with form for a focus on substance. How does where one works, when one works, and how long one works really, really impact key results? And he needs to see that Gen Xers have a point: There is more to life than toil; a lot of work and very little play make Jack and Jill wear out.

There seems to be an opportunity here to restructure teams and give people a chance to work with people who are different from themselves. Although there is comfort in "birds of a feather" and working with someone who is different clearly can be as awkward as taking in-laws on a honeymoon, important growth and valuable progress come through change. Besides, we all have comfort zones about two sizes too small. Charlie should heroize team mates who effectively team with people who are different.

Finally, Charlie needs to take the lead in honoring results while valuing differences. When team members complain about "She's not pulling her weight," Charlie should ask, "What weight is she accountable for pulling and what evidence do you have that it's not being pulled?" Team members watch leaders' moves, not their mouth. Walk the talk. Be patient. Don't lower standards. And, find joy in the creative tension of unique people bringing unique talent in unique ways.

Judy Corson's Response

Judy is partner and cofounder of Custom Research Inc., a Baldrige Award winning national survey research and data base firm, based in Minneapolis, Minnesota. Judy is a Boomer.

First of all, Charlie should never have let this situation get to this stage. I believe if something is worth worrying about, it is worth talking about, and the sooner the better. Everyone involved has to be in on the discussion. Nipping things in the bud is the way to prevent the kinds of problems Charlie is now facing with his team. Things have gotten out of hand, and it is very difficult to deal with them once entrenched attitudes have become so negative. The old adage, "an ounce of prevention is worth a pound of cure" is still true, maybe even more so, with a diverse workforce.

As the leader, Charlie needs to install passion in the mission of the team's responsibilities. It has been my experience that, when everyone is excited and passionate about the mission of the team, it doesn't matter what the generation gap differences are. When everyone is pulling together to accomplish a common goal, they can work extremely well together. The same thing seems to be true when faced with a crisis. If the team is threatened by some business change or a member of the team experiences a personal crisis, the members of the team can use this situation to focus on the goal and work together in a way they haven't been able to before. It is human nature to "rally round" when faced with a crisis.

Charlie also has to have a performance management system in place. This system has to incorporate financial, team, and personal performance goals tied to specific rewards. Individual performance standards also have to be in place for each position within the team so that people know exactly what is expected and understand how they will be evaluated for promotion, salary increases, and the like. Team members need individual development plans so that they get the skills needed to do their jobs and the company develops people for future promotions.

Once these things are in place and a team begins to have problems, we encourage informal team building. Informal team building seems to open lines of communication to be able to voice and articulate differences in work style and values among team members. Again, if the team can agree on the outcomes they all want to achieve, they can come up with ways to achieve them while still preserving differences among team members in work styles and even differences in levels of commitment. Different team members have different personal life situations. Not everyone is going to be in the same place at a given time.

Try and get the team to understand intergenerational differences and conflicts. It is best if this can be introduced in a fun way, with people looking at stereotypes that they can laugh about but still see the differences, too. At the same time, the team can develop a common language for how to deal with differences and still retain mutual respect for these differences. It is important that the team do these team-building meetings on a regular basis, at least once a month so they can talk about how they are working together as a team and get problems aired when they are small rather than letting things build up.

In addition to team building, we have found it useful for the team to work on process improvements. Beginning with simple team processes, the team can break apart the processes and then examine each process and the handoffs that occur within the team. Expectations can be clarified and improvements made so the team owns the improved processes and there is agreement up front as to each team member's contribution and accountability.

Finally, the team has to back their leader. Yes, leaders are responsible for leading teams, but teams have to be responsible for practicing "followership" too.

Larry Bourgerie's Response

Larry is director of human resource development at TCF National Bank and adjunct faculty at St. Thomas Graduate School of Business in Minneapolis, Minnesota. Larry is a Boomer chronologically, but an Xer in spirit.

Charlie is facing a classic case of diversity in the workplace. In this instance it's age diversity. The face of today's workforce has two sides— the diversity of the new workforce versus the homogeneity of the past. Charlie is more comfortable with the past and has difficulty adjusting to the changing workforce.

Team two has the "advantage" of all members being cut of the same mold. They know each other and they think alike; thus, they have less conflict on the team. They are able to handle the conflict that does arise quite well because they share a common value system. The down side of the situation is that Charlie and this team may have a harder time dealing with the change. They have been focused on climbing the ladder and advancing their careers in the organization. Because of this, they have more vested in the organization and suffer more of a sense of loss and frustration. The chaos that is resulting from the impending changes will probably not affect the Xers as much as older team members, because they grew up in an era of downsizing, layoffs, and frequent change.

Team nine is experiencing the growing pains of a diverse workforce. Because they have many different types of employees, they have different values to deal with and a diversity of talents. They have more difficulty dealing with inevitable conflicts due to their differing perspectives and values. They need to understand and work with the differences on the team; in fact, they need to truly value the differences and learn to leverage the talents of all members of the team. Charlie also must deal with the fact that his values about work ethic are different from the members of team nine. He cannot assume that what he values and what motivates him can be transferred directly to all of team nine's members.

To effectively address the situation and deal with the diversity on the teams, Charlie needs to go back to basic management principle, supplemented by understanding what will motivate and reward team members who differ from him. His approach should include the following:

- Get each team focused on the work at hand. Reiterate the team mission and purpose. Nothing gets a team working effectively like working toward a common goal, getting work accomplished, and achieving results. (It also leaves less time to focus on peripheral issues.)

- Maintain open communication about what is happening in the organization. Let employees know where they stand. Regardless of their differences, all team members will respond to honest and direct communication.

- Charlie needs to shift his frame of reference and understand that management is no longer a "one size fits all" situation. Charlie needs to expand his management approach to recognize the values and motivational requirements of the different employees on staff. The younger Gen Xers are not likely to respond to the family atmosphere and focus on the larger good of the organization that has been fostered in team two. They will respond to growth opportunities and skill acquisition that benefit the individual.

- Look at new ways to motivate and recognize the employees. Talk to them and get their ideas on specific rewards that they will respond to. If Charlie tries to solve the problem himself, he will be limited by his paradigms and fail to turn the situation around.

- Look at different ways to staff the organization. Explore flex time, telecommuting, and other options. This could increase motivation and productivity at a time when it is badly needed. It also could increase revenues and decrease costs.

Bottom line is that Charlie needs to go back to basic good management practices coupled with an appreciation for the changing workforce. He needs to recognize that team nine is the team of the future and will be the key to future successes. Engage them in a vision, meaningful work, recognition, and face time with Charlie, and their performance will most likely turn around. Also, he should be sure there is frequent contact with the team in the form of feedback on their efforts, communication of information, and a constant focus on maintaining positive team morale.

CHAPTER EIGHT

MAKING THE CROSS-GENERATIONAL WORKPLACE WORK:

Twenty-One Often-Asked Questions—and Some Very Practical Answers

Not every organizational problem, foul-up, shortcoming, and faux pas has a cross-generational origin. It would be more than disingenuous—it would be dishonest—of us to suggest such a thing. But when you do have a cross-generational problem, you know it. It can permeate everything that goes wrong, from slow product design and introduction to lousy customer and employee relations.

What follows are twenty-one questions—about managing and motivating, job growth and enrichment, building teams, sales and service, and training—that represent the kinds of cross-generational problems people most frequently report encountering. The problems—turned into questions—were gathered in interviews, focus groups, online chat groups, surveys, and seminars. They come from real managers and real employees struggling to make their way in the multigenerational workplace. Although we've edited them to make them more universal, they are the real thing, and the answers are our best advice. It is advice based on what we have seen, working in generationally confused and generationally friendly organizations.

These twenty-one questions—and problems—are separated into five groupings. Within each grouping, they are further tagged by the complaint they engender and the conflicting generations addressed in the question:

MANAGING AND MOTIVATING

1. Tom and Linda: Losing the Xers Who Report to Them — Boomers and Xers
2. Li: Looking for Respect From George — Xers and Veterans
3. Tom and Linda: Demanding a Different Schedule — Boomers
4. Devon: Suddenly Supervising His Buddies — Xers
5. Dorothy's Pep Talks Fail the Yawn Test — Veterans and Xers
6. Linda Is Accused of Micromanaging — Boomers and Xers
7. George Wants to Know: "How Do These Young Techies See Me?" — Veterans and Xers

JOB GROWTH AND ENRICHMENT

8. Keeping Devon and Li Around When There Seems No Place to Go But Out — Xers
9. George and Dorothy Don't Want to Swap Jobs — Veterans
10. Are Tom and Linda Becoming Stagnant? — Boomers
11. Devon and Li Are Looking for the Path to the Top — Xers

BUILDING TEAMS

SALES AND SERVICE

TRAINING

RECRUITING

Managing and Motivating

1. Tom and Linda: Losing the Xers Who Report to Them

Boomers and Xers

Q. We're a high-tech company. We hire "the best and brightest" technical people straight out of college; they make up about 70 percent of our total workforce. By and large, they're managed by people in their forties. Our managers are baffled by the new recruits. They say they aren't loyal, won't make a commitment, and have no work ethic. We must motivate and retain our young technical employees. They are our future. It's very expensive to replace them, and, when they leave, they take our developing technology to our competitors. What can we do?

A. The Boomers—those fortysomethings—grew up with the notion that they were the be-all and end-all…that they were the generation the proverbial torch was being passed to…that they were the *new* generation who would change the world. Consequently, when it comes to the Xers, Boomers have been a bit like the older child who, when his parents announced a new baby on the way, hid all his toys. The Boomers also have a feeling they changed everything for the better in the 1960s and 1970s, that their values and beliefs have created a better world and certainly a more fair and humane workplace. These young Gen Xers showed up at work wearing an entirely different set of filters. They are skeptical of the Boomers' optimism, self-reliant in the midst of the Boomers' affinity for teams, committed to having a life outside of the driven work ethic the Boomers' had fueled, and suspicious of the Boomers' authority. The Boomers have been baffled by this younger sibling, allowing themselves to become self-righteous and judgmental of those who haven't embraced their ways.

What's needed is a means for the Boomers to develop empathy, to understand that the X Generation has a valid perspective that is neither better nor worse, simply different. A training program that educates managers about their younger colleagues is a reasonable option. If your target audience is Boomers, this should be a relatively easy task, because Boomers thrive on personal development. The market for virtually all self-help books, they're eager to learn new things and increase their skill base. Develop a program that helps them understand and develop empathy for their younger cohorts. You may want to include a segment in which Gen X associates discuss and give their perspectives on such work issues as balancing work and personal life, loyalty between companies and employees, the importance of fun, and the ideal work environment. The program should be customized for technical managers, and it should include some specific recommendations for managing Gen X technical associates. Involve younger associates in the design and delivery. Survey your managers to find out what format—seminar, audiotape, CD-ROM, video, workbook—best suits their needs.

2. Li: Looking for Respect From George

Xers and Veterans

Q. I'm a twenty-seven-year-old manager in the financial services industry. Although this is my third job since I graduated from college, I've been with this company for four years—four years in which I learned the business at warp speed and moved quickly along the fast track. I now have twenty account managers in three cities reporting to me. Each of them challenges me in a different way, but I am pleased to say I've found effective ways of working with each of them as individuals—all, that is, except for one. He is sixty-three and works in another city. I visit his office once a month, and I speak to him or send him e-mails two or three times a week. He is courteous, even overly courteous, to customers, but he treats me like the girl who came across the street to mow his grass. How can I establish credibility with this man who is old enough to be my grandpa?

A. Begin by "walking a mile in his shoes" and imagining how he must perceive you. When George first entered the workforce, age and rank correlated. You would not have had your job in those days. Although you were promoted to management because of your competence, he likely looks at you as an unseasoned, inexperienced young person, and it's true—you don't have the wealth of knowledge he has accumulated over the years that lend that extra edge of experience to customer interactions and critical decisions.

Give him that much. And there may be some gender issues at hand here. Your sixty-three-year-old employee grew up with clear distinctions between the roles of the sexes. Remember, there were no women in management when he began his career. Making the issue even more complex is his location in another city. Whereas your younger employees probably handle your virtual department with great ease, barely even noticing you're in different physical locations, your Veteran may be struggling with what he perceives as an absentee manager who, by the way, seems to be getting credit for his hard work.

Take time—in person, not via e-mail—to get to know this man as an individual. Slow down your pace when you're around him, as he probably feels you're traveling at the speed of light. Take him to coffee—don't order a latte—but don't allow yourself to be patronized. Be friendly but firm. Take your cues from him as to whether you talk about his life outside of work. Focus your conversation on his experience, his track record, and his contributions, along with the long-term strategy of the company.

He probably prefers a manager who is slightly more directive in style than is currently popular. He is likely, also, to be looking for consistency from you, especially in how you stand behind and implement policies and procedures.

Keep your expectations for change on his part realistic. You are asking for a shift in lifelong perception from this employee, and that may be quite a stretch for him. It may be possible for him to produce the results you require without ever changing his perception of you. And that's what you're after, not a new buddy.

Remember that older workers often don't fit the stereotypes. Mark Dowley, thirty-three-year-old chief executive of McCann Erickson's Momentum Marketing Unit, says that, when he inherited a CFO in his sixties, he worried the man would be unresponsive to new ideas and unable to keep up with the fast pace. "Little did I know this guy had done everything from government weapons contracts to working with the biggest corporations," he says. "I used the hell out of his experience, and learned so much from him."[1] When it was time for the CFO to retire, Mr. Dowley was unwilling to get along without his expertise and experience, so he brought him back as a consultant.

3. Tom and Linda: Demanding a Different Schedule

Boomers

Q. Our fiftysomething Boomers seem to be changing their work ethic: drawing the line on weekend hours, early-morning meetings, and challenging deadlines. We thought we could count on them to pitch in and do the right midnight-oil thing when needed, but we're finding it increasingly difficult to get them to say "yes." What gives?

A. The Boomers' work habits are finally beginning to catch up with them. In her book, *The Overworked American,* Harvard University Professor Juliet Schor tells us that, in the last twenty years, the average. American worker has increased the amount of time he or she spends on the job each year by a full month.[2] The Boomers, along with growing corporate pressure to produce more, faster, and with fewer resources, are primarily to blame. They entered a highly competitive job market and have had to compete with their seventy-six million cohorts for the good jobs. Add to the equation that they've depended on their professional lives to create their personal identity and you have a recipe for a group of driven, stressed-out, overworked people. Schor says, "the time squeeze surfaced with the young urban professionals. These high achievers had jobs that required sixty, eighty, even a hundred hours a week. On Wall Street, they would regularly stay at the office until midnight or go months without a single day off. Work consumed their lives. And if they weren't working, they were networking. They power-lunched, power-exercised, and power-married." And, of course, corporations grew used to and fond of this very work ethic.

As the oldest Boomers prepare to turn sixty, watch their parents die, witness heart attacks and strokes among those in their own age group, and prepare themselves to move into elderhood, they're questioning their decision to work themselves like oxen. After all, their parents on their deathbeds have not said, "Why, oh, why, didn't I work more hours?" The Boomer women, too, decided years ago to "go for the gold" at work, while continuing to be the primary person at home in charge of the children, the housekeeping, and the kitchen. On reflection, they're saying, "Enough is too much." For once, the Boomers are realizing that there really is a life beyond work, and the grass looks quite lovely over there, thank-you very much.

Thus, they've begun to draw some lines in the sand: no meetings after 5:00 and the like, and they and their companies are beginning to test the strength of those boundaries. Those businesses that choose to ignore the Boomers' change of heart, and the attitude about balance Xers bring to work, can expect major problems with plummeting employee morale and skyrocketing turnover.

It's time to stop thinking of employees as disposable lighters: Burn them until the fire runs out, then toss them and find another. With the tight labor market, people aren't a dime a dozen, waiting with bated breath to step into a lost employee's job. We truly must begin to treat employees like customers, respecting their needs and working with them to find creative solutions to their challenges. If you need an expert on the topic of balancing work and life, see your local Gen Xer.

4. Devon: Suddenly Supervising His Buddies

Xers

Q. I've just taken my first management position; I will be supervising twelve chemical technicians who were previously my lab mates. We get along great. We often get together after work for a burger and hockey game at the brew pub down the street, and we pretty much respect each other's abilities in the lab. My buddies are glad I was promoted and, although a couple of others applied for the position, nobody seems to resent me for getting the job. My question is: How can I stay part of the team without giving away all my authority?

A. Management consultants a decade ago would definitely have given you a different answer than we're going to. They would have told you it was time to make a choice between the job and your friends. The implied "right" answer would have been to dump your friends. That would have required no longer hanging out with your buddies. Perhaps this actually was the right answer if you had been working in a hierarchical organization, or if your buddies were Veterans, or you had to order them to the battlefront.

Today, at least where Gen Xers are concerned, that answer is dismally short sighted. Evan DeFoe, 28, became a manager at a restaurant in Baltimore when he was twenty-two. Because he had been pals with his staff for 2½ years, he assumed he needed to "do the power trip thing." He says he went out of his way to catch people making mistakes. "I acted like a boss." But his turnabout failed. "People argued with me, and I even made a couple of them cry. Now I'm their co-worker until they ask me to be a boss. I allow people to make their own mistakes and then fix them themselves."[3] This attitude jibes well with Gen Xer's predilection for popping in and out of work roles at the drop of a hat. A software designer at Microsoft thinks nothing of dropping out of the programming team to "try out" management for a couple of years and then dropping back into the same group as a designer. Switching jobs with your boss is not extraordinary at Microsoft.

Gen Xers feel differently about authority than either the Veterans or the Boomers. Veterans automatically gave their respect to those in authority roles. They witnessed very powerful leadership from fiery figures like General Patton and Vince Lombardi, and they were taught to revere leaders as a special category of human being, one that existed on another level from us "regular folks." The Boomers, on the other hand, have had a love/hate relationship with authority. While activists and campus protesters in the 1960s claimed they were "antiauthority," the Boomers have been drawn to leadership roles, using them as another means to prove their worthiness. But Xers attach no special status to leadership. They grew up watching authority figures, including their own parents, getting demystified. Companies like Bell Northern Research in Dallas, where the majority of employees are Generation X, are finding that promotion into management lacks the appeal it had a decade ago. "Why take on the extra headaches," many of their employees are asking, "when my real interest lies in doing the technical work I was trained for?"

So authority is less an issue than it would have been just a few years ago. Ease into your new role as manager. Observe the effectiveness of varying interactions with your team. Be cautious about letting quality standards be influenced by your friendship. Talk to your team about how they want you to behave. And keep the dialogue going. You'll all be learning together what works and doesn't.

5. Dorothy's Pep Talks Fail the Yawn Test

Veterans and Xers

Q. My pep talks are flunking the snicker test. My staff seems to be sneering as they leave our staff meetings. I've been at this for nearly thirty years. When I look for inspiration, I look back on the best manager I ever had. What made him unique? He breathed fire into us by calling a meeting and inspiring us, right down to our toenails. He ranted, he raved, he motivated us, he challenged us; and it worked. We nearly doubled productivity in the seven years we worked for him. But something's not clicking in my approach. My pep talks seem to backfire with my mostly twentysomething staff. They don't seem motivated at all. They seem, well, put off by my efforts.

A. Check with your staff, but we think pep talks are outmoded. The Veterans, shaped by World War II, revered leaders like Franklin D. Roosevelt, Churchill, and Eisenhower. When that generation went to work, their civic values were kindled by fiery speeches that tapped into "can do" attitudes and "nothing less than full victory" behaviors.

But your younger associates grew up seeing and hearing inspirational efforts that turned out to be mere hyperbole. Today they turn a cynical eye on anything that seems jingoistic. Our guess is that your staff doesn't consider your well-intentioned pep talks sincere. They would probably prefer you simply talk to them in a straightforward, less emotional fashion.

This doesn't mean they can't be inspired. As a matter of fact, that is still an important role of the leader. How they get inspired, though, is an entirely different matter. Because this generation is very task oriented, inspire them around the task and the importance of shipping the product, delivering the service or finishing the project. And if the task itself bites, be honest about it and schedule some fun celebration after the onerous project is completed. These young workers are motivated by fun; use that when you must. Consider having different staff members lead staff meetings. On each project they tackle, encourage them to decide as a team what their goals are...how they want to work together... what they want to accomplish...how they will measure it. When they share in creating the big picture, that picture is far more inspirational than when someone else delivers it to them.

6. Linda Is Accused of Micromanaging

Boomers and Xers

Q. I'm the quintessential Boomer manager: single mom, history of fifty- to sixty-hour workweeks, hooked on lattes. My staff is primarily Gen Xers. Here's my problem: They constantly ask for more feedback, but when I give it, they accuse me of micromanaging, and I'm being held to very stringent quality standards by my management. Help!

A. This is a tough one! You may have to go to them, or ask someone with a neutral perspective, to find out. We're only guessing here, although we've heard the complaint before. Perhaps your feedback is based on your goals and your picture of what good performance looks like, rather than on a common picture that you've developed mutually. Developing a shared set of goals requires a substantial amount of time, but it will be well worth it in the long run. Work individually with each of your employees to develop a career map for them. Find out what their destination is for the foreseeable future (probably no more than three to five years; if it's for only six months, that's okay). Then help them to inventory the skills, characteristics, and knowledge they have and those they need to develop. Finally, decide together what excellent performance in their current role will look and sound like, listing as specifically as you can the way they want to perform such functions as communicating with customers and coworkers...how their written reports will look...how they will handle deadlines. It helps if you can frame your performance criteria in terms of "This is going to be on the test." That's a phrase Xers resonate with. If you can explain why certain performance will be on the test, even better.

Now you have a basis for feedback, based on their own unique personal goals and the behaviors you've outlined together. If they've messed up, ask their permission, privately, to give them some coaching. Then, tell them clearly and specifically exactly what they said or did that was ineffective, the effect it had, and how they can do better next time. ("When you arrived at 1:20 for the 1 :00 client presentation to ABC Widgets and then interrupted Stan while he was talking about the G5 release, he looked frustrated, and it may hurt the outlook for the sale. Next time, arrive a little early and talk to Stan ahead of time about what he intends to present.") When they've done something well, specify exactly what behavior was effective and spell out the effect it had. ("The customer who had his flight canceled was very angry. But you were patient and courteous to him, and found an alternative that seemed to please him. I think you may have saved that account and kept his business with our agency.") By tying your feedback in to your coaching conversations and an individual's career plan, you'll be contributing to their personal success, and with any luck the feedback will be interpreted as valuable coaching, not micromanaging (keep your fingers crossed).

7. George Wants to Know: "How Do These Young Techies See Me?"

Veterans and Xers

Q. I'm your standard issue Veteran, complete with Korean War experience, managing a bunch of Gen X techies. This year, come performance appraisal time, they'll be evaluating me. I find them bright, creative, somewhat aloof, and demanding. How do you suppose they perceive me?

A. Gen Xers, more than any other generation, judge you first and foremost on your technical competence. Do you have patents? A history of creative technical contributions? These things, more than your people skills and management savvy, are important to young technical associates. Then, too, they don't automatically respect you simply because you're the manager. Previous generations were taught to respect those in leadership positions, but Gen X was taught to never automatically just do what an adult said, but to ask, "Why?"' first. Expect to be forced to work for and earn their respect, possibly at a snail's pace.

Gen Xers tend to see Veterans as nonthreatening. They're not competing for the same jobs, and, besides, they aren't as technologically savvy as their younger coworkers. They find them rather conservative, "old school," and "by the book." On the other hand, lots of Xers admire and emulate Veterans for their genuineness. Whereas Xers accuse Boomers of being highly political—of giving lip service to politically correct concepts and then not following through with aligned actions—they feel the Veterans have a history of doing far more practicing than preaching and following through on the promises they make. Show a little respect for their skills—and growth, when you see it—and they'll be a delight to work with, if somewhat perplexing from time to time.

Job Growth and Enrichment

8. Keeping Devon and Li Around When There Seems No Place to Go but Out

Xers

Q. In our company, the Baby Boomers have most of the good jobs. They're the vice presidents, division managers, and district managers. In the last five years, we've hired lots of young people. For the most part, they're working in clerical and entry-level jobs: as secretaries, in the mail room, and at the front desk. Most of them are college educated, and they expect to move up quickly. The trouble is, the people in the jobs they want will be there another twenty years. How can we keep our young people and keep them happy, or at least patient and around?

A. This issue—companies fully staffed at the upper levels with people who are likely to "stay put" for years to come—is growing increasingly common, particularly in those industries Boomers traditionally considered attractive (law, medicine, accounting, finance). In these industries where the retention rate for mid- and upper-level employees is bullish, retaining those very important entry-level people, the ones who meet and greet clients and who generally keep the company afloat, can be a daunting challenge.

In fact, you may be forced to accept high turnover among the front ranks. This may require shifting the mind-set of longer-term employees by preventing them from labeling those who move on as "not committed" and "disloyal." If you find you must live with high turnover, you may want to upgrade and streamline not only your hiring process but your orientation and training programs. Some quick-serve restaurants we know have made an art form of this, by producing learning aids, reminder cards, and checklists that assist anyone to virtually walk into any job and perform it satisfactorily.

But don't give up hope on reducing turnover yet. Air this issue publicly within your company. Talk openly with not only your entry-level people but your more senior ones as well. Is the issue as you have perceived it? Are your front-line people frustrated and feeling stuck? What ideas do people at all levels have for dealing with the challenge?

Many companies, realizing they cannot offer upward mobility to front-line associates, do such a good job of delivering other benefits to this group of employees that they find promotion a nonissue. Specifically, they develop people to the max. They often create a career web instead of a career ladder. If people feel that they're challenged, learning, and growing, it's unlikely they will feel "stuck," even if their actual day-to-day job is relatively easy for them. The most compelling method for developing employees in this situation is mentoring. A recent issue of *Fast Company* tells how Boomers are mentoring Xers at Ivillage, Sony, and StrideRite.[4] Such programs pair front-line people with upper-level associates who teach them about business strategy, company history, and decision making. Mentors help their protégés to develop a career plan (knowing that it may require changing firms and even industries) and deliver regular feedback to their protégés. Front-line employees tend to stick around because they're getting "more real-time, practical skills and knowledge than is available in an MBA program."

9. George and Dorothy Don't Want to Swap Jobs

Veterans

Q. Five of my people are in their early sixties. They're great at customer service. They can answer virtually any question because, between them, they've been with the company for more than one hundred years. The problem is that our company is pushing job swapping. They want everybody who has worked in a position for more than five years to train for another job on their own level. Four of my five are dragging their feet. They don't understand why, as long as they're performing well, they need to learn other jobs. I have a feeling they just want to stay put for another few years until it's time for retirement.

A. Members of the Veterans tend to prefer a work environment that is stable, consistent, and low risk, so it makes sense that four of your people are dragging their feet. Do you have a say in your organization's human resource policies? If so, perhaps you can influence others to see that job swapping shouldn't be mandatory. As we mentioned in the Acorn Imperatives, one of the key principles at work in successful cross-generational companies is flexibility. The younger the employee, the more likely he or she is to embrace the notion of trading jobs laterally. Your Gen Xers may thrive on such a program, but many of your risk-averse older people will find it threatening and just plain unpalatable.

That doesn't mean, though, they can't be encouraged and persuaded to change roles and make a big success of it. Many managers operate under the mistaken and disparaging notion that "you can't teach an old dog new tricks." In fact, many older employees embrace the challenge of learning new skills, technology, and roles. Some senior citizens took to the Internet gleefully and while away many an hour surfing from web site to web site.

If you can't waive the policy or make a good business case for the rotation issue, find out what your four associates object to. Are they afraid of looking foolish in front of others? Do they worry their experience will not be acknowledged and respected? Are they concerned this is actually a means to "move them out"? Once you better understand what is holding them back, you'll be in a much better position to help them get with your program. You told us that one of your sixtysomethings was willing to make the swap; enroll that willing colleague in your cause.

Then, keep in mind that convincing someone of the Veteran Generation takes a different set of messages than convincing someone of, say, Generation X. Sell your message based on how:

- Job swapping ties into the organization's long-term goals
- This program benefits the greater good
- Learning a new role ultimately contributes to the success and smooth running of the business

Also, as people grow older, their passion for teaching people what they know increases dramatically. The "teacher inside" each of us wants to stretch his or her legs as we age, so enlist the foot draggers as trainers in your job swapping program. When you set them up as the gurus of their particular job competencies, they are much more likely to show some ownership of the whole program.

10. Are Tom and Linda Becoming Stagnant?

Boomers

Q. Our most seasoned employees are members of the Baby Boom, a generation of people who have tended to get much of their identity, self-confidence, and personal satisfaction from their work. Job enrichment is high on their list of priorities. We have continued to enlarge their jobs. But how are we doing at enriching their jobs? Is this population feeling stagnated? How do we reward them and make them feel important?

A. It is true that the Baby Boom generation has been driven by a need to prove themselves worthy as human beings and that most of them have used their jobs as the means to that end. Therefore, work is a critical issue in the personal satisfaction quotient for most Boomers. Whereas hordes of them have lost jobs to the downsizing trend in the last decade—losing not only their major means of financial support, but also their personal foundation—a much larger segment have found their span of control increased. That means they have power over more people, which is something they like, but it also means they have increasingly been expected to work longer hours, be more productive, make more decisions, write more performance reviews, deliver more feedback, and take responsibility for more and greater results. Moreover, some of these Boomers have discovered a "new" method of proving themselves worthy human beings: parenthood. This makes workaholism a less attractive path than it's been in the past for Boomers.

It is no great surprise, then, that stress among this cohort is at near-record highs. According to J. Walker Smith and Ann Clurman, Yankelovich Partners and authors of *Rocking the Ages*, Boomers are the most stressed generation in history.[5] Yankelovich research shows the Boomers are beginning to yearn for simplicity in their lives more than any other cohort group. Boomers have a tendency to keep themselves challenged (some would say "over-committed") and to speak up for themselves when they're not. But it is critically important in retaining them to let them know they are valued and that their contribution is making a difference. How can you do that? Well, tell them regularly, to start with. And reward them with stress-reducing perks, things that make life a bit easier for them. Think comfort and convenience, particularly during business travel. Boomers really appreciate riding in business class on that long flight, using the hotel fitness center and spa on a free afternoon of a particularly busy week, or having a company cell phone that keeps them out of the long lines at airport pay phones.

11. Devon and Li Are Looking for the Path to the Top

Xers

Q. We've just paid some very expensive consultants to run a company morale survey and do competency modeling at the executive level. My department—the IT group—gave the lowest employee satisfaction rating of all, and we have the highest turnover in the company. My people constantly gripe and complain. They say they're kept in the dark about what it takes to succeed here. Is there a way I can reduce turnover, or is it inevitable in the IT department?

A. The results of the competency modeling could be very valuable to you in this situation. The consultants who did the work should be making at least some segment of that information public. Ask for an executive summary of their findings. Share that information with people in your department; it is a way to show them what skills and behaviors are necessary for executive positions in your company.

Then you need detailed information from the employee satisfaction survey. What specifically is it about the IT department that is demoralizing? The consultants should be able to give you detailed information. Work with your people to get specific examples, and, most importantly, get them involved with you in coming up with solutions. You need their thoughts on how to make their work more interesting and more satisfying. People in IT departments typically feel that IT is a dead end, that the skills they develop there do not translate into positions outside the department. Sometimes that is the case, but in others not. IT work doesn't necessarily lead to low morale and high turnover.

Don't assume that everybody aspires to the executive ranks. Instead, work with the individuals in your department to create career plans, and inventory their skills and qualities. You can help them decide if they need to study another skill set, if they have transferable skills, and if they need to find ways of increasing their personal satisfaction while maintaining their current job. Help them to understand exactly how people get compensated in your organization...how to move along...how to develop a career. Finally, don't rule out poaching. There are a lot of recruiters out there with their sites on your IT professionals. Bounties and signing bonuses are common now, so your people may just be having a case of "the grass is greener" syndrome.

Building Teams

12. Dorothy Meets Li: Following Tradition vs. Breaking the Mold

Veterans and Xers

Q. We have a cold war going on here between our older and younger staff members. The younger people want to make changes and move ahead quickly. They feel the older staff drag their feet on everything. The older ones feel the younger ones make hasty decisions without researching what has and hasn't worked historically. I can't convince either group to listen to the other.

A. You and your company have lots of company! This is an issue that lots of managers are wrestling with these days, but knowing you're in good company doesn't ease your frustration, get you any closer to a solution, or pay for a cup of good coffee. Understanding the historical perspective and improving communication with your team will make a difference.

First, it is important for you to understand that, although this is an age-old challenge, it is exacerbated by differences in world perspective between the Veterans and the Gen Xers. Yes, younger employees have always wanted to "get on with it" and have been more willing to try new approaches. Longer-term associates have been notorious for quashing every creative idea with, "We've never done it that way before," and "This is just the way it's done here," or "Been there. Done that." But the generations' past-versus-future orientations throw a bright, shiny, newfangled top-of-the-line monkey wrench into the picture.

History is a key part of the Veterans' sociology. They were the final generation of, and the group who put the finishing touches on, the development of this nation as an industrialized society. They are justifiably proud of their accomplishments in the fields of commerce and industry. And history was their guide. They are the last of our current American generations to hold the past in such high esteem. In their view, the future is created by the past. Thus, when your older associates begin to work on a project, their tendency is to make decisions based on what has worked historically. As they see it, precedents lend stability and predictability to a world that is changing and not necessarily improving, to their experienced eyes, at the speed of light.

On the other hand, Generation X came of age as the United States shifted from a manufacturing economy into the information age and service economy. Companies, families, and even schools shifted from traditional hierarchical manufacturing organizational models to new flatter models where, at least theoretically, every voice counts. Xers were told in school they were capable of creating any future they wanted. As they began to approach adulthood, they learned they could not count on the older generations and historical assistance programs, with Social Security as a good example. They have decided that if they are going to have a pension, it will most likely be the one they fund on their own, for themselves. Then, too, they've never struggled with change. As children, many mastered a change of parents on weekends, and they've grown adept at adapting to "whatever." Thus, they believe they control their own destiny, but on a very individualized basis. They are, as Neil Howe describes them, collectively pessimistic but individually optimistic.[6] Each Xer believes he or she can beat the system and become successful, but as a generation or even as a society, they don't have much hope for the future.

It's not that either is right or wrong, of course, but it's not worth it to try to get everyone to see things from one perspective. Both viewpoints have tremendous payoffs, and they bring balance to any decision or project. So when Dorothy, the senior engineer, sits down with Li, the kid just out of MIT, to work on a project, your challenge is to make the most of both perspectives. That might mean asking Dorothy to define the project and explain what has worked and what has not worked in the past with similar problems. Then hand "what's worked in the past" to Li and ask her why this isn't working now, what needs to be tweaked with the old methodologies to get them to work, or how the team might be able to take chunks of past solutions and cut and paste them into a new fix for the problem at hand.

But we've still not attacked the silence gap, getting your people to talk and listen to each other. There is a tendency to leave generational work issues unspoken, allowing them to fester and escalate. Promoting open, honest discussion can be helpful. Get your staff together and talk briefly about the problem at hand. Then ask them to divide themselves, at their own choosing, into two groups: those who tend to see themselves following historic precedent and those who see themselves as more future oriented, making it clear that both perspectives are valid and valuable.

Once people have divided themselves into two groups (it's not important the groups be of exactly the same size), ask them to discuss two questions for five minutes. You may want to give them an easel with flip-chart paper to record their answers.

1. What do they find frustrating about working with the opposite perspective?
2. What do they appreciate about the other perspective?
3. Then ask each group to discuss their answers with the other.

Next, discuss the importance of working together effectively and ask the whole group to come up with guidelines or "working agreements" about how they want to communicate with each other on coming projects. The more specific the agreements, the more likely they will "hold up" over time.

An optional activity, one that could be part of another meeting, would call on the best of both perspectives by asking the group to:

- Outline the history (even if it's just two or three years) of the organization, company, department, or team. List what they are proud of (events, people, accomplishments, reputation).
- Create a mental picture of what your staff wants to accomplish.

These discussions can clear the air, give validity to differing perspectives, develop empathy and understanding among staff members, and, most importantly, get the warring tribes listening to each other.

These are long-term fixes—proven to work. If you're going for the short-term solution, require your employees to read our chapters on the Veterans and the Xers!

13. Dealing With Devon's Intimidating Technical Competence

Xers and Boomers

Q. I'm a twenty-four-year-old computer engineer working on a committee with two fortyish guys to recommend a new software switching system for our communications department. I know I was appointed to the team because of my technical expertise, but, in meetings, I have a hard time getting the other two to listen to me. They act like they know far more about the company, and I feel like they're ignoring my suggestions. How can I get them to listen?

A. Technology and education have worked together in the last couple of decades to produce increasing numbers of very successful young professionals such as yourself. As you and other talented young people take on increasing amounts of responsibility, there is a flattening out, even a reversing, of our traditional roles where older executives worked primarily with older executives, middle-aged mid-level managers worked with other mid-mids, and so on. Those two fortyish guys you're working with are likely feeling threatened because their expertise in some areas is not as great as yours. You're the "young hotshot" in this situation, a role most of us must take on—whether we like it or not—at one time in our lives. Keep in mind your other two committee members may have an agenda you are unaware of. Boomers frequently see each other as competitors and, indeed, may be. They may be withholding information to avoid "giving away all the marbles." On the other hand, the collective years of experience these two guys share is worth acknowledging and tapping into. All things considered, you've got the formula for a great collaboration among the three of you, as long as everybody can find a way to work together.

Meeting initially with these two on a one-on-one basis might help your situation. When you're all together, the two may support each other's lack of willingness to listen to you and your ideas. Provide them with any written information you can to bring them up to speed with where you are technically. Consider positioning this information as a competitive advantage. If you learn from a third source that these two are competitors, try positioning the project as something that can make you all look good if successful. This will give them the privacy they need to increase their knowledge without having to appear uninformed in front of you and each other. Try making a list of issues each person on the team would like to be briefed on. This gives you the opportunity to ask them to fill you in on some of the corporate history, department culture, and precedents, and, hopefully, it will cause them to tap into your expertise. If you find yourself "teaching" these guys, be very subtle. Allow them to save face and keep their egos intact.

14. Linda Tries to Keep Their Fires Burning

Boomers and Xers

Q. I'm managing a team of bright, enthusiastic Gen Xers. How do I provide direction without putting out their fire?

A. The fact that you are concerned about keeping your Gen Xers' fires burning says a lot about you as a savvy, perceptive manager. Work with your Xers to create a picture of what you want to accomplish together, then chunk that vision down into do-able, tangible, results-producing steps. Build in milestones and celebrate when you reach them. Give individuals and the team lots of positive feedback about their creativity. Make certain that you are genuinely validating their ideas and accomplishments while continuing to assist them in laying down "do-able tracks" that get results.

Mindy McCune, operations manager at Motorola's Phoenix Design Center, has 105 engineers reporting to her, the majority of whom are in their twenties and thirties. She enjoys their fresh ideas and has created a "supercasual" work environment to accommodate their preferences.[7] She says these workers actually crave direction, as long as it's "general" and "high level." Her people seem to disdain micromanagement every bit as much as their cohorts in other industries. Once she has given her people the high points, she lets them come up with the specifics. Together, they schedule checkpoints, reporting methods, and project reviews, all of which give her a means to steer projects back on track when needed. If the status report does not meet her expectations, she continues to avoid "telling people what to do." Instead, she uses questions: "What can I do to help?," "Where are the problems?," "What do you need in order to get this done?" Mindy feels it's her job to give them what they ask for...to let them know she's behind them...to give them her confidence, support, and feedback.

15. Li Wants to Know: "Devon doesn't work the hours I do, but you pay him more..."

First-Half and Second-Half Xers

Q. We're a mid-size computer animation studio in a large midwestern city. We are wrestling with a workload problem that is proving particularly vexing. We have a lot of older Xers who are beginning to settle down, acquire mortgages, and have children. The other half of the workforce is young, out-of-college Xers who don't have a lot of the same time constraints and can work a lot of late nights to get projects out the door. Mixing the two is very, very difficult. How do you compensate them? You have people who have been around awhile, they're very good, they work fast, but they can't work fifty to sixty hours a week. Others are willing to work seventy to eighty hours, but they're newer and not quite as fast.

They stand in the hallway and show each other their pay stubs. The younger ones complain, "How come I'm working all these hours and making less than this guy who is working fewer hours? It's not fair." How do you maintain fairness in an environment where people's outside lives are fundamentally different?

A. We're finding this challenge—resolving compensation and work-load issues—to be most common in the industries that Gen Xers have been most attracted to, namely the high-tech industry. Repeat "mid-size computer animation studio" three times in public and watch Gen Xers' and Gen Nexters' eyes light up. In jobs viewed as less desirable, the Gen Xers simply have not been willing to put in seventy- to eighty-hour weeks. But where they have found the work stimulating and congenial, they've been willing to work the hours the Boomers did when they were in their twenties. Where the generations differ, though, is in their thirties, once young families are at stake. The Boomers in their thirties gritted their teeth and then tried to do it all: Be a superstar at work and a loving and industrious mother or father and partner at home. The Xers witnessed the results of trying to do it all—neglected children and marriages, high stress, health problems—and have determined they won't be part of such a losing game. Thus, they're opting out of the eighty-hour workweeks.

The Xers, too, don't believe in keeping what we once called "personnel issues," such as the amount of your paycheck, private. In the "old days," some companies even had rules prohibiting employees from divulging salary information to each other. Whereas the Boomers played their salaries "close to the vest," Gen Xers subscribe to a form of honesty so straightforward that they're in the break room and out in the hallway playing blackjack with their paystubs.

We believe this will be one of the major issues businesses will face in the new millennium—balancing compensation and work demands. Companies are in the habit today of expecting their personnel to do twice the work they're actually compensated for. It's an unwritten, even unconscious, rule that has developed gradually over the past twenty years. The Boomers bought into it, donating a little more time each month in order to get the work done and stay ahead of the highly competitive masses who might want their very jobs.

The rules are changing. Soon the majority of employees will be willing to give only forty hours for forty hours of compensation. It's just that simple. Some companies are biting the bullet and hiring more people. (See the profile of Chevys in Chapter 6, for example.) Ultimately, you will need to pay overtime to those who are willing to burn the midnight oil. Gen Xers never heard of "Win One for the Gipper," nor would they respond to it if they had.

Sales and Service

16. George and the Missus Eat Out—and Are Taken Aback

Veterans and Xers

Q. I manage a restaurant, and I often get complaints from my older customers that they're being treated disrespectfully by my waiters and waitresses. On closer examination, I find it's not really disrespect; it's just very informal, casual communication. I can't afford to lose my older clients, so I need to do something. What do you suggest?

A. Different generations have unique and distinct preferences about service, and those preferences are starkly different between Generation X and Veterans. The best servers understand and adapt to these differences intuitively; most need training and coaching to learn to deliver the kind of service each customer wants. The On Border restaurants, a division of Brinker International, trains servers in generational communication via a program developed by MasterCard International. A half-day program teaches servers about the generations and the type of service each responds to most. Then participants practice gearing their approach, language, pace, and attitude to different generational scenarios.

Members of the Veterans are "turned off" by the chummy, casual service younger people sometimes deliver. We know of one older gentleman who took his wife out for a romantic evening at a new upscale French bistro in his midwestern town. The server actually sat down at the table with the couple to discuss the menu with them side by side, a technique some Boomers would actually find rather appealing. But the customer was so astounded at what he considered to be disrespectful behavior that he won't be returning to the restaurant again.

Make sure your servers understand that their eldest customers may prefer "dignified" service, with lots of polite language like

"Sir," "Ma'am," "Mr.," "Mrs.," "please," and "thank-you." Veteran consumers appreciate good grammar and clear enunciation; servers need to remember that some members of this generation don't hear as well as they once did. If parts of the menu are in French or include "exotic" items (arugula and chipotle, for example), watch for cues that customers are baffled. But warn your people never to assume that gray-haired customers are de facto "unhip." They may, in fact, be very cosmopolitan consumers. Be sure that you practice translating unusual menu items from hip to mainstream language with your servers so that the language they use with unsure customers doesn't come across as condescending.

In studies at Cornell University, this type of customized, targeted communication and service has been proven to render larger tips.[8] But it takes practice. Allow servers to role-play the way they would approach members of each generation, and give them feedback to increase their skills.

17. Li Needs Some People Skills

Xers

Q. My youngest sales rep, the penultimate techie, just told a fortysomething attorney, "If you still don't see that this is the best software for your practice, I might as well talk to a client who's smart enough to understand what we're offering here." Within an hour, they were both on the phone complaining—to me. I'd like to keep the customer *and* the employee. Any suggestions?

A. For the time being, you had better send another sales rep to meet with your client, a sales rep with good people skills and a track record of dealing with attorneys and other professional people. Probably better call the attorney and apologize, as well.

As for your out-of-bounds sales rep, we're guessing her technical skills make her a real asset to your business. Have you worked with her on a career map? Members of her generation tend to think of themselves as "free agents" and "marketable commodities." They know their resume is their passport to job security. This employee needs "people skills," for which the Boomers are renowned. If she doesn't see this need, perhaps it is because she hasn't looked at the importance of communication and rapport skills in getting where she wants to go. A good look at her plans will resolve that.

Get her all the help you can—a mentor and coach, regular feedback, seminars, books, and tapes—so that she can learn to create rapport with customers as skillfully as she can communicate about technical matters. Teach her to approach nontechnical clients in a way they feel they're not being condescended to...to talk about technology in a way that nontechnical people can understand...to read a customer's cues in order to tailor her communication so that it fits the client. Today, it's the "soft skills" that get the big results. These skills are real resume builders; once she can honestly include them on her list of assets, she'll be far more marketable than she is today.

18. Cohort Marketing: A Key to Mixed Generation Customers

Veterans, Boomers, Xers, and Nexters

Q. We own a car dealership in a large midwestern city, and we've recently seen the term "cohort marketing" in our trade publications. What is it, and is it worth pursuing?

A. Dealerships today are in a highly competitive market, and it's absolutely necessary for the marketing budget to be focused and effective. Some companies are accomplishing those goals via cohort marketing—sharpening their focus so that their marketing resonates with a specific generation, relating to its history, lifestyles, attitudes, and current needs. As cohort marketing has grown more popular, there is a growing body of evidence that shows just how well it works.[9] Recently, Nostalgia Television, Inc., a cable network in Washington, D.C., sent out a direct mail piece meant to appeal specifically to their target market—the Veterans. It included graphics appealing to their unique history: stars and stripes and WWII-era photos of Generals MacArthur and Eisenhower. Response was more than seven times their regular rate. Smith and Clurman, Yankelovich Partners, concluded, "based on years of research and analysis, that generationally determined lifestyles and social values exercise as much or even more influence on buying and purchasing than do more commonly understood demographic factors like income, education, and gender."[10]

Your dealership would be smart to target generational cohorts for your marketing efforts. Which generation do your customers typically come from? Which generation has spent the most money at your dealership in the last five years? Is there a generation that might create an excellent customer base that you've been missing?

Some *Veterans* are retired today, and many are moving toward retirement. They're generally out of debt, and they have the time and good health to relax and enjoy some of life's luxuries now that their nests are empty and their careers complete. They like to travel and mix with people of other ages. Their financial style is, and always has been, conservative—to save and pay cash. When they make a major purchase, they are attracted to stability and history. "In business since 1920" is a phrase that appeals uniquely to them. They prefer to not be thought of as "old." A recent study by the AARP shows they perceive themselves as fifteen years younger than they actually are, and the gap is widening.[11] They've done a lifetime of shopping, and they want their experience to be respected. They want details and quality assurance. Trial periods, warranties, and refunds are very successful with this cohort. Many advertisers and sales people approach this generation too seriously; Veterans actually appreciate easy-going, light, humorous approaches. At their stage in life, they've stopped taking things quite so seriously, although, as we said earlier, they do appreciate being treated with respect.

The Boomers, now preparing to turn sixty, will be very different older people than their parents. Having grown up with all the benefits of modern medicine, healthy diets, and active lifestyles, they will stretch middle age well into the first couple of decades of the new millennium. Today's Boomers are cocooning, scaling down, and simplifying. Many have promised themselves this will be the year they work less; they will garden or golf more. They're moving into smaller but more up-scale dwellings—townhouses, condos, and lofts. They used to eat out more than they ate in (four to five times each week), but that has shifted; more and more, they're eating at home. Their financial priorities are to save for retirement and pay for their kids' education. Their financial style has always been to use the credit card, and to—very willingly—go into short-term debt in order to accumulate what they think will personally satisfy them. They are the single strongest force and buying power ever to pass through any society in history. And they are swarmers—they tend to migrate like lemmings toward whatever is trendy at the moment: In the 1980s, it was running, fernbars, and mineral waters; today, it is golf, microbrews, and cappuccinos. Be quick and mobile with this market. Speak to their youthfulness and invincibility. They'll probably still be listening to the Rolling Stones and eating pizza when they're in their eighties.

Generation Xers are getting established in their careers and beginning their families. They have strong interests outside of work—family, friends, hobbies—and they are demanding a balanced lifestyle. Their financial priorities are to pay the rent, buy a funner car, and finance their education. They tend to be fiscally conservative as they struggle to make ends meet. Their primary buying need is to make their lives easy and fun without adding to their debt. If you target this cohort, you need to remember these are smart, media-savvy consumers who are deeply skeptical of marketing. Advertising that tries to imitate what's cool without paying attention to their issues will fail. A classic example is a Subaru TV commercial that took a hip grunge approach, showing young people with flannel shirts and baseball hats on backwards. Xers were insulted by the slacker image. The Saturn commercial that portrays a young woman buying her first car from a respectful Saturn staff has been far more popular. To succeed with this generation, you need to show potential customers "what's in it" for them, which requires knowing their needs.

The oldest *Nexters* will soon purchase their first cars. They'll graduate from high school and college and begin their careers. They are sophisticated about money and have been involved in family purchases from the time they were little tykes. But savvy marketers are quickly learning that their buying style is unique from the generations that precede them. In clothing, sports equipment, and entertainment, they are not attracted to the brands the Boomers loved. Instead, newcomer brands have become hot names. And with the large size of Gen Next, they will pack a wallop in the consumer market. Their preferences today for a new kind of product and a new style of advertising will likely stick with them as their generation comes of age. According to *Business Week,* "They respond to humor, irony, and the (apparently) unvarnished truth. Sprite has scored with ads that parody celebrity endorsers and carry the tag line, 'Image is nothing. Obey your thirst.' Arizona Jeans brand has a new campaign showing teens mocking ads that attempt to speak their language. The tag line? 'Just show me the jeans.'"[12] To succeed with this generation, you will need a great web page, e-mail accessibility, and a growing number of satisfied Gen Next buyers. They're very pragmatic. They like making commitments and coming up with five-year goals for themselves. Learn all you can about this cohort and tap into their personal plans, and you'll own a new generation of buyers.

Training

19. Coping With—and Adapting to—Differences in Generational Learning Styles

Veterans, Boomers, Xers, and Nexters

Q. Do the generations have different needs when it comes to training? We run the training department in a national fast food company. We have learned that our training programs, methods, and materials work best when they are targeted to our learners' specific tastes, styles, and preferences. Our industry hires the youngest employees; we depend on high-school students and others in their late teens as our primary source of new labor. What can we expect from Generation Next and how can we prepare our department to serve their needs?

A. Yes, each has its own learning style, determined, more than anything else, by the way they were taught when they were in school.

Veterans respond well to a traditional classroom environment and to lectures and presentations given by topic experts. They respond best to language that is logical and nonemotional, and to information that is organized, well researched, and supported by facts, figures, details, and examples. This cohort does not like to be in learning situations in which they might be made to look foolish in front of the group because they don't know an answer or handle a hypothetical situation "right." Training materials should be printed in a font that is easily read by "sixtyish eyes" and in a format that is simple and easy to follow. On-the-job training works well with this generation when it is respectful, nonthreatening, and risk free. Veterans like their information in summary form. *Reader's Digest* Condensed Books are more popular with Veterans than with any other cohort.

Because part of their generational personality consists of a value for lifelong learning and because they see education and development as a means to climbing the ladder, *Boomers* respond well to a variety of training formats. Their predilection for teams is accommodated by training seminars and workshops, particularly when they include team-building opportunities. They like books, videos, self-help guides, and audiotapes they can listen to on morning and evening commutes. In the training room, Boomers enjoy a more casual atmosphere than the Veterans, and they prefer a more participative, interactive format. For some reason, though, Boomers as a group do not respond well to role-playing, albeit engaging and practical. Training materials aimed at Boomers should be scannable, so that the reader can glance at a page or section and see what it's all about. The material should include plenty of information. Boomers see information as a reward, and they're always looking for new ways to "win" on the job. They like their information to be well-organized, so that they can delve into an area and get more information if they're interested. The way information on the Internet is organized is a good example. There's an overview of the information available, and then you can click on an area you wish to delve into. *USA Today* and *People* magazine are favorite Boomer publications.

Statistically, *Xers* don't read as much, so they're far less likely to visit the self-help section of the bookstore to develop a new skill or increase their knowledge of a topic. On the other hand, Xers are far more comfortable than the other two generations learning from a computer. Many of the most successful computer game companies are now hauling in the big bucks by developing computer programs that teach employees everything from accounting to zero-based budgeting. If your training department sticks primarily to the traditional classroom format, you're missing lots of opportunities; CD-ROM, interactive video, distance learning, and Internet courses are just a few of the ever-expanding world of possibilities for training Xers. Not that standard classroom training isn't also popular with this group—it is. Whereas the Boomers have avoided role-playing like the plague, trainers in a variety of industries tell us they just can't build in enough role-playing for their Gen Xer learners, who appreciate the opportunity to practice their skills and get feedback and coaching on the spot. Xers want their information organized in such a way that they can sample it. Because they learn by doing, they prefer the most interactive and participative of materials. Printed materials appeal to this generation when each page has lots going on: think *Spin* magazine, where graphics, type, sidebars, headlines, subheads, cartoons, and other items compete visually for the reader's attention. Xers claim this format stimulates, not confuses, their learning, and it taps into their capacity for "multitasking."

Because *Generation Next* has already begun to join your industry, you're doing the right thing by gearing your training to meet their needs and preferences. When designing training for this new generation of employees, here are some points to keep in mind:

- They read more than the generation ahead of them. Publishers say the annual sales of children's and young adults' books have quadrupled in the last ten years.

- They are used to learning in a highly interactive way. If you went to school in classrooms where kids sat in straight rows of orderly desks and you've been assuming that picture still exists, think again. Kids spend lots of time working on projects in teams. To the proverbial "man from Mars," today's classroom looks like barely contained chaos.

- The popularity and productivity of role-playing and other interactive activities work in inverse proportion to their age. The older the employee, the more uncomfortable they are with acting out roles in front of a seminar room full of their peers. The younger the employee, the more likely they are to ask for even more role-playing.

- The experts say that the Millennial Generation will make Xers look like technological dinosaurs. Business learners more and more will get their knowledge and skills via the Internet, online, and from CD-ROMs.

Engage the services of someone who has had regular, ongoing exposure to this new generation, perhaps a particularly outstanding middle- or high-school teacher. Education and industry need to work side by side as partners in preparing young people for the world of work. Focusing on the transition is well worth the effort.

20. Li and Devon Go to Management Training

Xers

Q. We pride ourselves on hiring only the best and brightest new business graduates. My job is to shepherd them through their first eighteen months, from orientation to first permanent assignment. Our management trainee program is somewhat traditional. We want to expose trainees to all of our business operations so they can make better decisions when they go on the job; that's our theory, anyway. So for the first year we rotate them through several departments, alternated with seminars that cover everything from senior management talking about a strategy with them to public speaking. Several problems have arisen lately. The trainees treat our program like an option, which it isn't. They come to seminars when they feel like it, and often they come late. The chairman was doing a strategy briefing, and two of them strolled in thirty minutes after he started. Later, when I spoke to them, one of them flatly stated, "I'm not interested in what he has to say. It's all noise." The other told me, "Mornings aren't good for us."

A. First, we would recommend you hold a focus group with ten to fifteen people who have graduated from your management trainee program in the past year or so. Get someone to facilitate it who is nonconfrontational and nonintimidating and with whom the group feels comfortable, because you need the truth. Find out all you can from the group about the effectiveness of your program. Did they learn skills and information that are useful in their current jobs? Which parts of the program were most useful? Least useful? Why? If they could change the program, what would they change? Remember you are talking to *survivors* of the management trainee program. It would be well worth your while to conduct five or ten phone interviews with those who dropped out of the program and to ask the same questions. Their answers may be quite different and even more valuable.

Your goal of exposing trainees to all your business operations is a good one, and it appeals to younger employees who prefer learning the big picture and a variety of skills rather than just being trained in one very specific job. We're wondering, though, if the fieldwork takes on the flavor of "dues paying." Are trainees expected to perform grueling, entry-level labor for ten to twelve hours, including evenings and weekends? Those are the unwritten expectations of many management trainee programs. Some managers tell us, "That's the way I started. These young people have to pay their dues, too." We don't agree. It's time we gave up the "dues-paying" story, unless we can afford to lose good trainees. Changing the culture on this issue may require some training of those old-school managers who think everyone must "pay their dues." We're also wondering if those seminars need updating and if they're the best format to be using with your new recruits. Should you be assigning mentors instead? What about computer training? It may be time to revamp the whole program.

We're as horrified as you by the fact that some of your trainees show up at the seminars when they feel like it. We recommend making the program requirements clear during the hiring process, even getting a signature from your new hire. But something's wrong when the seminars don't seem important to the participants. Do they actually need public speaking skills in their jobs, for example? If so, not only may you need to update the course, but you may need to "sell" it in the hiring process and help new hires see the importance of the skills they'll get there.

Now, what about the chairman's strategy briefing and your new hires calling it "noise"? Remember that Generation Xers feel markedly different about authority than do older employees. They don't automatically "give away" their respect—it must be earned. Does the chairman come across as sincere? He or she may need some coaching about adapting his or her presentation style. If it seems like hype, the Xers won't buy it. Maybe, too, there's a better format for this meeting, such as an interview video, a written document, or a question-and-answer session rather than a rehearsed speech.

Finally, when your trainees tell you, "Mornings aren't good for us," don't buy it. This new employee is ready for some one-on-one coaching—from you—about what you expect and how to succeed in your organization.

Recruiting

21. Finding the Best and the Brightest

Veterans, Boomers, Xers, and Nexters

Q. What is the single best method for recruiting new employees?

A. Unquestionably, the best method for recruiting new people is to do a great job with your current staff. Create an environment that accommodates their needs, is nontraditional, and has flexible management that is respectful and focuses on retention.

Start there.
Then, if you still need to go looking:

When you're recruiting Veterans, you'll need to:

- Be patient about their learning curve. Once they've got it, they've really got it. Aging only mildly impairs the short-term memory. Mid- and long-term memory are fully intact and may be even better than a younger person's because older employees have more experience with which they can contextualize the things they are learning.

- Provide lots of flexibility in scheduling. Unless they are really strapped for cash, many of these older workers aren't looking for full-time work. Part-time work is great with them, and, in some cases, they've already got their own health and retirement plans when they come to work for you.

- Play up the leader of the company as a person of integrity, one who wants the whole enterprise to excel together. These workers like to be part of an organization that's striving to be number one.

If you're trying to land Boomers:

- Show them how they can be one of the stars in your organization. Boomers use their jobs to prove their worthiness. At this stage in their lives—read "middle aged"—they feel they should be excelling.

- Demonstrate respect for their experience and achievements.
- Speak to the "status markers" included with the job, anything from a nice office to airline upgrade certificates to an impressive title.
- Emphasize the relational aspects of the company—warmth, caring, trust, and friendship.

If you're attempting to recruit Xers, especially for technology-intensive jobs:

- Stress that your corporation is not like all the others, that you do things very differently and that anyone with a good idea will be heard, regardless of seniority, title, or age.
- Institute casual dress all year round and try to incorporate fun activities into the work environment.
- Make sure they have access to the Internet and, if you can afford it, the latest in computer technology.
- Make sure you get the message across that Xers will be able to move around—across if not up—into a lot of different jobs if they join the company.

To recruit Nexters, our newest generation of candidates:

- Be tolerant of "swiss cheese scheduling"—an hour or two here, a half-day there.
- Make your recruiting efforts appeal to parents as well as Nexters. Emphasize that your work environment is safe, for example.
- Institute employee discounts.
- Emphasize they'll be assigned an older mentor.
- Work with local high schools, community colleges, and universities to offer student internships.
- Get involved in high-school career days.
- Send recruiters to job fairs.

AFTERWORD:

Predicting the Cross-Generational Future

Predicting the future is a strange business. It would be hyperbole to even call it an inexact science. Nevertheless, you rolls the dice and you takes your chances. And predicting what the future workforce will look like based on generational personalities is probably no worse than any other method and quite a bit cleaner than sifting through chicken entrails.

So here goes.

When you look at past and present business environments, you see connections. One might expect the Veterans, for example, to create a predominantly top-down, semimilitaristic, centrally controlled, paternal, bureaucratic corporate structure. The Boomers, for their part, have spent a lot of their corporate existence tearing down the bureaucracy and flattening the hierarchies. Their predilection for "changing the system" has led them through a cornucopia of business fads during the 1980s and 1990s, as they continually search for solutions to their companies' real and perceived problems. Boomers also don't wear the mantle of authority easily. When they end up as leaders, they attempt to personify the humane, altruistic, concerned executive in tune with the feelings of the troops. If the Veterans personify and admire the George S. Patton staunch hero vision of leadership, the Boomers see themselves more like Albert Schweitzer. As Boomers move from middle management into the ranks of executive level decision makers, they will attempt to achieve guru status. Remember, this is the generation that loves gurus, from Jack Kerouac to Timothy Leary to Peter Drucker. It wouldn't be surprising to find them coveting positions where they could sit quietly on the top of a corporate mountain and be consulted from time to time for business wisdom.

That brings us to Generation X. They're now actively moving into leadership positions in their organizations. So it's still anyone's guess what they will be like on a macro level. Those who are currently in management and executive positions have gotten there in two primary ways. Many have jumped in at ground level in small, start-up companies. These Xers have an entrepreneurial mentality that will preclude them from ascending to management positions in traditional organizations. Other Xer leaders, like Steve Buege at West Group (see Chapter 6), have climbed the ranks of the information technology (IT) department to find themselves not only at the top of their field but suddenly in charge of one of the more influential departments. As technology has taken a more central role in organizations, it has dragged the IT department and technology-adept Xers along with it. Often they lack people skills commensurate with their technical acumen.

There's also a possibility that there won't be a predominately Xer corporate culture, except in pockets of Silicon Valley, Seattle, and Cambridge. It's difficult to imagine the kinds of wild, chaotic business climates described in *Fast Company* and *Wired*—touchstones of business cool for Xers—migrating into blue chip companies like General Electric and Procter & Gamble. One might postulate that the small start-up companies will be the primary sanctuary for Xers who want managerial roles and responsibility. If Howe and Strauss are right that Xers are the ultimate free agents and contract workers, then it's hard to imagine how they will ever have the patience to get a foothold in large corporations as they currently exist. Perhaps the reins of power will be passed on to the Nexters, and companies will skip right over Generation X. It wouldn't surprise Gen Xers much to be skipped over yet again.

On the other hand, there's every chance Xers will find their place in corporations as both managers and leaders. The Fortune 2000 show no signs of imminent demise and will need a large steady supply of replacement workers well into the next decade as the Veterans and pre-Boomers muster out of the workplace. And it's quite likely that their "task orientation" will dictate their management styles and the corporate cultures they create. As leaders, they will be much more concerned about getting work done than just about anything else. Their question, "Will this be on the test?," will dominate the way they manage, and they will eschew corporate politics, bureaucratic machinations, and anything that gets in the way of the task at hand. How they manage the human resource and other soft side functions of tomorrow should be interesting.

Bureaucracy will be their Achilles heel, the source of constant frustration and the wall they constantly bang their heads against. Corporate bureaucracies have clearly stood the test of time, thriving under the Veterans, and if any generation could have destroyed bureaucracy, it would have been the Boomers. They tried to outsource, flatten, and downsize it away, and still it survives. It's probably time to admit that no amount of generational effort will do away with it. The Xer approach to bureaucracy will probably be more subversive than that of the Boomers. They prefer to ask forgiveness rather than permission, doing an end-around when obstacles present themselves, quickly changing direction to find a different path to a solution, even if it's against the rules and impolitic. In corporate environments, this has gotten senior leaders in a lot of trouble. Over time, the smart ones will learn either how to operate in step with the bureaucracy or, more likely, bend the rules without breaking them.

Jonathan Swift excoriated the sins of absentee landlords in his satiric piece, *A Modest Proposal*. Generation X will likely be the first corporate cohort to be accused of "absentee management." There are already signs of this group doing a lot of work with fewer meetings and more e-mail. Business books about managing in absentia will top the charts as Xers assume the ranks of managerial power. They like the idea of working from home, so corporations will probably be beset with a whole crop of at-home managers who interact with their direct reports via e-mail, teleconferencing, and voice mail.

This will not sit well with the Nexters. They are a generation that, for better or worse, are used to being doted on. Stay-at-home managers will bug the fertilizer out of their new workforce. Pouting Xers, who think corporate politics is the worst kind of waste of time, in charge of Nexters looks like a recipe for trouble. The Millennials will be the most politically active generation we've seen since Franklin D. Roosevelt was elected four times by the Veterans. Whereas the Xers are collectively pessimistic and personally optimistic about their future, the Nexters are collectively very optimistic about their future and less individualistic overall. Howe calls them the "Nobody Gets Left Behind" generation—they will work hard so that everyone moves forward into the future together.

This will ring a bit dissonant to Xers who never really had a collective sense of their generational selves. Their personal optimism gives them an "every person for himself" mentality that will certainly clash with Nexters. Finally, Xers will resent the hell out of all the attention paid to Nexters, just as they resented how everyone focused so much attention on the Boomers before them. Worse yet, managers and supervisors will be "expected" to pay a lot more attention to these young workers. Xer managers will resent that even more.

All in all, mixing Xer managers and supervisors with a Nexter workforce looks like a recipe for a future disaster. But it probably won't be any worse an explosion than those we've seen between the Boomers and Generation Xers. There will be a lot of tension and work style dissonance between each generation and the cohort immediately preceding it. It's been said that the only thing you can count on about a generation's personality is it will be a polar opposite of the generation that came before it. So the general disconnect between the generations at work will probably repeat itself over and over in the future. And although the gap in understanding and behaviors will probably always exist, the specific issues will be as diverse and complicated as the generational personalities that create them.

INVENTORY

How Cross-Generationally Friendly Is Your Work Group,
Department, Business, or Organization?

Accommodating Employee Differences

1. There is no one successful "type" in this organization: Managers, leaders and those in the most desirable jobs are a mix of ages, sexes, and ethnicities.

1	2	3	4	5
Completely false	Somewhat false	Somewhat true/some-what false	Somewhat true	Completely true

2. When a project team is put together, employees with different backgrounds, experiences, skills, and viewpoints are consciously included.

1	2	3	4	5
Never	Rarely	Occasionally	Usually	Always

3. Employees are treated like customers.

1	2	3	4	5
Never	Rarely	Occasionally	Usually	Always

4. There is lots of conversation—even some humor—about differing viewpoints and perspectives.

1	2	3	4	5
Never	Rarely	Occasionally	Usually	Always

5. We take time to talk openly about what different cohorts—and the individuals within them—are looking for on the job...what makes work rewarding...which environment is most productive...what types of work load, schedule, and policies work best.

1	2	3	4	5
Never	Rarely	Occasionally	Usually	Always

Creating Workplace Choices

6. Our atmosphere and policies are based on the work being done, the customers being served, and the preferences of the people who work here.

1	2	3	4	5
Completely false	Somewhat false	Somewhat true/some-what false	Somewhat true	Completely true

7. There is behind-the-back complaining, passive-aggressive behavior, and open hostility among groups of employees.

1	2	3	4	5
Always	Usually	Occasionally	Rarely	Never

8. There is a minimum of bureaucracy and "red tape" here.

1	2	3	4	5
Completely false	Somewhat false	Somewhat true/some-what false	Somewhat true	Completely true

9. The work atmosphere could be described as relaxed and informal.

1	2	3	4	5
Completely false	Somewhat false	Somewhat true/some-what false	Somewhat true	Completely true

10. There's an element of fun and playfulness about most endeavors here.

1	2	3	4	5
Completely false	Somewhat false	Somewhat true/some-what false	Somewhat true	Completely true

Operating From a Flexible Management Style

11. Managers here are a bit more "polished" or professional than in most companies.

1	2	3	4	5
Completely false	Somewhat false	Somewhat true/some-what false	Somewhat true	Completely true

12. Managers adjust policies and procedures to fit the needs of indi-viduals and the team.

1	2	3	4	5
Never	Rarely	Occasionally	Usually	Always

13. Managers here are known for being straightforward.

1	2	3	4	5
Never	Rarely	Occasionally	Usually	Always

14. Managers give those who report to them the big picture along with specific goals and measures, then turn their people loose.

1	2	3	4	5
Never	Rarely	Occasionally	Usually	Always

Respect for Competence and Initiative

15. We assume the best of and from our people; we treat everyone—from the newest recruit to the most seasoned employee—as if they have great things to offer and are motivated to do their best.

1	2	3	4	5
Never	Rarely	Occasionally	Usually	Always

Nourishing Retention

16. We are concerned and focused, on a daily basis, with retention.

1	2	3	4	5
Never	Rarely	Occasionally	Usually	Always

17. We offer lots of training, from one-on-one coaching to a varied menu of classroom courses.

1	2	3	4	5
Completely false	Somewhat false	Somewhat true/some what false	Somewhat true	Completely true

18. We encourage regular lateral movement.

1	2	3	4	5
Completely false	Somewhat false	Somewhat true/some what false	Somewhat true	Completely true

19. Work assignments here are broad, providing variety and challenge, and allowing each employee to develop a range of skills.

1	2	3	4	5
Never	Rarely	Occasionally	Usually	Always

20. We market internally, "selling" the company to employees and continually looking for ways to be the employer of choice.

1	2	3	4	5
Never	Rarely	Occasionally	Usually	Always

If Your Score Was

- **Under 70**   Your organization is in danger. The high costs of losing, recruiting, and training employees will seriously damage your bottom line, if they haven't already.

- **70-79**   You're typical of most organizations. Although you're doing some good things, you must make major improvements to your work environment if you're going to survive and thrive in today's competitive market.

- **80-89**   Your turnover is probably lower than the industry average. You are doing a good job, but there's room for improvement.

- **90-100**   Congratulations! Not only is turnover lower than the average for your industry, but the work atmosphere you've created is so attractive to employees that recruiting nearly takes care of itself. Good job.

WEB RESOURCES ACROSS THE GENERATIONS

As in all things, there is a wealth of information about the different generations out on the World Wide Web. Information, communities, zines, and organizations center around generational studies, so many, in fact, that most of the sites we are going to recommend are links pages (a type of web site that primarily provides links to related sites, a directory of web sites if you will). Three very general sites—ones that should appeal to members of any of the generations—are very good places to start your journey.

- *The Fourth Turning* at *www.fourthturning.com* is centered around the book of the same title by Neil Howe and Bill Strauss. Howe and Strauss are preeminent generational scholars and have done most of the pioneering work in this field. This site discusses all matter of generational issues, from predictions for the future to workplace issues to questions for the authors to political issues. Interestingly enough, Howe and Strauss are using these discussions to help them frame and write their next book on the Millennial generation. It's an experiment that bears watching.

- *The Generational Inquiry Group (GIG)* has a web site at *www.millennials.com* that primarily talks about who they are and what they talk about, i.e., the five living generations as defined by Howe and Strauss. It also includes an easy-to-join listserv, a community of people who discuss generational theory.

- *Speaking of Generations* at *www.generationsatwork.com* is Claire Raines' web site. It includes all the issues of *Generations™, A Newsletter for Managers,* which has addressed issues such as recruiting by generation, marketing to Generation X, the Boomers versus the Busters, and Generation X managing Generation X.

Veterans

- *The American Association of Retired Persons* has a web site at *www.aarp.org,* but that's not surprising for such a ubiquitous organization. The web site has information about the organization, member benefits, computer tips, consumer alerts, and political issues. As more and more older people get on the web, this could become a very important portal site.

- *Senior Organizations* at *www.seniors.com* is purely a links site, a jumping-off place to find organizations this cohort might be interested in. It includes links to the Grey Panthers, the Older Women's League, and some union groups.

- *SeniorNet* at *www.seniornet.org* is an organization primarily dedicated to helping older adults become more familiar with computer technology and providing formal computer education for this generation. Its web site, however, is much more than that. It includes book club discussions, computer discounts from IBM for seniors, software discounts from Microsoft, online investment education from Charles Schwab, and a Time Capsule (sponsored by ABC News) where this cohort is encouraged to share their stories.

This site was declared "Best Community Site for Seniors in 1998" by Yahoo! and boasts many other nominations and awards. There also exists a SeniorNet web ring, a series of interconnected sites set up by regional SeniorNet organizations.

Boomers

- *The National Association of Baby Boomers* at *www. babyboomers.org* is a membership group that promises networking opportunities and political power. It is itself an alternative to the AARP (for those Boomers who aren't yet ready to make that plunge).
- *The International Association of Baby Boomers Plus!* has a web site at *www.boomersassoc.com* that, at first glance, doesn't provide much of anything except the dancing baby video and a bunch of other silly Internet tricks. A little digging, however, reveals a real organization with member benefits, a registry for blood, organ, and tissue donors, and a political agenda regarding saving Social Security. Members also receive the periodical *Boomer-Ang*.
- *Boomers International Club* has the mother of all Boomer web sites at *boomersint.org* and offers different versions of the same web site depending on which browser you use. The full-frame version is 18 pages if you were to print it out, and it's chock full of what can only be called pure nostalgia. Links will take you to the *Boomer of the Month*, the club's newsletter, a discussion forum, a web ring for Boomers who want to talk business and a host of other things. This page has it all.
- *Boomers Business Web Ring* is a whole series of Boomer-related web sites that have bonded together into a kind of web community. Each site that wants to participate loads an icon on its page, and the ring master eventually includes them in the loop. For the generation that turned "network" into a verb, this might be the latest and greatest expression of this predilection.

- *Boomers Site of the Month* is a short, one-page set of links to other Boomer sites of merit (according to the owner of this page). Some links are not bad.

*Editors Note: It's instructive to note that generational differences extend even to the web pages you will find herein. Boomers, the generation who decided it could "have it all," seem to design pages that emulate that philosophy. The web pages take forever to load, have links to an eclectic mix of sites, and include all the bells and whistles (The National Association of Baby Boomers web site plays "Stairway to Heaven" and "Come Together" when you finally get its pages loaded on your browser). Likewise, Generation X web pages tend to be sparse, utilitarian, and full of attitude.

Generation X

- *Adam Rifkin's Generation X Page* at *www.cs.caltech.edu/~adam/lead/genx.html* should be your first stop when searching for Gen X resources on the Internet. It has more than seventy-five links to sites that might be of interest to this cohort. Some of the links aren't that current, but there's plenty here to keep you browsing for hours, if not days. It also includes a list of recommended books and movies that will give deeper insight into this cryptic generation.

- Because Xers don't tend to "join" organizations, there are a dearth of associations on the Internet for Generation X. About the only one that's had any shelf life is *Third Millennium*, a political group that tries to organize Xers around important political and policy issues that will affect this generation's future. It's at *www.thirdmil.org*, and it simply describes the organization, its issues, how to join the group, publications, and page that allows you to send a message to Congre

- Another links page is called *GO Network: Generation X*, and it's part of a larger portal site. It's at *www.go.com/WebDir/People/Society/GenerationX*. It has a lot of interesting sites for Xers. This page also rates the sites so you know where to begin.

Nexters

- *The Fourth Turning* at *www.fourthturning.com*, as mentioned earlier is currently in the middle of doing research on this generation. If you want to be part of some very definitive research and discussion about this youngest cohort, join the discussion there.

- *Love Those Millennials* at *www.millennials.com/ltm/ltm.html* is a newsletter that studies the next generation coming down the pike. The newsletter is created by Frank Gregorsky, and some articles from back issues are on this web page. Articles are both by and about the Nexters, so you can hear from these young people in their own words.

- *The Northwestern Mutual Life summary* of a study of the graduation class of 2001 is at *www.northwesternmutual.com/2001/summary-main.html*. This is an excellent look at the attitudes and opinions of the leading edge of the Millennial generation.

- *www.growingupdigital.com* is the web site of Don Tapscott, author of *Growing up Digital: The Rise of the Net Generation*. It includes lots of information *about* Nexters along with areas for them to visit and participate in, such as "Question of the Week" and "Forum of the Week."

ENDNOTES

Chapter 1: Old Farts and Upstarts: Crisis in the Cross-Generational Workplace

1. J. Walker Smith and Ann Clurman, *Rocking the Ages* (New York: Harper Business, 1997), p. xvii.
2. Norma Carr-Ruffino, *Managing Diversity* (Stamford, CT: Thomson Executive Press, 1996), p. 4.
3. David K. Foot, *Bust & Echo* (Toronto: MacFarlane, Walters and Ross, 1996), p. 2.
4. David K. Foot, *Bust & Echo* (Toronto: MacFarlane, Walters and Ross, 1996), p. 7.
5. William Strauss and Neil Howe, *Generations* (New York: Quill Publications, 1991), p. 23.

Chapter 2: The Veterans: What Will the Colonel Do Now—Work? Retire? Consult?

1. Tom Brokaw, *The Greatest Generation* (New York: Random House, 1998), p. 37.
2. Alvin Toffler, *The Third Wave* (New York: Bantam Books, 1991), p. 118.
3. M. Scott Myers and Susan S. Myers, "Toward Understanding the Changing Work Ethic," *California Management Review* XXI (1974):7.

4. Susan Mitchell, *The Official Guide to the Generations* (Ithaca, NY: New Strategist, 1995), p. 216.
5. Neil Howe, interview by Bob Filipczak, October 1998.
6. Kristin Anderson and Ron Zemke, *Coaching Knock Your Socks Off Service* (New York: AMACOM, 1997), p. 110.
7. "The Hunt for America's Oldest Worker," *Training Magazine*, February 1999.
8. The National Older Worker Career Center is based in Washington, D.C.

Chapter 3: The Baby Boomers: Peter Pan Grays at the Temples

1. The Boomer Institute, based in Cleveland, Ohio, in a study conducted on their Web site, August 22, 1998.
2. The Boomer Institute, based in Cleveland, Ohio, in a study conducted on their Web site, August 22, 1998.
3. Robin Maranta-Henig, "Adult Ed Groupies Grope for 'Aha' Moment," *USA Today*, 2 March 1998.
4. Sue Shellenbarger, "Families Are Felling the Generation Gap in Work-Family Issues," *Wall Street Journal*, 11 February 1998.
5. William Strauss, interview by Bob Filipczak, October 1998.
6. Anne R. Carey and Kevin Rechin, "More Gray Hair in the Workplace," *USA Today*, 21 March 1996.
7. Sabra Chartrand, "In Retirement Planning, Boomers and Xers Are Universes Apart," *The New York Times on the Web*, 22 August 1998.

Chapter 4: The Gen Xers: Absence and Malice

1. Claire Raines, *Beyond Generation X* (Menlo Park, CA: Crisp Publications, 1997), p. 36.
2. Howard Schultz, *Pour Your Heart Into It* (New York: Hyperion, 1997), p. 94.
3. Nina Munk, "The New Organization Man," *Fortune Magazine*, 16 March 1998.
4. Nina Munk, "The New Organization Man," *Fortune Magazine*, 16 March 1998.
5. Marc Prensky, vice president of Bankers Trust, *Across the Board Magazine*, 5 February 1998.
6. Margot Hornblower, "Great Xpectations," *Time Magazine*, 9 June 1997.

7. David Plopus, interview by Neal Conan, *NPTC News, Dallas,* 25 October 1997.

8. Roberta Maynard, "How to Motivate Low-Wage Workers," *Nations' Business,* May 1997.

9. "Industry Report 1998," *Training Magazine,* October 1998.

10. Lawrence J. Bradford and Claire Raines, *Twentysomething: Managing and Motivating Today's New Workforce* (New York: MasterMedia, 1992), p. 39.

11. Amy Joyce, "Some Companies Pick up the Tab for Help Hired to Run Employees' Errands," *Los Angeles Times,* 18 October 1998.

Chapter 5: The Nexters: Chilling Out and Cheering Up

1. Dan Tapscott, *Growing Up Digital: The Rise of the Net Generation* (New York: McGraw Hill, 1998), p. 2.

2. 1995 National Survey of Preteens, conducted on *www.kidspeace.org.*

3. 1995 National Survey of Preteens, conducted on *www.kidspeace.org.*

4. T.L. Stanley, "Get Ready for Gen Y," *Brandweek,* 15 May 1995.

5. John Ryan, "The Millennial Generation," *San Francisco Chronicle,* 13 December 1998.

6. Landon Jones, *Great Expectations* (New York: Ballantine Press, 1980), p. 44.

7. Neil Howe and Bill Strauss, *13th Gen* (New York: Vintage Press, 1993), p. 63.

8. Neil Howe and Bill Strauss, *Generations* (New York: Quill Publications, 1991), p. 335.

9. Al Lewis, "Kids Get Upscale Touch," *Rocky Mountain News,* 22 November 1998.

10. Susan Mitchell, *The Official Guide to the Generations* (Ithaca, NY: New Strategist, 1995), p. 124.

11. Kathy Boccella, "New Baby Boom? Nope, It's a Parent Boom," *Denver Post,* 28 March 1997.

12. Heather Knight, "U.S. Report Shows Mixed Trends," *Denver Post,* 3 July 1997.

13. William Porter, "For Gen Y Pop Culture is Pluralistic," *Denver Post,* 25 April 1999.

14. Melinda Beck, "Next Population Bulge Shows Its Might," *Wall Street Journal,* 3 February 1997.

15. Barbara Dafoe-Whitehead, "The Girls of Gen X," *American Enterprise,* January/February 1998.

16. Neil Gross, "Zap! Splat! Smarts?" *Business Week,* 11 November 1996.

17. Jonathan Kaufman, "At Age 5, Reading, Writing and Rushing," *Wall Street Journal,* 4 February 1997.

18. Susan Mitchell, "The Next Baby Boom," *American Demographics,* October 1995.

19. According to educational consultant, Judith Armstrong, Tiburon, California.

20. Bill Strauss, interview by Bob Filipczak, August 1998.

21. "1997 Reader's Digest Survey," *Reader's Digest,* 8 July 1997.

22. Harold Hodgkinson, Institute for Educational Leadership, Washington, D.C.

23. Bill Strauss, interview by Bob Filipczak, August 1998.

24. 1995 National Survey of Preteens, conducted on *www.kidspeace.org.*

25. "Generation 2001," a study conducted by Milwaukee, Wisconsin-based Northwestern Mutual and New York City-based Louis Harris in 1998.

26. David Krane, executive vice president of New York City-based Louis Harris Research, in a study entitled "Generation 2001" released February 3, 1998.

27. "Generation 2001," a study conducted by Milwaukee, Wisconsin-based Northwestern Mutual and New York City-based Louis Harris in 1998.

28. Neil Howe, interview by Bob Filipczak, August 1998.

29. Susan Mitchell, *The Official Guide to the Generations* (Ithaca, NY: New Strategist, 1995), p. 388.

30. Cheryl Dahle, "HP's Mentor Connection," *Fast Company,* November 1998.

31. Cheryl Dahle, "HP's Mentor Connection," *Fast Company,* November 1998.

32. Neil Howe, interview by Bob Filipczak, August 1998.

33. Neil Howe and Bill Strauss, *Generations* (New York: Quill Publications, 1991), p. 338.

Chapter 6: Where Mixed Generations Work Well Together

1. Industry of Choice Executive Overview, conducted by the Foodservice Research Forum, sponsored by Coca-Cola Company, 1997.

Chapter 7: The Plight of Charlie Roth: A Cross-Generational Workforce Case Study

1. In discussing his response, Chip, a Vietnam War veteran, used this analogy: "In Vietnam, there were sometimes powerful racial issues at play between soldiers. But when we went into battle, these issues were put aside for the common good—survival. Charlie needs to be clear that survival is the overarching issue here. He can and should subjugate the cross-generational problem to the need for his department to survive. Then he can deal with the generational diversity problems."

Chapter 8: Making the Cross-Generational Workplace Work: Twenty-One Often-Asked Questions—and Some Very Practical Answers

1. Carol Hymowitz, "Managing Your Career," *Wall Street Journal*, 21 July 1998.
2. Juliet Schor, *The Overworked American* (Boulder, CO: Basic Books, 1991), p. 132.
3. Claire Raines, "Generation X Managing Generation X," *Generations: A Newsletter for Managers*, Fall 1997.
4. Pamela Kruger and Katharine Mieszkowski, "Stop the Fight," *Fast Company*, September 1998.
5. J. Walker Smith and Ann Clurman, *Rocking the Ages* (New York: Harper Business Press, 1997), p. 6.
6. Neil Howe, interview by Bob Filipczak, October 1998.
7. Mindy McCune, operations manager at Motorola's Phoenix Design Center, interview by Claire Raines, 18 November 1998.
8. Michael Lynn, "Seven Ways to Increase Servers' Tips," *Cornell Hotel and Restaurant Administration Quarterly*, Summer 1996.
9. Michael M. Phillips, "Selling by Evoking What Defines a Generation," *Wall Street Journal*, 13 August 1996, and Faye Rice, "Making Generational Marketing Come of Age," *Fortune Magazine*, 26 June 1995.
10. J. Walker Smith and Ann Clurman, *Rocking the Ages* (New York: Harper Business Press, 1997), p. 6.
11. Patrick Flanagan, "Don't Call 'em Old, Call 'em Customers," *Management Review*, October 1994.
12. "Generation Y," *Business Week*, 15 February 1999.

ACKNOWLEDGMENTS

Our Thanks

This book was born, became a toddler, and reached adolescence in dozens of conversations and dialogues with scores of people who were interested in, encouraging of, and enthusiastic about the ideas of a workforce filled with quiet cross-generational conflict. We were blessed with the opinions, perspectives, and insights of hundreds of the people out there working every day in the midst of the cross-generational chaos. It was our good fortune that they were paying close attention to how the issues we address here affect the way organizations do their work. There are many, many people to thank for helping us with this project over the past two years.

First are Neil Howe and Bill Strauss, who were generous not only with their time but with their invaluable insights into the character and conflicts of the generations. We need also to heartily thank Kevin Bradley of Chevys Fresh Mex; Anne Varano of TGI Friday's; Sean Greenwood of Ben & Jerry's Homemade Inc.; Patrick Sexton; Brian Hall, Steve Buege, and Ed Gilbert of West Group; and Laurie Lamantia and Lari Washburn of Lucent Technologies for sharing their trials and triumphs with us. Special thanks to Larry Lamb and Jeff Thingvold of Lamb and Co., another ACORN company that we learned much from.

Another very special "thank-you" goes to those stalwart souls who responded to our case study— Bruce Tulgan of Rainmaker Thinking, Gloria Regalbuto of Bath and Body Works, Deidra Wager of Starbucks, Sandy Mazarakis of Mazarakis & Associates, Pat Crull of McDonald's, Chip Bell of Performance Research Associates, Larry Bourgerie of Twin City Federal, and Judy Corson of Custom Research, Inc.

Many thanks also go to Marjorie Allison, Judy Armstrong, Tom Connellan, Chrysta Wille, Steve Zemke, Jason VanderVelde, Lindsay Willis, Jeff Pope, Oren Harari, Gordon and Margaret Filipczak, and Mae Zemke for reading and commenting on the manuscript. Thank you Stevy Merrill for providing information, sharing perspectives, proof-reading—and generally keeping us up to date on Generation Next.

Two people on the home team need special commendations— Wendy Webb who wrote and edited many of the cases, and Jill Applegate who not only typed and retyped the manuscript, but who was the keeper of the book's heart and soul and the chronicler of our where-abouts.

Our spouses, Susan Zemke, Amy Filipczak, and Allen Alderman, were models of patience, perseverance, and support during this two-year journey—and are still speaking to us. Thank you.

We're certain we've left important contributors off this list. If you're one, please know that, as you read this, we're burning with guilt and humiliation since we remembered we forgot to include you, and that, oafish as we are, we are, nevertheless, deeply grateful for your as-sistance.

To each and every one of you, "Thank-you. We hope you'll enjoy reading the book and finding your contributions. We're proud of what all of us accomplished together!"

Ron Zemke
Claire Raines
Bob Filipczak

INDEX

ABOUT THE AUTHORS

Ron Zemke proudly represents the Veterans. Ron's award-winning writing, consulting, and research with organizations such as Ford Motor Company, Roadway Express, Dayton Hudson Department Stores, Beverly Enterprises, Microsoft, Southern California Gas, the Audubon Institute, Harley-Davidson, Wendy's International, Courtyard by Marriott, Motorola, and Wendy's International bring him face to face with the problems and opportunities of the cross-generational workforce and marketplace. As senior editor of Minneapolis-based *TRAINING* magazine and contributing editor of the *Training Directors' Forum* newsletter, he has covered the emergence of the nation's growing service sector as well as other major issues in American business and management. Ron is the author or coauthor of 23 books, including the best-selling *Knock Your Socks Off Service* series (AMACOM) and *Knock Your Socks Off Selling* (AMACOM, 1999). He is also the coauthor with Karl Albrecht of *Service America!,* a book credited with starting the U.S. customer service revolution. Ron can be reached at *Zemke@aol.com* or *socksoff.com.*

Claire Raines is considered one of the nation's leading experts on generations. She is the coauthor of *TWENTYSOMETHING: Managing*

& Motivating Today's New Work Force (Mastermedia, 1992), named one of the thirty best business books of 1992; author of *Beyond Generation X: A Practical Guide for Managers* (Crisp Publications, 1997); and commentator of videos *The X Factor* (CorVision, 1998) and *The Boomers vs. The Busters* (CorVision, 1999). She is the editor of *Generations: A Newsletter for Managers,* which is published quarterly. Her dynamic speeches and workshops focus on better understanding the generations and creating workplaces that attract and retain employees. Clients include McDonald's, Sprint, MasterCard, Toyota, and Coca-Cola. Claire has been featured widely in the media, including *USA Today, Training, Working Woman,* and *Personnel Journal.* Claire resides in Denver, Colorado. She can be contacted via e-mail at *ClaireRain@aol.com.* Visit her web site at www.generationsatwork.com.

Bob Filipczak is an honorary member of Generation X, although some argue that his 1962 birth year makes him too old to make the claim. He himself has no trouble grouping himself with the Xer cohort and has always identified strongly with them. He took his first plunge into writing about generational issues as staff editor for *Training Magazine.* His early editorial "Working for Boomers" was followed by a cover story entitled "It's Just a Job: Generation X in the Workplace" in April 1994. That was so well received, especially by Xers, that he started talking to Ron Zemke about the book you now have in front of you. In the course of collecting a basement full of information about Gen X and the Millennial generation, some of it sank into his brain and here are the results.

He followed the traditional path through school, high school, and college, finally graduating with a liberal arts degree from St. John's University in Collegeville. That's when the abysmal reality of a workplace where there wasn't any room for him and his cohort became clear. He is essentially a writer, writing business articles, fiction, and poetry. He currently works for the regional brokerage firm, U.S. Bancorp Piper Jaffray, and pursues a variety of hobbies and vices typical to his generation: home brewing, single-malt scotch, cigars, and the Internet. Bob can be reached via e-mail at BobF@uswest.com.